HARD AND NOBLE LIVES

*A Living Tradition of Cowboys and Ranchers
in Wyoming's Hoback Basin*

PAUL JENSEN

Cover Design: Sue Sommers
Original Maps: Sue Sommers
WRWS Design
wrwsdesign.com

www.pronghornpress.org

Western culture and character, hard to define in the first place because they are only half-formed and constantly changing, are further clouded by the mythic stereotype. Why hasn't the stereotype faded away as real cowboys became less and less typical of Western life? Because we can't or won't do without it, obviously. But also there is the visible, pervasive fact of Western space, which acts as a preservative. Space, itself the product of incorrigible aridity and hence more or less permanent, continues to suggest unrestricted freedom, unlimited opportunity for testing and heroisms, a continuing need for self-reliance and physical competence.

Wallace Stegner,
The American West as Living Space
University of Michigan Press, 1990

To Sherrill and Lilian,
who share my life in Wyoming,
and let me work as a cowboy.

To my older children, Luke and Hadley,
who joined me in my discovery of Wyoming.

In memory of my mother, Inkeri Vaananen-Jensen,
who later in her life became an author and
translator of Finnish literature.

And to the early cowboys and pioneers
who, against the odds, settled the Hoback Basin.

Acknowledgements

Many, many people have contributed to *Hard and Noble Lives* —most through interviews, handwritten family histories and family photographs. Others contributed through conversations. All gave generously of their time and personal memories. Since I cannot recognize all of them here, at the very beginning of my book, I would like to thank them. Many are listed in the book's Notes and Sources section.

A few individuals deserve special recognition.

First, I would like to thank my wife, Sherrill Hudson. Not only did she encourage me and offer sound editorial advice, but she gave me immeasurable assistance with the manuscript and photographs. The book could not have been completed without her or our daughter Lily's patience and enthusiasm.

Second, I would like to thank Norm Pape, his wife Barbara, and two sons, Fred and Dave, for hiring me as their roundup rider in the Hoback Basin and continuing a long standing Pape Ranch tradition. Also, I would like to acknowledge their early and generous financial support.

Next, I want to thank Tom Filkins who rides for the Hoback

Stock Association. He introduced me to the Basin years ago and recommended that the Stock Association hire me as the second rider in 2005. Lou Copeland, Tom's brother-in-law and my friend from Maryland, gave the book early and much appreciated financial support.

Similarly, I would like to recognize Kevin Campbell of the Campbell Ranch and Gerry Endecott of the Little Jennie Ranch for helping me along the way. The Little Jennie and the Wagstaff family, who owned it, gave the book project a welcome financial contribution.

Gil Ordway, owner of the River Bend Ranch, made an equally generous and timely contribution.

Fifth, I would like to thank the Green River Valley Museum in Big Piney, Wyoming. It sponsored the book and made available their invaluable collection of historical research and photographs. More specifically, I want to recognize Barbara McKinley, who carefully read my manuscript and offered suggestions. Due to her assistance and attention to detail, *Hard and Noble Lives* is a better book.

I would also like to thank the Wyoming Community Foundation and specifically its Gail McMurry Kinnison Donor Advised Endowment. Their grant to the Green River Valley Museum allowed me to finish the manuscript, design the book's cover, acquire photographs, complete the original photography, pay copyright fees, and develop the specifications for the book's maps.

Some of the nearly forgotten history of the Hoback Basin and its ranchers was fortunately found in the records of the United States Forest Service. From the Bridger-Teton's Big Piney Ranger District, Ranger Greg Clark and Steve Harmon, who supervise the Hoback Allotment, freely made available their historical files. They were helpful, informed, and congenial. They represent the best of the USFS tradition. I would also like to recognize Jamie Schoen, the Bridger-Teton archeologist, who made available homesteading records that dated back to 1900.

I am particularly grateful to Jim Fallows, a friend of thirty years, who is National Correspondent for the *Atlantic Monthly* and a nationally recognized author. Jim served as senior advisor to the book project. Not only did he help edit the manuscript, but he gave the best advice on ways to enhance the book's structure, flow, and readability.

Victor and Jo Mack, Bondurant ranchers and residents for nearly sixty years, read the book for fun and historical accuracy. I appreciated their constructive comments, but also enjoyed the conversations and stories. Some of them easily found their way into the book.

After much editing and rewriting, Albert Sommers, who ranches along the Green River, read the manuscript. His comments improved the history and prompted me to simplify and rewrite still confusing sentences and paragraphs. During the summer of 2004, I worked for Albert and rode the Green River Drift. I learned a lot from him, and we became friends.

I would also like to thank Albert's wife, Sue, who designed the book's cover and maps.

A special thanks goes to Katherine Campbell Bond whose photos of today's cowboys added much to the book's visual appeal, including the cover photo.

Finally, I would like to thank the Charles Redd Center for Western Studies at Brigham Young University for their timely grant that underwrote the design and completion of the book's maps.

Of course, any omissions or other shortcomings are entirely my responsibility.

Table of Contents

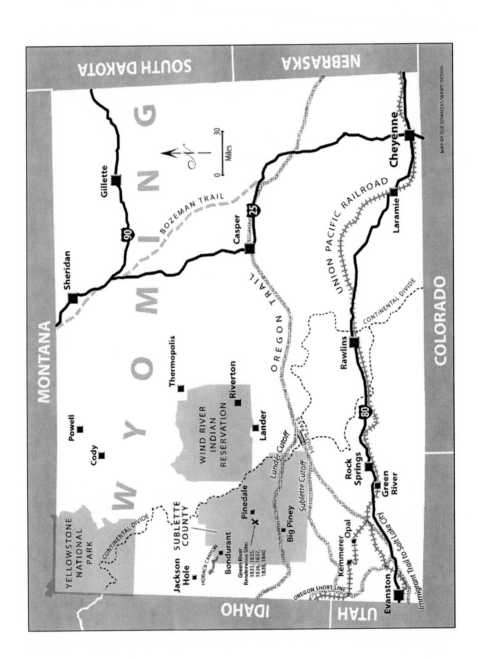

Part One

A Guided Tour of Wyoming History

PAUL JENSEN

My romance with the American West began fifty-five years ago when I was five and living in Ames, Iowa. Just like kids all across the country then, my older brother and I would dress the parts and play "Cowboys and Indians." In a black cowboy hat, a black mask or bandanna and with toy pistols in my holsters, I dreamed of riding the Western plains.

And it didn't matter that I couldn't tell anyone their location.

Later, my Uncle George made me a fringed leather vest complete with bullet holes in the back, chaps with holsters and a near pony-size rocking horse named Midnight. I was magically transported to the ridges and mountains of my West.

Three years later when television began to make its way into most American households, the Saturday morning westerns—*The Cisco Kid, The Lone Ranger, Wild Bill Hickok, Hopalong Cassidy, Gene Autry* and *Roy Rogers*—further enlarged the West in my generation's imagination.

A few years later the cowboy made it into prime time with *Gunsmoke, Bonanza,* and *The Rifleman.*

The more recent popularity of Larry McMurtry's *Lonesome Dove,* Norman Maclean's *A River Runs Through It,* Kevin Kostner's *Dances with Wolves,* Clint Eastwood's movie, *The Unforgiven* and Wallace Stegner's writings speak to the endurance and cross-generational appeal of the West.

While the frontier and the image of the cowboy are tightly woven into the American psyche, most learn to set those impulses aside and let other ambitions and city life prevail. Eventually, those pioneering images will reassert themselves, but most likely in the form of outdoor adventures like skiing, snowboarding, kayaking, camping, hiking, mountain biking, fly fishing, rock climbing, horseback riding or other more extreme sports.

Through public school, college, graduate school and a nearly thirty year professional life in Washington, D.C., my life had the exterior of the more typical way of city living. Like my friends, my dreams of another way of life gave way to professional ambition, money, and my children's education.

However, my brain was hardwired for the West—and not for the cities like Denver, Las Vegas or even Bozeman, but cowboy country in Wyoming. My travelogue started in 1970 with a cross country trip to Jackson Hole, Wyoming, during my first year in graduate school and ended a few years ago with a move to a new custom log home on over forty acres near Daniel, Wyoming. With approximately one hundred year-round residents, Daniel is in the middle of ranch country, and the surrounding county, Sublette County, is sometimes called the "last frontier of Wyoming." I share my life here with my wife, Sherrill, and my youngest child, Lilian, who is eight.

Along the way, that journey to Daniel has had many side trips, rest stops, testings, friends, mentors, and a horseback education. During the summers and fall I now work as a cowboy and ranch hand. During the past four falls I have had the privilege of continuing a long-standing tradition riding roundup in the Hoback Basin for the Pape Ranches near Daniel. From June 1, 2005 through November 1, 2005, I had the opportunity to work as the second rider for the Hoback Stock Association, and that included the first two weeks in October when I still rode roundup for the Pape Ranches. At last, my dream of "cowboying" in the West had been realized.

So this is the story of the homesteaders, ranchers and cowboys in the Hoback Basin. To the extent that I have become a small part of that tradition, it is my story as well or at least a definitive chapter in it.

Paul Jensen. *Photo by Sherrill Hudson.*

Why This Story?

When coming into the Basin from the south on U.S. 189 and over the Rim, the daylight view that stretches for miles but lasts for only seconds is almost spiritual—even by the standards of northwestern Wyoming, which is known for its scenery and views in Teton and Yellowstone National Parks. Whether it is natural beauty, rugged mountain terrain, creeks, meadows, the geology, the Elkhorn Bar or the homesteaders, cowboys, and ranchers, the Basin has character—even a "style." And, like some other ranching communities in the Rocky Mountain West, real characters have populated its more than one hundred year history and still populate its life today.

Some of those characters include: Charlie Noble, a clubfooted orphan from Missouri and one of the first ranchers in the Basin, who led the way for others; Dead Shot Swenson, a Danish immigrant who always wore a pistol, and although short in stature, made up for that with a sizeable imagination; "Mother" Williams, a very good cowboy and gambler, who looked after youngsters and helped them learn about horses, cows, and life; Johnny "Peck" May, who worked for the

Papes for forty-seven years; and the Campbells, a third-generation ranching family that still uses horses to mow hay. Each character in the Basin is distinctive and can range from eccentric to courageous, humorous, or just plain determined. More than a few were "tough as boots" cowboys.

Above all, this history will be about those characters who ranched and rode in the Basin, and those who keep that tradition alive today.

These characters tell a good story, but until now no one has given them a voice. Like many similar ranching communities, the recorded history of the Hoback Basin, the Hoback Stock Association, its ranchers and riders is nearly nonexistent. Not only are the original homesteaders long departed, but a few of those who lived or could vividly remember that history have recently died. The first was Eileen Fronk Dockham, a ranch woman, artist, and self-trained historian whose parents homesteaded in the Basin in 1918. The other was Harve Stone, who worked as the Stock Association rider for many years and raised his family at the cow camps. Fortunately, some old timers are still around and their memories, together with other sources, paint a true and colorful historical portrait of the Basin. But before they vanish and the history is lost, a more complete story of the Basin, its ranchers, and cowboys is timely and engaging.

The life stories of these characters are the stories of ordinary people who did extraordinary things. They remind us of how the West was really won, and how much of even our most recent history has been shaped by the courage and determination of "ordinary" people. Their stories deserve telling.

While the Basin is a small slice of American Western history, it is representative of the last one hundred years of that history and speaks of its translation into the twenty-first century. Today, when the West is romanticized in Western lifestyle magazines such as *The Western Horseman* (I am a subscriber) or movies, it is refreshing to find one place where authenticity and tradition still matter.

My interviews with the "old timers" revealed a feeling I recognize in myself—namely that riding the Basin was one of the best parts of their lives. Some of it is nature's making. Some of it the characters. Some the carefree days of youth. And some an intuitive sense of being part of history. But most of all the Hoback Basin is a place where anyone tough enough could—and still can— be a cowboy.

Wyoming's Frontier

The story of the Hoback Basin and Stock Association begins in the late 1890s. But the best way to appreciate the Basin's settlement and early life is first to look at it through the broader prism of Wyoming history and western expansion.

Beyond Yellowstone, Teton National Park, Jackson Hole, and Devil's Tower, most seasonal visitors and tourists can't help but notice the bucking horse on the Wyoming license plate. For visitors and even year around residents it symbolizes the "Cowboy State." That image draws on Wyoming's better-known and most flamboyant characters from the almost mythical mountain men like John Colter, Jim Bridger, and Kit Carson to Buffalo Bill Cody, who debuted his Wild West Show in 1883 and saw it play to worldwide success until 1906. Mingling within that historical stretch of time was Cattle Kate (Ella Watson), a 170 pound outlaw, prostitute and cattle rustler who, in 1889, was the only woman ever hanged in Wyoming. Then came Tom Horn, who was a cowboy, a first class steer roper, an army scout trailing Geronimo, a deputy sheriff, a livestock detective, but most notably he was a hired killer who ended his life at the end of a rope in 1903. And Butch Cassidy, the Sundance Kid and the Wild Bunch— outlaws whose exploits and uncertain dates of death have created a romantic fascination with them, and who remain an iconic part of the West.

All of these well-known characters shaped Wyoming's culture and its settlement, and further accentuated the state's image as a wild country with a frontier sensibility which was broadly enhanced by movies such as Sam Peckinpah's The Wild Bunch, and with Paul Newman, Robert Redford, and Katherine Ross, respectively, playing Butch Cassidy, the Sundance Kid, and Etta Place against the backdrop of Burt Bacharach's music.

At the same time, similar but much less well-known characters tell a more accurate, but less glamorous story of Wyoming's settlement and western expansion. John Kendrick, a young Texas cowboy, who built a huge cattle company and later became governor and a U.S. senator; Alexander H. Swan and the six hundred thousand acre Swan Land and Cattle Company; Charles Carter and the Bug Ranch; Otto Franc and the Pitchfork; Abner Luman, Sublette County pioneer who initially settled a very long stretch of land starting north at the Green River Lakes running south nearly to Rock Springs; Daniel Budd of Big Piney; and James M. Noble of Cora are very familiar names to students of Wyoming history. However, except in the communities where they ranched, few would recognize them, just as few would recognize the early ranchers and cowboys in the Hoback Basin. Many other ranchers and cowboys "made Wyoming their own," but history has not yet recorded their lives and may never do so.

Wyoming's springs, rivers, and the woodlands along them suited the beaver and the mountain men in the early to mid-1800s. But due to its aridity, altitude, wind, and vast expanses of sagebrush and mountains, few of the thousands of overland immigrants, who crossed Wyoming along the Oregon, Mormon and California Trails, chose to stay. It was said that Wyoming was "hell on women and horses." In 1870, the Census found only 9,118 people in the Territory, excluding the Indians.

The construction of the Union Pacific Railroad across southern Wyoming in the late 1860s propelled the organization of the Wyoming Territory and that territorial status was finalized on May 19, 1869. The Wyoming Territory was created mainly from Dakota Territory and then squared out from small portions of Idaho and Utah. Generally, the railroad had followed the settlement of the West and established population centers, but in Wyoming it created civilization. The railroad led to the first real cities in the Territory such as Cheyenne, Laramie, Green River and then later Rawlins, Rock Springs and Evanston. Yet by 1880 Wyoming still had just barely over twenty thousand non-Native American residents.

Reflecting the virtues of the open range and warmer winters, the 450,000 cattle in 1879 jumped to a million and a half by 1885—a ratio of one person to seventy-five head of cattle.

Yet even the cattle boom of the 1880s did not entice a rush of people, and except for the coal needed by the railroads, the development of the state's energy resources was further in the future. Between 1880 and 1890 the Territory grew by 40,000 and its population by 1890 stood at 62,555 people. By comparison, Kansas had 1,400,000; Nebraska 1,000,000; Colorado 400,000 and South Dakota 350,000 people.

Despite this limited growth, which would characterize its entire history, Wyoming achieved statehood on July 10, 1890. This late development explains why, when compared to the rest of the West, Wyoming's history is relatively recent. It means that the first ranchers and cowboys are not a long look back in history's rearview mirror. And that today their ancestors by blood or tradition are not that far removed in time or space.

In 1893, Lander, Wyoming, held the first commercial rodeo

including entry fees, tickets, money purses for the winners, and advertising. In September, 1897, Cheyenne celebrated its first Frontier Days, and cowboys suddenly became socially acceptable and began to play the part. In 1902, influenced by his summers on a Wyoming ranch, Owen Wister, an easterner, published *The Virginian* which firmly rooted the mythic West and its hero in the American imagination. The Wyoming cowboy had started his journey to become one of America's most enduring icons.

Beginning in the 1890s, the first ranchers and cowboys settled in the Hoback Basin. They built on Wyoming's tradition of the cowboy, but made that tradition their own.

Wyoming and the Rest of the West

Other happenings in the West in the last half of the nineteenth century forged life in Wyoming and the Basin. A quick look at them can advance the understanding of Wyoming and the Hoback Basin's place in the West.

First, the Civil War that wracked the nation and ended in late spring 1865 ironically benefited Wyoming and the rest of the Great Plains and Rocky Mountain West. It accounts for the growth of the cattle industry and the emergence of the cowboy. After the war, beef was in short supply, particularly in the East. The mining towns and army forts in the West added to that demand. The construction of the transcontinental railroad and its work force further increased the need and desire for more beef.

With the destruction of much of the South, including Texas, Confederate soldiers had few opportunities beyond working and trailing Texas cattle. At first, these longhorns of Spanish descent were the most readily available supply of beef. Thus began the legendary cattle drives on the Goodnight-Loving Trail to Colorado, the

Chisholm Trail to Abilene, Kansas, and the Montana Trail farther north.

Eventually the demand for higher quality beef and the completion of the railroad and its spurs led to America's adoption of English breeds like the Hereford and Angus and prompted the growth of ranching in Wyoming and Montana. The relatively short distance to the rail hubs did not require the toughness of the longhorn and that allowed the production of better beef. With both domestic and foreign investment flooding into the cattle business and the open range, the 1880s heard the cattle boom echo across the West, but particularly in Wyoming and Montana.

Overgrazing on the open range and the killer winter of 1886-1887 when drifting cattle died by the thousands, brought a big change to the cattle industry. Improved breeds of cattle, hay production and winter-feeding, water rights and fencing ushered in a new era of ranch management. The arrival of sheep and more homesteaders accelerated these trends; particularly the barbed wire fence that was designed to keep sheep and other livestock off the bigger ranches and ranges. Those same trends led to the formation of local stock associations that could protect the interests of cattle ranchers and eventually to the creation of grazing permits on public land.

The Civil War provided another stimulant to the growth of the West. In 1860-1861 the pro-slavery South withdrew from the Union. As the South had opposed the growth of free states in the West, its secession allowed the Congress to pass and President Lincoln to sign the first true free land act, the Homestead Act of 1862.

Under that Act any U.S. citizen, who was over twenty-one and not an enemy of the United States Government, could file on no more than 160 acres of unappropriated public land. The land could only be used for settlement and cultivation and had to be lived on for five years. At the end of those five years, two witnesses were required to verify that the land had been "proven up."

As settlers finally arrived in the more arid parts of the West like Wyoming, Montana and Utah, 160 acres or a quarter of a section was way too small for cattle ranching. Roughly forty acres were required per animal so 160 acres would allow just four head. Under the Timber Culture Act of 1873, a person could get 160 acres free if he or she agreed to plant and keep growing trees on forty acres for eight years. Then came the Desert Land Act of 1877 where for twenty-five cents an acre, a person could buy up to 320 acres of desert land—land that could not be cultivated without water. After three years and an additional dollar per acre, the person could gain title, but they had to irrigate part of it to receive the patent.

Even though some settlers took advantage of the Timber Culture and Desert Land Act, the Homestead Act gave the greatest impetus to western expansion. Throughout the West 1,623,691 homestead claims were carried to patent.

In order to further improve the transfer of public lands to settlers in the West, Congress passed the Forest Homestead Act of 1906 that allowed settlers to claim forest reserve land at a cost of $2.50 per acre. Then came the popular Stock Raising Homestead Act in 1916 where settlers could claim 640 acres of public land designated by the Secretary of Interior. Those settlers were required to make permanent improvements like buildings, wells and fences that amounted to at least $1.25 per acre.

Except for reclamation projects, the Homestead Act was finally rescinded by the Taylor Grazing Act of 1934 and its companion Executive Order. That law allowed the Department of Interior to keep the bulk of its remaining land. Administered by the department, grazing districts were established on 173,000,000 acres of withdrawn land with approximately 16,000,000 of those in Wyoming. This acreage did not and does not include the national forests and the grazing permits issued on them. The national forests and their grazing policy were established much earlier in the twentieth century.

Nevertheless, the lax enforcement of the homesteading laws,

particularly the Homestead Act, allowed double entry, relatives filing entries, and even cowboys filing for their bosses. Eventually these patents could be purchased back by the rancher or he could buy out the other surrounding homesteaders who decided to leave. In this manner, the larger ranches were created.

Not surprisingly, in Wyoming the explosion in land filings came in the 1880s. For example, in the 1870s only 365 entries were filed compared with 10,962 in the 1880s. But like other territories, many did not lead to patents and by the time of statehood, not more than ten percent of Wyoming land had been patented or cultivated and lived on for five years.

Despite Wyoming's rough country and lifestyle, the completion of the coast-to-coast telegraph in 1861 and the transcontinental railroad in 1869 created a communication and transportation network that could support some future economic and population growth.

Starting in the late 1870s, the dime novels, particularly those published by Erastus Beadle in New York City, helped as much as anything else to develop the image and broaden the appeal of the Cowboy State. The novels introduced to a mass audience romantic Western heroes like Deadwood Dick, Calamity Jane and finally, Buffalo Bill Cody.

The creation of Yellowstone National Park in 1872, the first national park in the world, and the advent of the great Western painters and illustrators, Thomas Moran, Charlie Russell, and Frederick Remington further established the beauty of the country and portrayed cowboys, ranchers and Plains Indians in a manner that resonated with the rest of America. By then the frontier life, the West, and the cowboy began to seep into America's imagination, and Wyoming was becoming the stage for these mythical dramas.

The photographer and painter, William Henry Jackson, amplified these images, and then authors and novelists like Owen Wister further embedded them. More recently that artistic and literary tradition has been carried forward by people like Lynn Thomas in Boulder, Wyoming, Kay Meeks from Daniel, Tucker Smith in Pinedale, Fred Pfulghoft also of Pinedale, Jo Mack in Bondurant, Wyoming, the writer, Gretel Ehrlich, now of Cora, Wyoming, with her book, *The Solace of Open Spaces*, published in 1985 and Teresa Jordan, who wrote *Riding the White Horse Home* in 1993.

The Wyoming Cowboy

For almost sixty-five years after the exploration and opening of the West by Lewis and Clark, most settlers and development skipped Wyoming. The aridity, land, and its harsh climate were just too intimidating.

Even the latter stages of the traditional pattern of frontier settlement bypassed Wyoming. In much of the West the buffalo trail gave way to the Indian trail. The hunters and traders arrived and were followed by the ranchers, who came for the grasslands and open range. Next, the rich soil of the river valleys attracted the farmers, who built roads, bridges, mills, schools and churches. The next wave brought the entrepreneurs who, with investment capital, began manufacturing, built factories and diversified the economy. The property of the original settlers increased in value, and they could sell at a sizable profit. Then, as a person of capital, they might move to the next edge of the frontier and contribute to or begin that community's cycle of development.

For most of the nineteenth century and beyond—with its land

unsuitable for farming—Wyoming passed from the mountain men to the ranchers or coal miners and did not move to the more technologically advanced and diverse stages of development.

What early growth and economic stability did occur was primarily attributable to ranching, where Wyoming's grasses, rivers, open spaces, and range comprised its comparative advantage. The railroad provided the means to transport cattle to large and far away markets like Omaha and Chicago. So began the evolution of Wyoming's natural resource based (and boom or bust) economy which always relied on ranching, but which continued with energy development that was first tied to coal, then to oil and finally to natural gas. Today, Wyoming's energy industry is dominated by natural gas and coal.

Next, the strength and vitality of Wyoming's cattle industry and evolving towns can be traced to the availability of the public lands where, during the summer, cattle grazed. And the public domain continued to play an increasing role in the development of ranching, the dude ranch industry, the energy industry, and tourism.

Wyoming has been and remains something of an anomaly. First, it is a state with a small homogeneous population. It is the least populated state in the U.S., and failing to diversify, its economy is still dependent on natural resources. At the same time Wyoming is a state with a beauty, history and characters that have been romanticized by artists and in turn the public.

Ironically, the very features of the country and its wildness that earlier discouraged development are the same ones which animate the present Western mythology and the state's real Western appeal.

These contradictory forces bring forward the last observations on the broader role of the Western frontier. Like his predecessors further east, the Western homesteader found new opportunity, escape from the dictates of the past and an ever-changing society that required experimentation in contrast to tradition and custom.

Mobility was the essence of the frontier West. Otherwise no one would have settled it. Free land and an absence of hereditary or economic class structures fostered a belief in equality and democratic institutions.

These beliefs and experiences forged in the Western frontier became the quintessential features of the American character. Add a sense of freedom and independence and the cowboy jumps off the page. That helps explain America's love affair with the West, the cowboy, and Wyoming's part in it.

Wyoming Today

According to the 2000 Census, Wyoming claimed 493,782 of the 281,421,906 residents in the U.S. When compared to the populations of every other state and the District of Columbia, Wyoming has the fewest number of people. Montana had 902,195 residents and Idaho 1,293,953.

According to the Wyoming Game and Fish Department, in 2004 the state had a total population of 457,00 pronghorn antelope. In 2004 Wyoming had 1,400,000 cattle, nearly three head per person.

The Census estimates for 2005 shows Wyoming growing three percent between 2000 and 2005, compared to a U.S. population growth of five percent in the same period.

Wyoming has a land area of 97,100 square miles and it is estimated that sixty percent of that is sagebrush. With respect to population density, Wyoming has 5.1 people per square mile compared to the average density of 79.6 for the country. Compared to every other state in the continental U.S., Wyoming has the fewest people per square mile. Montana has 6.2 but almost 50,000 more

PAUL JENSEN

square miles than Wyoming. Idaho has 15.6 people per square mile. And the densest state in the U.S., New Jersey, has 1,134 people per square mile.

In 2000, Wyoming's population was 92.1 percent white compared to the country's average of 75.1 percent.

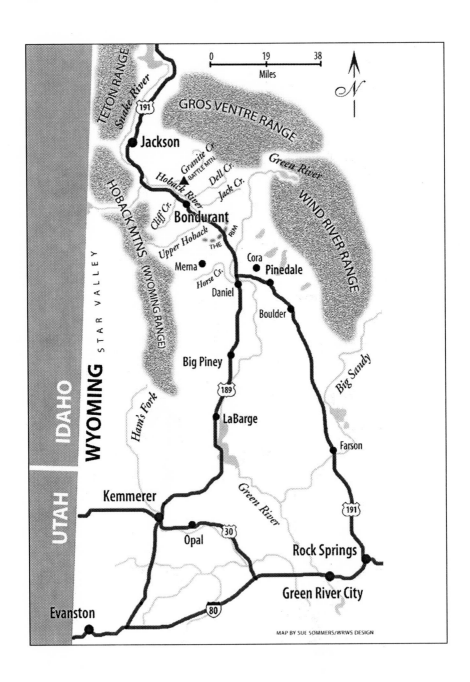

MAP BY SUE SOMMERS/WRWS DESIGN

Part Two

The Place:
Its Exploration and Ranching Heritage

PAUL JENSEN

The vastness, the space, the sheer bigness of the Western landscape shaped the life and character of those who settled the Hoback Basin and still live there. The aridity, matched with the altitude of its mountains and the flatness of its deserts, gives colors, clarity and ever-changing light that inspire painters and photographers. Those same visual displays stick in the memory of all who take time to see.

But like all places in the West, nature's gift can quickly change its wrapping and bestow punishing weather, isolation, and hardship.

The Hoback Basin lies forty miles north and west of Pinedale, Wyoming, near the town of Bondurant, which is home to about one hundred people. It is about thirty minutes south and east of Jackson Hole through the mountainous Hoback Canyon. Although known as the "Little Hole" during the mountain man era, by the late nineteenth century, it was called the Fall River Basin.

The Basin is the headwaters of the Hoback River, also formerly known as the Fall River, which flows into the Snake and Columbia Rivers and finally the Pacific Ocean. Coming north from Pinedale after thirty minutes, a traveler will meet the eight thousand foot Rim of the Hoback Basin, a small pass that is the topographical divide between the Green and the Colorado River drainages, and the Snake and Columbia River drainages. The Gros Ventre Range frames the northeastern side of the Basin. That mountain range encompasses the

Gros Ventre Wilderness and the Shoal Creek Wilderness Study Area.

The main tributaries of the Hoback River are Fisherman Creek flowing from the east; Shoal Creek, whose headwaters are in the Gros Ventre; Jack and Dell Creeks originating farther northeast toward the Gros Ventre; Cliff Creek northwest of Bondurant and just above the mouth of the Hoback Canyon; and Granite Creek even further up the Canyon flowing from the northeast. Lesser tributaries in the Upper Hoback like Jamb Creek, Creased Dog Creek, and Kilgore Creek flow into the Hoback River.

The Basin terrain varies from rolling gentle slopes to very rough and steep slopes including mountainous terrain. The elevation ranges from seven to over eight thousand feet, and the soil varies from sandy loam to gray gumbo clay. Sagebrush, aspens, and conifers dominate. Unless sprayed and controlled, certain areas throughout the Basin are suitable for high growth larkspur and, since the early days, its poison has posed a deadly threat to cattle.

The Basin's average annual temperature is 33.3 degrees Fahrenheit. The winters in the Basin are normally more severe than surrounding areas, with average winter temperature reaching 10.5°. The average annual snowfall is 138.4 inches or about 11.5 feet. The average summer temperature is 54.4°, and the average fall temperature drops to 35.5°. Frost can and does occur within any given month throughout the year.

Historically, these temperatures and the snowfall insured that only the hardiest pioneers settled and ranched in the Basin. This ordeal by weather drove away the adventurers and dream seekers.

Precipitation averages between twelve to twenty-two inches annually, with most of it coming in the form of snow during the winter months. The snowmelt and spring runoff is normally intense. The Basin has an annual average runoff of almost seventeen inches.

Although known at the beginning of this century as the Fall River Basin, since 1811 (and named by John Hoback), the upper end of the canyon near Jackson Hole and today's Hoback Junction may always have been known as the Hoback Canyon. Nevertheless, two competing explanations for the name, Fall River, have been offered: First, the very heavy spring runoff dramatically raises the water level and after the snowmelt, the level of the river drops or "falls" precipitously. The other holds that from its headwaters, the river steeply descends into the canyon, and the elevation of the river "falls" significantly. Whatever the explanation, the name, Fall River, persisted for over thirty years.

The Basin: In the Beginning

In any setting, the people, their way of life, and their culture are influenced by natural resources, topography, landscape, and climate. The Hoback Basin permits a special look at the interplay of these forces and their geologic foundation.

As a matter of rock structure, the Rim and the Hoback Basin sit on top of the northern Green River Basin. That Basin is the rock icing on top of various other rock layers dating from earlier times. This would contrast with a river drainage that in today's parlance is also called a "basin." The northern Green River Basin is a sediment-filled basin between the thin-skinned overthrust belt to the west that includes the Hoback Mountains and the Gros Ventre and Wind River Mountains to the northeast, which, along deep-cutting thrust faults, expose much older Precambrian rocks at the surface. Those rocks range from two to three billion years old, when the most elemental life forms were just beginning to emerge.

The thrust faults were cracks or fractures in the Earth's crust that formed during the tectonic plate collision to the west and the resulting Sevier and Laramide mountain building events. That collision created the fissures in the surrounding rock that were further deformed as the two sides of the fracture started rubbing against each other.

The low hills and rock outcroppings surrounding the Basin and the Canyon are varicolored sandstone and shale, dropped as stream and flood plain sediment about fifty-five million years ago—in geologic time that was just yesterday. Over the intervening millions of years, basin filling continued, and coal, oil, natural gas and other minerals were created, along with the prospect of future wealth and conflict with other uses and values. The canyons of Wyoming were cut. Yellowstone erupted. The Tetons uplifted. And 200,000 years ago glaciers shaped the Wind River Mountains, the Hobacks and adjacent areas creating valleys, glacial lakes, and landscape as erosion and weathering of the mountains continued.

Moving into more familiar geologic time and history, the forces that formed the Hoback Basin, surrounding mountains, streams and rivers created a habitat very suitable for wildlife, including buffalo. Without extensive vegetative cover, the Basin and its lower elevations provided large quantities of pasture for the wildlife that first attracted the Indians such as the Shoshones, Crows and Arapahos and then, later, the mountain men. Soon the first ranchers came with their cattle and sheep. Within just a few years more ranchers and homesteaders arrived, and they became the more permanent residents of the Hoback country.

Not surprisingly, about two hundred years ago the Hoback Basin and its contours sat at the crossroads of America's earliest exploration.

During the 1830s and 1840s such singular mountain men as Jim Bridger and Tom Fitzpatrick and the mountain trading fairs or rendezvous on the Green River near Daniel, Wyoming, dominated the history of Rocky Mountain and Wyoming exploration. However, the Hoback Basin stood on the frontier of exploration and just behind Lewis and Clark.

The trek that brought the first explorers and white men to the Rim, through the Basin and down the Canyon, began in the spring of 1811—five years after the conclusion of the Lewis and Clark expedition. Wilson Price Hunt, a twenty-six year old St. Louis businessman with no mountaineering or outdoor experience, was chosen by John Jacob Astor to lead an overland expedition from St. Louis up the Missouri to the Columbia and on to Astoria, the American Fur Trade Company's settlement on Oregon's Pacific coast. This trip marked the second crossing of the continent. Astor, its architect, was a German immigrant, who had settled in New York and built a national business empire based on the fur trade. Even though the Astoria outpost finally failed, like many successful entrepreneurs, he reorganized the business.

Seeking knowledge of the middle Rocky Mountain wilderness and guides for the expedition, Hunt hired John Hoback, Jacob Reznor and Edward Robinson. Robinson was then a remarkable sixty-six year old who, during the earlier Indian wars in Kentucky, had lost his scalp. After that he always wore a handkerchief tied over his head. Together all three had trapped the headwaters of the Missouri and Snake Rivers from 1807 to 1810. They were friends from Kentucky, and when hired by Hunt, the three were on their way home. The Astorian party of sixty-two men, eighty-two horses, one woman and two children—the woman and children were the Indian family of Pierre Dorian, the expedition's interpreter— embarked up the Missouri well south of the Yellowstone River. After Sacagawea, Dorian's Indian wife was the second woman known to cross the continent.

After struggling through the Big Horn Mountains and over Union Pass, the Kentuckians led the Astorians to the Green River and camped just south of the Rim where they traded with the Snake or Shoshone Indians, killed buffalo, and further prepared for the next phase of their journey. Hoback, Robinson and Reznor led the expedition through the Hoback Basin, descended the river and canyon that led to the Snake River and southern edge of Jackson Hole. When Hoback and his party reached the upper end of the canyon near the confluence of the Hoback and Snake Rivers, they paused long enough for him to name that stretch of the river and canyon after himself. Some have claimed that it was Hunt, who named the river after his guide, but Hunt's diaries only refer to the Hoback as the "small river."

After crossing Teton Pass and reaching Henry's Fort on the Snake River in Idaho, the trio left the expedition to trap in their old hunting grounds—for the benefit of the American Fur Company and themselves.

During the winter and spring of 1812, the three were robbed twice by the Arapahos. Nearly destitute, they fortunately reunited briefly with another Astorian, Robert Stuart, who was returning to the East from Astoria. They took him up the Hoback Canyon to the Upper Green—just the opposite direction they took Hunt. Stuart's diaries were the first written reference to the "Hoback River."

A little later Stuart would discover South Pass, but throughout most of his lifetime he remained unaware of its importance as the route through the Northern Rockies. After leaving Stuart, the three Kentuckians successfully trapped along the Snake River from the fall of 1812 to the fall of 1813. During the winter of 1813 , all three were killed and dismembered by Indians. Hoback and Robinson were killed near the confluence of the Boise and Snake Rivers in Idaho. Farther up the Boise River, Jacob Reznor was killed in the company of Pierre Dorian and John Reed, another trapper.

Pierre Dorian's wife, whose Indian name has been lost to history, and her two children stayed at the base camp some miles from the murder scene. However, after seeing the dismembered bodies, she left immediately on horseback. Her young children sat in front of her. On their first night they ran into a snowstorm. They barely survived, but eventually ended up in Oregon where she remarried, took the name, Marie, and had three more children. Her family lived on a farm in the Willamette Valley, and she died in 1850.

Like John Colter, Hoback and his two friends were the precursors of most mountain men, who spanned just a single generation. Aside from the Kentuckians' geographic knowledge, which was not widely shared, Hoback's remaining legacy was the Canyon initially named by him and its importance as a connector to the Snake River running north and the Green River moving south.

Later, other mountain men crossed through the Basin on their way from the Green River rendezvous to the beaver-rich country north of Jackson Hole. In the 1840s Lieutenant John C. Fremont entered the Basin during one of his mapping expeditions. On August 29, 1835, the first Protestant sermon in the Rocky Mountains was preached by Reverend Samuel Parker at the head of the Hoback Canyon, where later the V-V Guest Ranch would be located. Parker came to the area in the company of 250 hunters and trappers. They camped on Saturday, August 28, and planned to stay until Monday. It has been reported that Jim Bridger, Kit Carson, and Jedediah Smith attended the service. However, Parker's diaries related that when he was nearly finished with his sermon, a herd of buffalo appeared on a hillside north of the camp. Within minutes his audience, save for some older Indians, left for the buffalo hunt, killing twenty-five animals. Later the collection plate was filled with buffalo steaks.

Wyoming Tribes

Historically, the Shoshone Indians formed the largest and most distinctive tribe in Wyoming. The precise origin of their name is unclear, but due to a tribal sign made by a snake-like motion of the hand with the index finger extended, white men called them the Snakes. Since other tribes called them Grass House People, it is likely that the serpentine motion signified the weaving of grasses into the frames of their houses.

The Shoshone lived mainly in central Wyoming and southern Idaho. The Western Shoshone, who occupied Idaho, shared a more primitive agrarian life and accordingly were often called the Diggers. The Eastern and Northern Shoshone were horsemen, hunters, warriors and finally peacemakers.

Initially, the Shoshone lived and roamed in an extensive geography that spread from Alberta, Canada, in the north through southwestern Montana, central and western Wyoming, southern Idaho and northern Utah. They shared some of this territory with the Bannocks, who were close allies—hunting together, fighting common enemies and intermarrying. Although culturally an identifiable tribe, eventually the Bannocks were absorbed by the Shoshones. In 1845 the Northern Shoshone numbered three thousand and the Bannocks one thousand.

With a horse culture and living in a geography teeming with buffalo, the Shoshone thrived and dominated this large area for most of the 1700s. When the Sioux or Dakotas pushed tribes like the Arapaho out of their native land in Minnesota into the northern mountains and plateaus, Shoshone territory became more circumscribed. Attracted by plentiful game, some Crows settled on the eastern side of the Big Horn Mountains, taking away more Shoshone land. The Blackfeet from Montana and Sioux from the Dakota Territory hunted and raided Shoshone country, forcing the Shoshone into Wyoming and northern Idaho

As the Arapaho moved into eastern Wyoming, they and the Shoshone became bitter enemies. The Cheyenne, who shared the Big Horns with the Arapaho, who had also been forced west by the Sioux, formed a firm and long lasting alliance. The Arapaho's culinary taste for dog stew led to their name, Dog Eaters, a term used derisively by the Shoshone and their allies. The final irony of this rivalry came about when the federal government's callous ignorance or malevolent design placed both tribes on the same reservation in Wyoming.

Lewis and Clark's expedition gained distinction as the first white men to meet the Shoshone. Of course, the best known Shoshone, Sacagawea, traveled with the expedition and assisted with Indian affairs. She served as an interpreter and secured horses, supplies and directions for their route through the mountains.

Next came the trappers and mountain men. Their rendezvous along the Green River near Daniel took place in Shoshone territory, and the Shoshone aided, traded and celebrated with the mountain men.

The almost neverending fleet of covered wagons floating through Wyoming brought the white man's first sizable disruption of

Shoshone life. Killing game, pasturing livestock and camping on their grasslands, the wagon trains prompted attacks by the Shoshone. Those attacks and retaliation against white settlers and overland mail coaches continued from the mid-1840s to the early 1860s. After a massacre of several hundred Shoshone by U.S. soldiers, they entered into a federal treaty in 1864 that established their first reservation around Fort Hall in Idaho.

Except for a renegade bunch of young Shoshone warriors who joined Bannock Chief, Buffalo Horn, in the brief "Bannock War" of 1878, the Wind River and Eastern Shoshone escaped engagement in the post-Civil War Indian Wars that ran from 1865-1891. Instead, they emerged as allies of the whites, fighting their old enemies, the Sioux. In order to retain their independence and culture, the Shoshone fostered this white alliance and navigated that difficult period under the leadership of Chief Washakie, a Shoshone of legendary proportions.

During the 1920s and 1940s the Shoshone created a helpful precedent for other tribes by successfully adjudicating their claims to their land and mineral wealth. Today, they live on the two million acres of the Wind River Reservation near Lander, Wyoming, and the one half a million acre Fort Hall Reservation on the Snake River in southern Idaho. In Wyoming, the Indian population totals 11,530.

The Origin of Sublette County

While still part of Dakota Territory, in January, 1867, the Territorial Legislature organized all of present day Wyoming into a single county, Laramie County, with Fort Sanders as the county seat. At that time a total of fifteen hundred whites lived in Wyoming. Fearing Indian attacks, most initially settled near the Fort. During Dakota's next legislative session from December, 1868 to January, 1869, the legislators carved two new counties, Albany and Carbon, from the western part of Laramie County. As long thin rectangles stretching from the southern border of today's Wyoming to the northern border, from east to west the line-up was Laramie, Albany, Carbon and later Carter County. The land bumping up against the large western part of the state continued as an unorganized part of Wyoming.

By then a Territory, the Wyoming Territorial Legislature, briefly composed of all Democrats, convened at noon in October, 1869, and created Uinta County from the unorganized strip on the western edge; changed the boundaries of the other three counties and renamed Carter County, Sweetwater. During this same session and overriding a veto by Governor John Campbell, who was a Republican from Ohio appointed by President Grant, the legislature voted to license gambling and prevent intermarriage between whites and those of "Negro or Mongolian blood."

It would take another fifty-two years and the addition of sixteen new counties before Sublette County would find its place in Wyoming.

Prior to Sublette County's creation, residents were first encompassed by Uinta County whose county seat was Evanston. After the addition of Fremont County, which was carved out of Sweetwater County in 1884, any Sublette citizen who needed to conduct county business had to travel to either Evanston or Lander, the seat of Fremont County. At the same time, that distance and dual jurisdiction limited the application or enforcement of any county laws or regulations.

Adding to the confusion, in 1911 when the legislature carved Lincoln County out of Uinta County, residents could travel to Lander or Kemmerer, Lincoln's county seat. At last, in 1921, when Sublette County had been formed, the citizens chose, by the narrowest of margins, Pinedale as the county seat over Big Piney, creating a rivalry that continues today.

The county's name came from "Billy" Sublette, who trapped and attended rendezvous on the Green River near Daniel in the 1820s and 1830s. A man of talent, energy, leadership skills, and kindness, Sublette became not only an accomplished mountain man but a very successful businessman. With Jedediah Smith, he rediscovered South Pass, which allowed trappers easy access to the unexploited Green River country. In 1826, with Jedediah Smith and David E. Jackson, he spearheaded the purchase of General William Ashley's fur company. Although he remained active in the fur and trading business, Sublette and his partners sold the company in 1830. In 1836 he retired to St. Louis where, as a gentleman farmer, he started a thriving business with a racetrack and hotel. Ironically, Sublette was an ardent Democrat. (Today, Sublette County is overwhelmingly Republican.) In the 1840s he became ill with tuberculosis. In 1845, on his way to Cape May, New Jersey, for treatment, he died in a Pittsburgh hotel. He was forty-six.

Sublette County contains 4,883 square miles and has 1.2 people per square mile. That density compares to Wyoming's 5.1 people per square mile and the U.S.'s 79.6. In 2005, the county's population totaled 6,926.

The First Ranchers and Cowboys

Like the mountain men, these cowboys and ranchers were explorers. They explored the Basin and embraced personal freedom, courage and self-reliance. They came from different backgrounds, but shared the vision of a better life. Some were colorful. Some were odd. Most stuck it out in the Hoback Basin. The "stickers" were ordinary men and women who won against the odds and settled the wilderness. These uncelebrated heroes built a distinctive ranching and cowboy heritage.

Those everyday heroes, who settled, built their ranches or worked as cowboys in the Basin, are the subjects of this book. Not only have they been united by their experience and the place they lived, but they have been tied together by the Hoback Stock Association. Although this story is mainly about people, it is also the story of this special Association. Some people and members of the Stock Association are more central to this story than others, and they will get more attention, particularly in the later chapters.

Throughout this chapter and the next three parts, I have tried to give each individual more life and texture than might be found in similar histories. Historically accurate anecdotes and stories help accomplish that. However, where no or little biographical information about a person had been previously published or was misleading, I incorporated a short biography. Although occasionally the biographies may interrupt the flow of the narrative, they preserve a history heretofore unknown and provide an important chronological context for that person's life and this history. I should also note that in Parts Two, Three, and Four, the characters have been mainly introduced in the order in which they settled or homesteaded in the Basin. For example, those who settled early precede those pioneers who came later.

At times, the reader may also want more information or stories about a family or individual, particularly the frontier women. More than anyone else, I wanted to present richer characters, but in most of those cases no verifiable history or even hearsay was found.

During the late 1870s, the early settlement of today's Sublette County started just outside the southern end of the county near Fontenelle and LaBarge and progressed north to Big Piney, Cottonwood Creek, Daniel, and finally to the Hoback Basin. Along the way, other settlers and ranchers established homesteads on the east side of the Green River, at Cora, Pinedale and Boulder. Many of those same settlers and ranchers helped shape the history of the Upper Green River Valley, but they have been the subjects of other histories.

From the 1880s to the 1940s the cattle from Big Piney, Cottonwood Creek, Daniel, and the Fall River or Hoback Basin were trailed to the nearest railhead and shipped east to the stockyards in Omaha or Chicago. The first shipping point was located in Granger, Wyoming, and from Big Piney it was a six to seven day ride south. After the completion of the Oregon Short Line Railroad in 1881, a lengthy northwestern spur of the Union Pacific, the cattle were trailed to Opal. If the cattle behaved and the weather held up, it was just a five day trail ride from Big Piney. Without cattle, one rancher rode from Opal to his ranch north of Big Piney in one day, but he killed his horse. By 1895, Opal shipped more cattle, sheep and wool than any other town in Wyoming. It was not uncommon for one or two ranchers to fill forty rail cars. Opal and its mercantile also served as the major trading and freighting center for the settlers in Big Piney and for those further north in Daniel and Fall River.

A wide range of ranchers, particularly those in Big Piney, played pivotal roles in the county's settlement and identity, but only a few stood as points of reference for early ranching in the Hoback Basin. Those Big Piney ranchers included Daniel Brockius Budd and his partner, Hugh McKay, who came to the Big Piney area in 1879. With somewhere between eight hundred and a thousand head of yearlings from his brother's estate in Nevada, known as the Empire Ranch, Budd and McKay started the 67 Ranch. Due to inclement weather and raucous cattle, it took a few months for Budd, McKay, and a Nevada cowboy, Amos W. Smith, to trail them to Big Piney.

Amos "Piney" Smith continued working for the 67 and later established the Muleshoe Ranch on North Piney Creek, and in 1884, he bought the 67 from Hugh McKay, who earlier had bought out Budd's share of the ranch. Later, one of Dan B. Budd's sons, Jesse, ran his cattle in the Hoback Basin, and the Muleshoe Ranch ended up with a special connection to the Basin, too. Finally and most important to this story, the Noble brothers, Eugene and Zach, established their ranches in Big Piney and later their brother, James, ranched in Cora and started a family dynasty there.

Zack Noble

The first recorded rancher who summered his cattle in the Hoback Basin was Big Piney's Zachary "Zach" Noble. In 1891, he bought his Basin ranch. The Noble boys—Zach, Eugene, and James—were born in Burlington, Iowa, and all became successful ranchers and businessmen.

Zach arrived in Chugwater, Wyoming, in 1880 where he worked for the Swan Cattle Company for two years. It was one of the largest ranches in Wyoming and had been bankrolled by Scottish investors. He then moved to Nebraska near the North Platte. During the next five years Zach and his family worked for three different ranches.

Between 1887 and 1888, the Nobles moved to Big Piney and during the first winter lived in a cabin on the Muleshoe Ranch. Initially he worked for a Big Piney ranch family, the Leifers, and their Circle Ranch. A little later Zach worked for their neighbor, the Swan family, who in 1878, were the first cattle ranchers in Sublette County. Their family and ranch were not related to the extensive Swan Cattle

Company in Chugwater.

In 1890, Zach Noble bought his own ranch on South Piney Creek from Walt Nichols, who with his wife, Julia, ran the first general store in Big Piney. The store was located about a mile west of town. Since she offered hot baths, homemade meals for the cowboys and made their red woolen long underwear, Mrs. Nichols became a local hero with the Big Piney cowboys—some who later rode in the Hoback or Fall River Basin.

The same year that Zach Noble bought his first ranch, 1890, Wyoming joined the Union as the forty-fourth state and the Wounded Knee Massacre ended the Indian Wars.

Zach was Charlie Noble's foster father, and in 1893 when Charlie turned fourteen he started working in the Basin. That year and for the next few he was the lone cowboy in the Basin, tending around two hundred head of cattle. It was on-the-job training with no mentor.

Charlie began building his own herd, and it has been reported that when he started running his cattle in the Fall River Basin in 1899 he already had about seventeen hundred head.

U.S. Forest Service homesteading records show that on July 29, 1901, Charlie filed his first homestead entry in the Basin and in 1911 added more acreage to it. Although getting a little ahead of the story, beyond that acreage, in 1913 he bought the Big Piney and Basin ranches from his foster father, who then returned to Iowa.

Elsewhere in the world, the Spanish American War was declared and ended in 1898. Riding the coattails of the Rough Riders and their "invasion" of Cuba, Teddy Roosevelt was elected governor of New York in 1898. In 1900 he accepted the vice presidential nomination joining the ticket of President William McKinley, who was running for a second term. Following McKinley's election and assassination in 1901, Roosevelt became president.

Joining Charlie for the 1899 initial trip to the Fall River Basin were two other Big Piney ranchers and cowboys, Elias H. "Link" Shideler and Johnnie Curtis. In the early spring of that year they moved their cattle up a narrow trail through high country and high water, over the Rim and down into the Basin. That cattle drive was sixty miles. Depending on how the cattle moved and the weather, it could take five days or more—a tribute to the grass and the open range of the Basin. After a few more trips, the trail widened out and it became known as the Noble Trail. Until the later development of the Sanford Trail, it served all of the Big Piney and Daniel ranchers who summered their cattle in the Basin.

Just down from the Rim and across Coyote Gulch sits a large basin where the early ranchers pastured their cattle when they first arrived in the Fall River country. Later it was named Noble Basin.

In the early years and wanting to get the cattle on summer pasture more quickly than is permitted today, the ranchers often trailed out before the snowpack had melted. In late March or early April, the snow softened and melted in the warmth of the day. That snow condition caused the cattle to work much harder and slowed them down. As a result, the ranchers waited until evening when the snow crust had frozen again. The cattle walked right on top of the snow crust, and they moved faster and with less stress

However, they often hit the Rim during May, and in those years calves were branded in the Basin. Generally the ranchers rounded up and cut out their beef no later than the first of November. The cattle were driven back on the Noble Trail to Big Piney and then to Opal—a one hundred and forty mile trip with the ranches along the way serving as rest stops.

Those first ranchers formed the Fall River Association, the predecessor of the Hoback Stock Association. Its boundaries appear to have been similar to those of the Hoback Cattle and Horse Allotment that contains the Upper Hoback, Cliff Creek and Shoal Creek. Its first officers were Charlie Noble, president, and Elias "Link" Shideler, vice president. In those very early days, Johnnie Curtis drove the mess wagon for the Association. Later, these ranchers were joined by Guy Carr from Big Piney, who until the early 1920s rode for the

Association. Later his brother, Bill, rode for Charlie Noble.

Although Charlie Noble reappears later in the story, the other two ranching pioneers will take their well deserved bows now.

Link Shideler roping, circa 1900.
Photo courtesy of the Green River Valley Museum.

Link Shideler

Link had a round face punctuated with a bushy moustache, worn throughout his life to hide a harelip. When on horseback, he wore his revolver. But Link was a good working cowboy and rancher, and to the delight of many, he played the fiddle and joined others who played for the dances in Big Piney.

The dances were first held in an octagonal log building near Piney Smith's ranch, the Muleshoe, where everyone "parked" their buckboards or buggies. From sundown to sunup, Link's fiddle sang out waltzes, polkas, schottisches and Virginia reels. The Christmas, New Year, and St. Patrick's Day dances were the social highlights of the year, and Link and his fiddle became a standard fixture. Also, on occasion during these dances, he was known to have pounded out piano chords.

When not playing at the dances, Link still liked to find the local action. Close to town, he rode to the Big Piney bar, the Bucket of Blood, and when his family needed to reach him, they called the bar. As a result, he became known as the "missing Link" in the Shideler family. That explains how his given name, Elias, gave way to "Link."

Link was born on October 10, 1873. His mother, Mary Ann, or Anna, with her first husband, Francis Angus, emigrated from Scotland to Canada. They were married in Montreal in 1861, and had two children: Margaret born in 1862 and John, born in 1864. After their father's death, their mother married Jacob Shideler and had seven more children, including Link. His step-brother, John Angus, came to Wyoming from Colorado after 1877, and worked for two Big Piney ranches: Ed Swan's PL outfit and Amos "Piney" Smith's 67. That connection brought Link, his mother and two brothers into Big Piney country and ranching. Like his step-brother, Link worked at the 67 Ranch.

Link married Emma Black, who came from Texas, in 1898—just a year before he started riding in the Basin. They homesteaded three miles west of Big Piney and eventually would have a son and four daughters. About twelve or so years later, Emma suddenly died and in 1912 Link went to Texas to find Emma's sister, Mae, who he married, only to discover that she was not as compatible as her sister had been.

Link was twenty-six when he started ranching in the Fall River Basin. Later, he also homesteaded in the Basin near Charlie Noble's place but on the other side of the river. Today that property is owned by Gil Ordway and the River Bend Ranch. Although now a hayfield, it is called the Shideler field. Approaching seventy-six, Link died on August 5, 1949.

One of Link and Emma's daughters, Lorena, married Guy Carr when he was riding for Charlie Noble. Guy was born in South Pass City, Wyoming and was one of fifteen children. Later, he worked for Link Shideler on his Big Piney ranch. Lorena served for thirty-five years as the Big Piney weather representative for the National Weather Service's predecessor, the U.S. Weather Bureau, and she became a local celebrity.

Johnnie Curtis

In 1863, Johnnie Bickford Curtis was born in Boston, Massachusetts. People who knew Johnnie said he was a real character, and he must have been. He worked as a fisherman on the Massachusetts and Maine coasts, and he never lost his Boston accent. Exactly when and why he landed in Big Piney, Wyoming, and started working for Charlie Noble remains a mystery, even to his family. He had whip marks on his back, but refused to talk about that part of his life. In fact, he never imparted much about his early life and strongly stated that no one should ask.

He always wore a handkerchief around his neck and tall cowboy boots. Save for his accent, none of the cowboys would have guessed that he grew up in Massachusetts. He drove the mess wagon, cooked and laughed with them for many years.

Johnnie married Daisy Kirkendall, Minnie Swan's sister. Later, they bought and settled on part of the Swan Ranch. They had four children: Everett, who never married, Lillian, Jack and Myrtle. When she turned fourteen, Myrtle suddenly died. Johnnie's son,

PAUL JENSEN

Johnnie Curtis circa 1900.
Photo courtesy of the Green River Valley Museum.

Everett, later rode for other ranchers in Big Piney and the Ryegrass Association.

One of Johnnie's most prideful purchases was a mountain cabin about fourteen miles west of Big Piney. He paid twenty head of horses for it, and the cabin is still in the family. Like many of his contemporaries and certainly the Irish, he enjoyed a good stout drink. He enjoyed it—perhaps too much—as he had to sell part of his ranch to pay the bar bills.

Compared to those with whom he worked, like Charlie Noble and Link Shideler, by virtue of age, Johnnie claimed seniority. In 1941, at the age of seventy-eight, he died in Big Piney.

Today, people change careers frequently and often dramatically. Yet Johnnie Curtis' move from a fisherman on the Massachusetts' coast to a Big Piney cowboy and then a cook for a Wyoming cattle outfit eclipsed any career change contemplated nowadays. And he certainly didn't do it for the money.

The Other Ranchers

Another Big Piney rancher who later followed Charlie Noble, Johnnie Curtis, and Link Shideler into the Basin was Jesse Budd, who was born in 1875 and died much later in 1952. But almost on the heels of Charlie Noble came two Bondurant ranchers, William "Bill" Bowlsby and John "Perry" Pfisterer. Although they later joined the Hoback Stock Association, at first Bill and Perry ran their cattle near Jack Creek. A little more than ten years after Charlie Noble's inaugural trip, the quality and availability of the Basin's water and grasses soon attracted Daniel ranchers and friends, Etheal Austin Richardson and Clarence Webb, and they joined the Association. Later, another Horse Creek rancher, Charles "Gordon" Jewett, started summering his cattle in the Basin and became a member of the Association.

About the same time as Austin and Clarence, other Bondurant ranchers, such as the Shel Baker and Lorenzo Campbell, worked their cattle in the Basin and later strengthened the Fall River Stock Association. The Bakers and Campbells also used Jack Creek pastures.

In the late 1920s, these Bondurant ranchers would create two other, but smaller associations. Not surprisingly, one was the Jack Creek Association and the other was the Fisherman's Creek Association

The Hoback Stock Association:
Its History and Evolution

This section presents the first recorded history of the Hoback Stock Association. That history also became a near perfect means for relaying the origin and role of stock associations, the history of U.S. public lands, and the early conflicts.

The post Civil War cattle boom which peaked in Wyoming during the 1880s brought a flood of investment, cattle, and wealth to the northern plains and mountain West. At the same time, the boom brought competition for grazing land, occasional overgrazing, cattle thieves, diseases such as Texas fever, carried by Texas longhorns, and confusion about range management and roundup schedules. The need to solve these problems together with the killer winters, prompted major changes in the cattle industry.

Two of the most readily recognizable changes were barbed wire fencing and the formation of "wagons" or local stock associations across all major Western grazing areas. Many states formed large scale or statewide associations, too. In Wyoming, by

1885, the Wyoming Stock Growers Association had four hundred members, who owned nearly two million cattle. The state and local associations were instrumental in advancing the welfare and political clout of the cattle industry.

In the Upper Green River Valley and the Hoback Basin, roundup wagons began forming in the early 1900s. Those wagons helped coordinate fencing, grazing, and roundup activity. They instituted practical measures to best manage the range such as, rotating cattle from one pasture to another so the cattle did not overgraze any one pasture or overwork a streambed. They served the self interest of each rancher who joined and supported the wagon.

With the creation of the National Parks and National Forests, by 1905 many grazing areas fell under the regime of public agencies. Eventually, those agencies and the Department of Interior's Bureau of Land Management expected the local stock associations to work with them to manage grazing on specific public lands or "allotments." The balance of this chapter explores the history of the Hoback Stock Association, the Hoback Cattle and Horse Allotment, and both within the context of the history of public lands.

The Early Years

The historical records of the U.S. Forest Service's Teton and Big Piney Ranger Districts established the approximate dates of early use and the number of cattle using the range. First, they suggested that trespass cattle—cattle whose owners grazed them without permit or official Association endorsement—may have come from as far away as Rock Springs and Green River. The U.S. Forest Service's earliest written records estimated that over three thousand head were run within the Association's boundaries. However, somewhat later permit allotment sheets suggested that closer to thirty-seven hundred head grazed the range. If horses and bulls were included almost four thousand head used it. The use period often started as early as late April and ended by November 1, roughly six months.

In 1899 and for just a few years beyond, Charlie Noble and Link Shideler ran most of the cattle in the Fall River Association. Towards the end of the early use period and primarily due to a long grazing season and trespass cattle, parts of the Upper Fall River may have been overgrazed.

Beyond the lush grasses and water, the Fall River Basin offered ranchers one other great advantage—it was open range until 1906 and as a practical matter, it remained as open range until the mid 1930s. Here is how that happened:

Officially across the West, a new era of public lands management began in 1891 with the passage of the Forest Reserve Act. That act gave the president the power to withdraw or reserve public lands from further use or abuse. Taking the first action under the law and reflecting a strong public reaction against the rapacious appetites of the big timber and railroad companies, President Benjamin Harrison set aside fourteen million acres, mainly in the West. That acreage included the Yellowstone Timber Land Reserve which encompassed land now in the Teton Wilderness. In 1897 President Grover Cleveland followed suit and his reserve proclamation created the Teton Forest Reserve. Neither of these Reserves encompassed the Fall River Basin.

Since the law and the two presidential actions were not wildly popular in the West, later in 1897 the passage of the Forest Management Act delayed forest reserve proclamations and restored some withdrawn land to public entry.

This unhappiness in the West reflected a broader national disenchantment with both Harrison and Cleveland, whom history has judged as undistinguished presidents. Both befriended Gould, Vanderbilt, Morgan, Carnegie, and Rockefeller—the "robber barons" of the day. Cleveland, a Democrat, was first elected in 1884, despite the admission that he had fathered an illegitimate child. (*"Ma,Ma, where's my Pa?" "Gone to the White House, Ha,Ha.Ha!"*) In 1888 he won the popular vote, but lost to Harrison in the Electoral College, who then lost to Cleveland in 1892. Forecasting a populist wave that eventually would sweep Teddy Roosevelt into office in 1904, the 1892 populist candidate, James Weaver, polled over a million votes and carried six states west of the Mississippi.

With the passage of the Transfer Act of 1905, Teddy Roosevelt set a milestone on public lands. That statute moved the authority over the nation's forest reserves from the General Land Office to the Department of Agriculture and created the U.S. Forest Service. That legislation also broke new ground by authorizing grazing fees. During its first year in 1906, grazing fees were set at twenty to thirty cents for each head of cattle or horses.

Again, to appease Western interests, in 1906 the Congress passed the Forest Homestead Act. As noted earlier, it authorized federal forest lands suitable for agriculture to be opened up for homestead entry. Between 1906 and 1915 the U.S. Department of Agriculture approved thirteen thousand of these claims.

In 1907, the name Forest Reserve was changed to National Forest. In 1908, the Yellowstone National Forest was divided into six separate National Forests including the Teton and Wyoming National Forests. The Fall River Basin fell into the Wyoming National Forest which later became the Bridger National Forest. Much later, in 1973, the Bridger and Teton National Forests were combined and formed the Bridger-Teton National Forest.

So it was only in 1908 that the Basin came under U.S. Forest Service management. Since any new legislation takes time to implement and the U.S. Forest Service faced a severe shortage of trained personnel, the initial impact of this legislation was limited, particularly considering the millions of acres of National Forest land across the country. Although the Hoback Basin's first federal grazing permits were issued to the John Perry Pfisterer in 1908 and 1910, the U.S. Forest Service records for the Wyoming and then Bridger National Forest confirmed that it was not until the mid-1930s that the range in the Basin came under any meaningful U.S. Forest Service monitoring and management.

At that time, the supervision of the Basin fell under the Hoback Ranger District which reported to the Supervisor of the Teton National Forest in Jackson, who had management responsibility for both forests. Ranger Charlie Dibble served in the Hoback District during some of those early years. He had been transferred from Horsetail Ranger Station at Kelly near the western side of the Gros Ventre. Aside from a reputation as a solid veteran ranger, two memories persist: First, in late June, 1925, during a torrential rain, a huge mudslide slipped into the Gros Ventre River, damming the river and creating a lake later known as Slide Lake. However, as the lake rose, it flooded out many homesteaders and ranchers including Charlie Dibble and his wife, Cap.

Two years later and fortunately during the day, the earthen dam broke, and Ranger Dibble was able to notify all residents downriver of the impending flood which brought trees and granite boulders through the canyon, bulldozing the town of Kelly. Only six died, but without Ranger Dibble's warning the number would have been in the hundreds. As an odd counterpoint to his act of near heroism, the most memorable visual impression he left with Basin residents was of his completely worn down teeth.

Roy Conner, whose family homesteaded near Merna in 1916-1917, also served as a Hoback Basin Ranger and may have preceded Charlie Dibble.

Eventually, jurisdiction for the Basin came under the Teton Ranger District, and in 1982, it was transferred to the Big Piney Ranger District.

When the Fall River Association was formed, the Basin was real open range and until the 1930s, as a practical matter, it remained open range. The Association served as a means to manage the range exclusively for its members in contrast to fulfilling a U.S. Forest Service requirement. Not surprisingly, a Fall River Allotment is not referenced in Forest Service records. Its early history is based on a few local histories and interviews.

As the U.S. Forest Service begins a more vigilant regime in the Basin in the 1930s, their records refer to the Coyote Horse and Cattle Allotment. It had the same boundaries as the Fall River Association and its successor, the Hoback Stock Association. The Forest Service presumably took the name from Coyote Gulch that sits at the southern end of Noble Basin. They continued to refer to the Coyote Allotment until 1960 and presumably, it was used by the Coyote Association.

Then in a May 3, 1960 memo from the Forest Supervisor H. H. Van Winkle to the Regional Forester, Mr. Van Winkle writes:

Over thirty years ago the Hoback Livestock Association organized with constitution and bylaws for handling the grazing business of the permittees running on the Hoback C&H Allotment.

During recent years local usage of the name Coyote Allotment and Coyote C&H Association has come into use resulting in considerable confusion in the files because no Coyote Association was ever organized.

Ranger Tom Brierley and I met with the Hoback Livestock Association at their annual meeting on April 30 and discussed this matter with the Association. It is the wish of the Association that the name "The Hoback Livestock Association" be used in designating correspondence and reference to business matters with the Association. It is also the wish of the Association that the name of the Allotment be designated Hoback C&H Allotment.

This memorandum is for explanation and to urge future reference to the Association and their allotment under the name of the Hoback Livestock Association or the Hoback C&H Allotment rather than making further reference to the Coyote Association or Coyote C&H Allotment.

A copy of the Hoback Cattle and Horse Association Constitution and By-Laws were attached to this memo. With the exception of a few later amendments, the Association's original Constitution and By-Laws are exactly the same as those attached by Mr. Van Winkle.

Further confirming this case of mistaken identity is an April 26, 1952 Cooperative Agreement between the "Hoback Stock Association" and the Teton National Forest. The agreement established a range improvement work fund managed by the Forest Service and funded by the Hoback Stock Association. This particular agreement called for an Association remittance of $319.29. Ironically, every other Forest Service document and map during the 1950s refers to the Coyote Allotment, but an additional review of local histories and newspapers revealed no reference to a "Coyote" Association.

Although no one has stepped forward to take the credit for misnaming the Hoback Stock Association, the decade long confusion about the name illustrates how easily history can occasionally try and trick us.

The 1930s marked a decade of change in the Basin. Aside from greater U.S. Forest Service scrutiny, the *Pinedale Roundup*, a local weekly newspaper, began referring to the Fall River and Fall River Basin as the Hoback River and Hoback Basin. For a few years these names were used interchangeably. Again, no records or oral histories can establish why this shift in nomenclature occurred. However, it would be reasonable to assume that as more and more people traveled the road to and from Jackson and Yellowstone National Park, the name, Hoback, simply moved up the Canyon to the river, and the Basin. As the southern route to Jackson and Yellowstone, the traffic progressively increased in the 1920s and 1930s. To simply avoid the confusion of traveling along the Fall River to the Hoback Canyon, the entire area eventually took the name Hoback. As most of this area was and still is in National Forest, it is conceivable that the Teton Forest officials encouraged this change, but no records have confirmed that.

The traffic volume along this corridor grew at such a rate that the Oregon Short Line surveyed its right of way in the Canyon.

Although the railroad was never built, in order to facilitate the traffic flow during the 1930s, the road to Jackson was rerouted from the east side of the Hoback River to the west side.

The Hoback
Cattle and Horse Allotment

The initial size of the Hoback Cattle and Horse Allotment was 74,835 acres of which 50,895 were suitable for grazing. That nearly seventy-five thousand acres translates to 116.5 square miles. That is almost twice the size the nation's capitol, the District of Columbia, which measures sixty-one square miles. As noted earlier, the U.S. Forest Service estimated that prior to 1937, an annual average of 3,132 head of cattle ran in the Basin, but the Allotment records show that an additional five hundred more head grazed that range. The use period ran five to six months. In 1938, the grazing season was shortened to four and one half months—from June 1 to October 15—and the number of cattle reduced to an average of 2,357 head. Again, the permit allotment sheets still show over thirty-six hundred head. Although the allotment sheets are the more reliable record, no one alive can explain the early discrepancy between the annual reports and the allotment sheets.

In the mid 1930s, the rangers also began enforcing the pasture

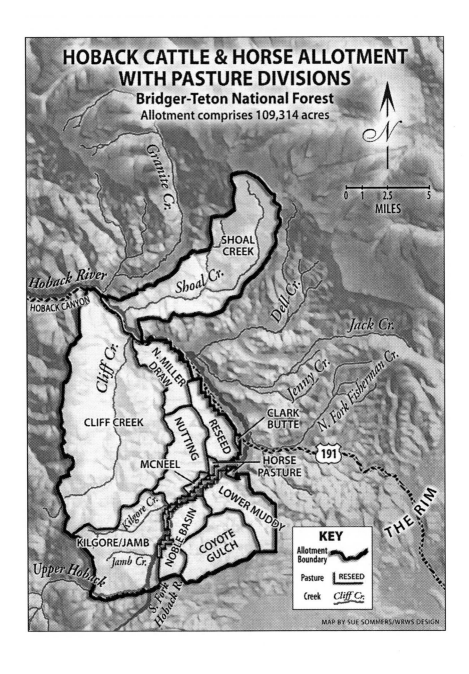

HOBACK CATTLE & HORSE ALLOTMENT WITH PASTURE DIVISIONS
Bridger-Teton National Forest
Allotment comprises 109,314 acres

MAP BY SUE SOMMERS/WRWS DESIGN

rotations and salting locations. In 1946, the grazing season was shortened again. The U.S Forest Service pushed the start date to June 11 and the season still closed on October 15. Since then the grazing season has remained the same.

This overall management regime lasted until 1954 when a slight increase in cattle was permitted. From 1954—1968 an annual average of 2,422 was allowed. In 1969 with the addition of several former sheep allotments, the Hoback Allotment boundaries increased by 31,715 acres. That growth (to a total of 117,583 acres) allowed another increase in cattle. Although the Allotment could carry 2,880 head of cattle, the next decade saw actual use average around 2,553 head. By the early 1980s the eleven permittees had livestock obligations totaling 2,882 head. Until recently, the current Association members have run somewhat less than that. Due to non-use in 2003 and 2004, the Association has run just under two thousand head. In 2005, that number rose to twenty-two hundred head of cattle.

Throughout much of this time, three small special use pastures were allowed within the Allotment—the McNeel, Game Hill and Upper Hoback. In 1980 the Upper Hoback pasture was established within the larger Hoback Cattle and Horse Allotment. In the 1980s all of the allotments totaled 129,577 acres, of which 43,456 were suitable for grazing. Today the Allotment incorporating the two special use pastures totals only 109,113 acres with twelve pastures; and eight permittees. The acreage of the Allotment equals over three hundred times the size of an average Iowa farm. Kevin Campbell serves as the Association's President and Norm Pape serves as its Secretary Treasurer. Both have held those positions for thirty years, and as long as anyone today can remember, the Association has met at the Pape Ranches twice a year: once in early May before turnout and then again in September before roundup.

The Association Members

Although the Big Piney ranchers dominated the Association from the early days through the 1940s, the first generation of Bondurant ranchers homesteaded just before the turn of the century and began using the range shortly thereafter. That first generation included the Pfisterers and the Bowlsbys. A few years later they were joined by the Bakers and the Campbells. Frank Van Fleck of the V-V arrived not long after. Much later they would be joined by Noah Booker, Julius Albert Miller, Elmer Nutting and Bill Stong. By this time, the Pape Ranches near Daniel had joined the Association, and eventually Lester Pape, Norm's father, would serve as the Association's Secretary Treasurer for over thirty years.

Details of the Association's life during the 1920s are sketchy. Through the 1930s, 1940s, and mid-1950s, its membership and their respective grazing obligations were remarkably stable. Charlie Noble ran eight hundred head; Gordon Jewett had eight hundred head; Walter Jesse from Ft. Collins, Colorado, grazed five to six hundred head; Clarence Webb ran four to five hundred head of cattle; Austin Richardson grazed three to four hundred head; Link Shideler had 225 head; Lester Pape and his father, Fred, ran two hundred head; Kenneth Noble, Charlie's son, pastured, fifty to eighty head; and Jesse Budd grazed sixty head. The Bondurant dude ranchers, Noah Booker and Frank Van Fleck, respectively, ran sixty-five and twenty head. The other Bondurant ranchers—Arthur "Banty" Bowlsby—Bill Bowlsby's son—Julius Miller and Bill Stong, respectively, had twenty-three, thirty, and fifteen head. Elmer Nutting, a Basin homesteader, ran ten.

Later the draw just above Nutting's homestead and near today's cow camp carried his name. Grazing conditions might vary from year to year as would the preferred number of cattle, but the total and each rancher's proportion of that remained fairly constant for twenty-five years. Also, the use of temporary permits allowed ranchers to raise the number of the cattle they grazed in any given year.

By the mid-1950s and 1960s a major change in membership took place. The Daniel ranchers then included Carroll James, the Koch Ranch, the Schwabachers, Harve Stone and the Pape Ranches. The Basin ranchers, who were members, included the Campbells, the Macks, the Little Jennie Ranch (initially built and owned by Tom Kearns from Salt Lake and then purchased by the Wagstaff family from Kansas City, Missouri), Gene Pfisterer, Gil Ordway, Bob McNeel, Bill Stong, Albert Feuz, Lot Haley, Lawrence Shaul and the Hicks. Another family, the Amreins, also joined the Association in the 1960s. The only Cottonwood Creek ranch running cattle on the Hoback Allotment was the Jewett Land and Cattle Company. No Big Piney ranchers had permits on the Hoback Allotment.

Today the Pape Ranches are the only Daniel ranchers who summer in the Basin. The Bondurant ranchers include the Campbells, the Little Jennie Ranch managed by Gerry Endecott, Bill and Tony Saunders on Gil Ordway's River Bend Ranch, the Pfisterer family,

Steve and Dallas Robertson and Victor Mack Jr. and his wife, Lucy, from Farson, Wyoming. No Big Piney ranchers run cattle on the Hoback Allotment today.

Hoback Association Riders, Cow Camps, and Roundup

From the late 1930s and throughout the 1950s, the Association riders and the roundup cowboys used three cow camps. Located on Muddy Creek, the first served as the main camp where the late spring or early summer season began. Before it served as the Association's main cow camp, the cabin had been Mont Johnson's homestead. He applied for his patent in 1926 and received it in 1932. Mont's one hundred sixty acres lies adjacent to and south of the Shideler place.

Later in the summer, the Association rider or riders would move by horseback to the camp on Cliff Creek and then to the Shoal Creek camp. The Cliff Creek camp was hailed as the most comfortable. The same cow camp rotation was employed for fall roundup where as early as September 25, roundup riders gathered at the main cow camp and pitched their tents or tipis. None of the camps had electricity, running water or indoor plumbing. In fact, until the mid-1950s, no one who lived in the Basin had electricity—unless the

Muddy Cow Camp.
Photo by Sherrill Hudson.

homestead generated its own power.

Prior to the extensive use of stock trucks and then horse trailers, these three cow camps composed the essential ingredients for the successful management of the Allotment and its stock. Harve Stone and his family were the last riders to use all three camps. In fact, in the late 1940s and before he became the Association rider, Harve helped build the Shoal Creek cow camp. Since it was a little bit off the beaten path, during the summers, riders pitched their tents closer to the cattle trails.

In the 1930s and 1940s, during the summer and fall, the school teachers in Bondurant, Daniel and Merna, adding spice to the cowboy life, organized weekend rendezvous or roundups in the Basin. Horses were plentiful as were the trail guides. A few like Charlie Noble, Bill Bowlsby, Noah Booker, and Lester Pape ended up marrying school teachers who taught in Bondurant or nearby. Since single women were scarce in the Basin, teachers greatly expanded the pool of those eligible for marriage.

One middle-aged and married rancher named Fritz became too excited about those young single women. Since his wife had planned an overnight visit with Pinedale friends, Fritz asked one of those young women to meet him in his bed that evening. The teacher told Fritz's wife about the plan, and unknown to Fritz, they switched roles. The teacher visited Pinedale, and with a different hair style, perfume, and nightgown, Fritz's wife went to bed. After a more than a few drinks, Fritz stumbled through the bedroom door. He eagerly embraced his partner in bed, and they went about their intimate business. Early the next morning, Fritz crowed that this was the best night he had ever had with a woman. His wife turned around and looking him straight in the eye said, "Fritz that is the best compliment you have paid me in years."

Today's Stock Association cow camp lies about two and a half miles up the Upper Hoback Road, the gravel road that is a left turn just after the Bondurant Post Office. The road was built in 1935 by

Today's cow camp tack shed and corrals. *Photo by Sherrill Hudson.*

Sublette County and the Forest Service. The cow camp sits near Horse Pasture Draw and north of the Hoback River. It was built in 1960 by the Association with many modern conveniences like electricity and a well with an outside pump. Many of the earliest homesteads and ranches were on this same road as are the newer homes of seasonal visitors and some year-round residents.

The three-room cow camp, tack shed, and corrals sit down in a draw as does the double-seated outhouse. Although badly sagging, the basic structure of the old Muddy cow camp still remains intact. Sometime in the 1960s, the U.S. Forest Service razed the camp on Cliff Creek and just a few remaining logs mark that camp's location. Although the Shoal Creek cabin still stands, it is no longer used. Now roundup begins in early October and runs until mid-October.

Back riding or searching for cattle not gathered during the roundup will continue until the first major snow. Usually back riding involves riding the high or back country where the more difficult cattle will hide. After the back riding that ends in mid-November, the Association has hired a private plane to fly over the Allotment searching for the remaining cattle. Each year a few are never found and often die.

Since 1994, Tom Filkins has been the Association rider and works from the first of June until mid-November. Tom will reappear in *Part Five, The Cowboys*. With the exception of the Pape Ranches and Bill Saunders of the River Bend Ranch, who both hire roundup riders, today the other Association members and their families ride the roundups.

Over the more than one hundred years of the Hoback Stock Association and its predecessor, the Fall River Association, many cowboys rode for it or one of its members. Others just rode "turn out' in the late spring or early summer and roundup in the fall. Although each rider collected his modest daily or monthly pay, the Basin gave each a richer reward of partying, renewing friendships and enjoying nature's handiwork.

Just a handful of cowboys built their lives and their family's lives on the foundation of the Association. As a young man, Guy Carr from Big Piney rode until he was called into service during World War I. After the war and until the early 1920s, he rode again. Starting in 1911, Phil "Morgan" Marincic worked as foreman for Charlie Noble's ranches and for the next eighteen years—with a two year interlude for World War I—he also served as foreman for the Association, living much of that time at Charlie Noble's ranch in the Basin. In 1927, he bought the Muleshoe Ranch and, ironically, with it a permit for the Basin's Fisherman's Creek Allotment not far from the Fall River or Hoback Association. Also he filed a claim for a Basin homestead. Phil will reappear in Charlie Noble's company in *Part Four: The Originals*.

Roughly riding up on the boot heels of Phil Marincic, Clure Smith and his wife, Lola, signed up with the Hoback Stock Association. In the 1920s, Clure worked on Gordon Jewett's Horse Creek ranch, and as Gordon and his family were Association members in good standing, Clure was a logical choice as the Stock Association rider. In 1927 Clure and Lola separated and later both remarried. During the next thirteen years Clure rode for the Association. In the 1950s he went to work for the Little Jennie Ranch. Clure will make another appearance with Gordon Jewett in Part Four.

Taking the reins from Clure Smith was Harve Stone, who rode for almost twenty years from 1954 until late 1973. Harve will take the stage as a star performer in Part Four.

For the next twenty years and until Tom Filkins took over in 1994, a bunch of different cowboys rode for the Association. In order to cover the Allotment's territory, the USFS also encouraged and expected the use of two riders—the primary rider or cow boss and a second rider. The use of two riders remains a common practice today. A record of primary riders or cow bosses that rode from 1974 to 1994 can be found in *Notes and Sources* at the end of the book. During the time each of these riders worked, they helped define the Association. And like me, they remember it as a special time in their lives. But their individual histories are beyond the scope of this chronicle.

However, one of those riders, Kent Snidecor, deserves a special mention. Not only did he ride with Harve Stone when Harve was cow boss, but he briefly married Havre's daughter, Cheryl. Kent and Cheryl rode together in the early 1980s. During those same years in the 1980s, Kent served as Tom Filkins' mentor and friend, and with their new wives and infant sons, they shared the cow camp.

Together just these five Association cowboys—Guy Carr, Phil Marincic Sr., Clure Smith, Harve Stone, and Tom Filkins—have ridden for nearly eighty years, most of the Association's lifetime.

A Roundup Tradition

It was early October and chilly in the Basin. That meant one thing. It was time for roundup, fourteen straight days of riding from first light until the day's work was done. And then moving the cattle to the home ranches. Weather didn't matter.

Each rancher with over two hundred head of cattle had to provide a roundup rider and every rancher had to provide horses for the riders. During the early decades the ranchers also shared the cost of a roundup cook and food.

But before riding, tradition called for the roundup cowboys to party for at least a day or two. Some would stay at the cow camp or go to Floerke's, the local bar. Others would drive up the Hoback Canyon to Jackson Hole.

One clear and cold fall day in the 1940s, late in the afternoon Fred Turner, who started working for the Pfisterer Ranch in 1935-1936, pulled his truck up to the cow camp and Rodney Pape and Charlie Stegman jumped in for the season's first trip to the Jackson bars. Fred, who was perhaps wiser and more tempered than his two cowboy friends, was the night's "designated driver." Still, they closed the bars in Jackson and then headed home with Rodney in the front passenger seat and Charlie squeezed in the middle. That night Rodney and Charlie drank enough to insure that the other cowboys would know that they had held up their end of the tradition.

Turning off the paved road and cutting through the River Bend Ranch to the cow camp, Fred had to drive across the Hoback River, then running more than a foot deep. In the middle of the river he stopped, turned off the lights and engine, shook Rodney and said to him, "We're home." With that Rodney stepped out of the truck right into the river and started flopping like a fish. Amid cursing and shrieks of rude surprise, Rodney, soaked but still drunk, climbed back into the truck.

Now down the road to cow camp with just one short stop to open and close the gate to camp. It was Charlie's turn. He got out, opened the gate and Fred pulled through and then waited for him to close the gate and get back in. And he waited. By now Rodney was shaking. Fred stepped out and found Charlie with both feet stuck in a badger hole. He could not move, and fearful that he might break his legs, he would not let Fred pull him out. Fred closed the gate and headed to cow camp where he built a huge fire so Rodney could dry out. An hour or so later—and cold as ice—Charlie walked in barefoot having left his boots in the badger hole and his socks on the way into the cow camp. Fred retrieved the boots, but the socks—never having been washed—were untouchable. It was finally morning and although warm, Charlie and Rodney had not yet felt the pain of sobriety.

So began another roundup in the Basin.

Courtesy of Victor Mack, Sr.

Jack Creek and Fisherman Creek

Aside from the Hoback Stock Association—by far the largest—two other allotments and associations were established in the Basin. They are the Jack Creek Cattle and Horse Allotment and Association and the Fisherman's Creek Allotment and Association. The U.S. Forest Service records show that all were operating and managed by the Forest Service in the mid-1930s. The *Pinedale Roundup* confirms that the Jack Creek Association was established on March 15, 1928, and the U.S. Forest Service records show 1931 as the date of the first improvement on the Hoback Cattle and Horse Allotment—the South Rim drift fence. To date no newspaper records have been found that can confirm an exact date for either the Hoback or Fisherman's Creek Association, but it does appear that all three were created at roughly the same time—in the late 1920s and certainly no later than 1930.

Similar to the Hoback Association, the Jack Creek Allotment was not meaningfully regulated until the 1930s. The Allotment contains a total of 38,425 acres of which 21,592 are suitable for grazing. That acreage has a grazing obligation of 1,004 cattle.

However, unlike the Hoback Association, the Jack Creek membership was mainly Bondurant area ranchers. They included the Campbells, Hearly Fronk, the Pfisterer family, William Crandall "Bill" Bowlsby, Eugene Holt, the Koontzes, Fred Watts and W. L. Jones. E. S. Robinson was the lone Daniel rancher. By the 1980s, the permittees were the Campbells, the Little Jennie Ranch, and the Pfisterers. These three ranches ran cattle on both the Hoback and Jack Creek Allotments.

The Fisherman's Creek Allotment encompasses 48,394 acres of which 17,965 are suitable for grazing. Recent grazing use allows up to 1,331 head of cattle. Like the Hoback Stock Association, its first members were primarily Big Piney ranchers, including Robert O'Neal, Phil Marincic, Sr.—who initially worked for Charlie Noble until he bought the Muleshoe Ranch in 1927—and the Chapels. Harve Scott was the single Daniel rancher who ran cattle in the Fisherman's Creek Allotment. By the 1980s, the Pfisterer family and the Kathy Miller of Daniel were the main Association members. More recently, Jim Eaton from Farson, Wyoming, joined the Association.

The Close

Some of the people briefly mentioned in this chapter will reappear in more detail and a brighter light in the next three chapters, particularly *Part Four, The Originals,* and *Part Five, The Cowboys.* But this chapter has created the context and hopefully an atmosphere that will allow the characters to emerge more as themselves than as historical artifacts—more the way other people knew them and less facts and genealogy.

In this chapter, however, one fundamental demographic and cultural fact underlies the history of these ranchers and cowboys: nearly everyone in Wyoming and the Basin came from someplace else, and many had been foreign born. Often they first came to places where friends or family may have homesteaded. Those immigrants from the British Isles, Scandinavia and Germany eventually found their way to Sublette County. Others came from Missouri, Iowa, Kansas and Nebraska. The 1880 Census reveals that of the roughly seven hundred cowboys in Wyoming, half were born in Ohio, Illinois, New York, Missouri, Iowa, Pennsylvania and Massachusetts. Only twenty-five had been born in Texas. Twenty-two had come from England. Only nine Indians and two blacks were listed as cowboys in 1880.

America had been the country of hope for the first immigrants. The West became the region of hope for their children and grandchildren, and in many respects it retains that attraction today. And ironically, while homogeneity now marks the life of Wyoming and its smaller towns, at the beginning it wasn't so. The isolated communities of Wyoming became mini melting pots and witnessed their share of social tension. That tension, however, was mitigated by the fact that the economic and social survival of small isolated communities demanded cooperation, not freelancing independence.

In the same vein and yet not fully appreciated, the Hoback Stock Association played a role as a unifier among a diverse group of county residents. For almost fifty years, it was the only institution that integrated ranchers, their families, and cowboys from Big Piney, Cottonwood Creek, Daniel, the Bronx, and the Hoback Basin. Despite wide gaps in background, education, wealth and income, the Association worked as an equalizer. The hired cowboy stood on the same platform as the owner of a several thousand acre ranch. That equalitarianism added a civic health and wealth that has served well this part of Wyoming and the West.

Old Jack Creek cow camp.
Photo by Sherrill Hudson.

Part Three

Bondurant and the Basin:
The Pioneering Settlers

PAUL JENSEN

HARD AND NOBLE LIVES

The newness and openness of the Western frontier attracted every type of booster, hope chaser, dreamer, and adventurer. Get-rich schemes abounded. They came for the boom, but usually got knocked down by the bust. No matter. Just move to the next town and start again. Wallace Stegner noted that the western thirst for the new was as much a curse as a virtue. It could cut people off from community and stability. He continued that the West could be more space than place.

But the rootless and the boom chasers did not make or settle the West. Those who did settle it Stegner called the "stickers"—the ones who stuck it out against the odds, "who settled, and loved the life that they made and the place they have made it in." (Wallace Stegner, *Where the Bluebird Sings to the Lemonade Springs*, pp xxvii, 7, 71-74).

The history of the Hoback Basin is mainly a story of the stickers, those, who weathered long difficult winters, sparse kitchen cupboards and isolation. Electricity finally arrived in the mid-1950s and telephone service beyond a local party line did not come to the Basin until early 1961, which made the long winters and isolation more profound. Of course, some didn't stay. Others couldn't settle down and saw the potential for riches down every new road. But even some of those returned or their families brought them back to a place they could call home: Bondurant in the Fall River Basin.

Many other people stuck it out to settle and develop other parts of Sublette County. But the Hoback Basin settlers—and more specifically those who built its ranching and cowboy legacy—are the subjects of this history. They've earned their place.

This section slightly broadens the scope of this history. First, two pioneer families, the Bondurants and Falers, created the Basin's early identity. Neither family ranched. Although their contributions were markedly different, without these families the flavor of the Basin's ranch and cowboy history would have been diminished. Today, ranchers still tell stories about them.

Next, some early trappers, ranchers, entrepreneurs and others found a unique place in this story—namely that much of the Basin and Hoback Allotment's defining topography bears their names. Those who first gave their names to posterity included the Kilgores, Sandy Marshall, the Kerrs, Hal Gibbs and the Sanfords. Even the Bondurants had a Creek named after them. Later, a few others gave their names to places in the Basin or simply gave the place a name.

Most of Part Three encompasses the people and institutions who had a direct connection to the Hoback Stock Association and its traditions. Many of those people were briefly introduced in Part Two. They were pioneer homesteaders and ranchers. At the end of this Part, a very brief section highlights some families and individuals who had no direct relationship with the Stock Association, but who were the close friends or neighbors of those who did.

The few earlier histories that have touched upon the town of Bondurant begin and end the story with the Bondurant family and particularly Mrs. Bondurant's soda biscuits. The more recent histories may include the Episcopal Church of St. Hubert the Hunter and the adjacent library. The Episcopal Church was completed in 1941 and a barbeque celebrated the occasion. That barbeque started an annual tradition that continues today. The adjacent library and a fully equipped first-aid dispensary were finished two years later in 1943.

A diamond ring paid for the church's $1,500 worth of

construction materials. A Mrs. John Markoe donated her diamond ring to Bishop Perry, the presiding Bishop of the Episcopal Church in America. She requested that the proceeds of the sale of the ring be used to build a memorial church. Bishop Winfred Zielger, the Wyoming Episcopal Bishop, having been stranded in Bondurant during a winter storm, knew of the community's need for a church. Bishop Perry agreed to sell the ring for that church. The Bondurant Episcopal Church, doubling as a community center, was listed on the National Register of Historic Places on January 24, 2002.

My history of the Bondurant homesteaders begins with the family after whom the village was named, because in good measure the most accurate early written history of the area starts with Benjamin Bondurant's diaries and the memories of his children or their spouses. Other fascinating characters were also part of that early history, but written and oral histories have ignored them. Some of those pioneers even preceded the Bondurant family. Yet despite my extensive research, a few of those early homesteaders appear more as shadows than well developed characters; however, in this story even those shadowy sketches are more than anyone else has portrayed.

The Bondurants

The wagons lurched forward and then stopped. The mules and horses were tired, and the two blind mules pulling the Bondurant's wagon would not take another step. Benjamin Franklin Bondurant's friend and business partner, Green Hunt, pulled the supply wagon alongside. It had been a long trip from Mayview, Missouri, to Kemmerer, Wyoming. With five children—Claire, Pearl Oscar, Rollie, Essie, Herschel and their Boston Terrier, Tip—Sarah Ellen Gouche, Bondurant's wife, welcomed the stop.

They had left their merchandise store and home in the spring of 1897 and were heading to Oregon with plans to open a new and more prosperous store. It was now fall of that same year, and snow was predicted for South Pass, their route to the next stretch of the Oregon Trail. They decided to spend the winter in Kemmerer, Wyoming, and repair the wagons, rest the livestock and relax themselves. Needing some extra money for the winter months, Bondurant and Hunt initially lent a hand to the Oscar Wright ranch on the Ham's Fork where the Bondurant family stayed, and later the two men worked briefly in the quarries and coal mines around Kemmerer.

During that winter Bondurant and Hunt heard stories about the bountiful wildlife, beauty, ranches, and emerging businesses in Jackson Hole, a place almost next door when compared to Oregon. They switched destinations, but needing more money for provisions, they traveled to Kendall, Wyoming, and worked in the tie hack camp. That camp was south of the Green River Lakes and near the northern end of today's Sublette County. Across the county at the turn of the century, a few camps like Kendall operated, cutting timber and partially finishing it for railroad ties. The ties were then floated down the nearby rivers or creeks during spring's high water. Compared to cowboy wages, the camps paid well and became a magnet for new immigrants—most from northern Europe—and those who, like the Bondurants, needed seasonal or temporary employment. They spent the winter of 1899-1900 at the Kendall camp.

With the visions of a rich new life in Jackson Hole giving them hope, the Bondurants and Green set out again. They headed north towards Jackson, but first they had to travel over the Rim, an eight thousand foot pass, and then drop down into the Fall River Basin. Captivated by the Basin's splendor and splendid isolation in that spring of 1900, they ended their trip right there—still about fifty miles south of Jackson.

As the Bondurants arrived and settled in the Basin, Wilbur and Orville Wright were completing the first powered flight at Kitty Hawk, North Carolina.

The Bondurants picked a site for their homestead on the east side of the river near Jack Creek, and Hunt located down river from the Bondurant place. After unloading the wagons and storing their belongings and provisions under a tent, they started building the barn, corrals and a five room hand-hewn log home with a dirt floor and dirt roof. After a wagon trip to Opal that resupplied their larder, they settled in for the winter.

In the spring of 1901, Bondurant, known by his nickname, "Bondy," and his son, Pearl, negotiated a contract to cut timber and dig ditches near Pinedale. By the next year, Bondy and Green Hunt launched a dry goods and general merchandise store. Hunt took responsibility for bringing the first year's supplies from Missouri, but after that, the store's supplies were haulled by freight wagon from either Opal, the closest railhead and well south of the Fall River Basin, or bought in Kemmerer, a larger city beyond Opal.

Aside from the two large stores, the Union Mercantile and Frontier Supply were owned by the Kemmerer Coal Company. Kemmerer also hosted the Southern Hotel, a whorehouse that was well-known and well-patronized in western Wyoming.

As the operation of their store and the creation of a customer base required regular mail delivery, Bondurant and others first picked up the mail in Kendall. But very shortly, the Postal Service mandated a change, and the Bondurants picked up the mail at Merna and more precisely at the Snider place, ten or so miles west of Daniel. As the Basin had no central location for mail delivery, Mrs. Bondurant applied for and was awarded a post office in Bondurant. She operated that office from 1903 to 1921. For most of those years, the Basin's mail still traveled from Daniel to Merna before finally reaching the Bondurant post office, a trip measuring more than twenty miles each way. During the summer the mail was delivered twice a week on horseback or with a buckboard pulled by a team of horses. During the winter the mail was delivered only once a week by dogsled, skis or snowshoes—then better known as "webs." A halfway station near the Rim offered a rest stop and shelter.

From 1902-1904, Bondurant supplemented the store income by working as one of the first Teton Forest Reserve rangers. In 1904 and shortly after Bondurant's Forest Reserve duty, Bondy and his sons built a substantial eleven room house and storage facility. In mid-1904 he started a hunting guide business, and by 1907 it had evolved into a dude ranch and lodging business.

In the wilds of the Fall River Basin, Sarah Ellen Bondurant garnered a reputation as a gourmet cook. Her soda biscuits and light bread were only rivaled by her cottage cheese with cream, nutmeg and sugar. Her steak and gravy created a near stampede to their lodge.

In the very beautiful, yet isolated Fall River Basin, the Bondurant family created a whole new vision of economic opportunity and became community leaders. From 1907 until 1927, they ran their dude ranching and hunting guide business.

Three of their sons homesteaded in the Basin—Claire on Jack Creek, Pearl Oscar on Dell Creek and Rollie on Jack Creek Flats. Essie later married Frank Hansen from Minnesota, and they homesteaded on lower Dell Creek. After selling his ranch to his father, Claire died of pneumonia in 1918. Nine years later, on his way to a friend's house in Kemmerer, Bondurant accidentally fell at a construction site and broke his hip. He never recovered from the fall and at the age of sixty-six, he died on October 15, 1927. The following year, on June 21, his wife, Sarah Ellen died at their home. Both were buried in the Bondurant Cemetery.

The Bondurants' Neighbors

When the Bondurants arrived in the Basin in the spring of 1900, they joined a small band of the earliest and hardiest of homesteaders. These residents lived throughout the Basin, but at the turn of the century, being within a few miles of each other equalled being considered next door neighbors. Among them were the Falers and John Rogers, a Civil War veteran, who was the Bondurant's' closest neighbor. The Bowlsbys, the Sanfords, and John "Perry" Pfisterer were also nearby. The Kerrs trapped on Cliff Creek. Alex Swenson and the Kilgores were neighbors. The Kilgores ranched on the Upper Fall River near a creek that was later named after them. And of course, Charlie Noble, who by then had been summering his cattle in the Basin for almost ten years, was included in this small group of "next door neighbors."

The Falers homesteaded in the Basin in 1892, ten years after the birth of Franklin Roosevelt. John Rogers settled there in about 1893, and his homestead sat just above today's Miller Draw and on the west side of the highway. After the Bondurant's arrival, Green Hunt lived with Rogers. In 1890 a trapper built a small log cabin on what shortly became the Roger's place, and he lived there for the next two winters. The trapper's cabin logs were so massive it took only six stacked logs for each side. Later he moved to Jackson Hole.

In 1909 or 1910, Rogers sold his property to Snell Johnson and Green Hunt. Noah Booker bought this ranch in 1919 and started a dude ranch business. Later Booker Ranch's loading pens and chutes served the Basin ranchers during the fall days when they shipped their cattle by stock trucks. In 1938 Roy Nealeigh and family bought the Noah Booker ranch and in 1946 sold it to the Hicks family.

Down the Hoback River from Deadshot Swenson's place, but just before the Noble ranch, sits the ranch originally owned by Mark Kilgore and his brother, Walter, which they'd homesteaded in 1901. Benjamin Bondurant notes in his diary entry of August 3, 1904, that in search of a small forest fire, he visited the Noble ranch and then went up the river to the Kilgore ranch where he camped overnight. Sometime shortly after that, the Kilgores sold it to the Winkle family, and then the two brothers moved out of the Basin. The Winkles sold it to Jesse Budd, the Big Piney rancher, and eventually Arthur "Banty" Bowlsby bought it.

In the very early 1900s, the Kerr family lived and trapped in the Cliff Creek drainage, a striking area surrounded by red rock cliffs. A Kerr daughter married Hal Gibbs, and he, too, "took up a place" on Cliff Creek. One creek in that area is known as Kerr Creek and another is called Gibbs Creek. Within a few years the Kerrs moved, and although excellent summer pasture, no others settled in that area. However, during the 1930s the Civilian Conservation Corps built a camp headquarters on the site of the old Kerr homestead.

The Real Bondurant Pioneers

Just as the few histories of Bondurant and the early settlers lead off with the Bondurant family, those same histories have placed the Falers second in the batting order of early homesteaders. The reasons for that will soon become apparent. However, in order to keep this history on the right chronological base path, those few who had a firm grip on the Basin prior to the Falers' arrival should be introduced first. Further, in the rush to tell the Faler story, the other histories and local folklore have overlooked these characters.

Like the Bondurants, before landing in the Basin many of the earliest settlers spent time in Kendall and the Upper Green River Valley. And some, like Al Sanford, finally settled in the Basin, but as younger frontier itinerants, they simple could not stay in a single place too long.

The Sanfords

Born and raised on a farm near Ottumwa, Iowa, Aldo "Al" Earl Sanford left home in 1880 and at age fifteen rode into Thermopolis, Wyoming, where he worked on area ranches. In 1889 he and a friend, Jack Haley, who later worked as a tie hack and rancher, wintered and trapped on the Upper Green River along Pine Creek.

In the spring of 1890 they moved to the Fall River Basin and continued running their trap lines. Like other trappers of the time, they trapped mink, coyotes, badger, beaver, muskrats, wolverines and lynx. Initially, fur companies like Northern bought the pelts for fur linings, fur wraps, hats and coats. Later Sears Roebuck and Montgomery Wards led the fur buying business. Mink and coyote furs commanded up to seventeen dollars a pelt. In today's dollars, those seventeen dollars then would be worth $414.58—a healthy sum to augment anyone's income.

Most trappers also hunted for deer and elk. Aside from the meat and the hides, the two ivory teeth from the lower jaw of the elk were particularly valuable. In fact, for a short time those ivories served as legal tender in Wyoming stores and saloons. Their value even prompted poachers to kill elk just for those two teeth. By chomping its upper and lower teeth together, the elk used them to make a clicking sound that warned other elk of impending danger

Jack Haley, with a reputation as a "tough customer," moved to Kendall Valley in the Upper Green, but Al headed to Miles City, Montana, where he settled and ranched. In 1891, Al met and married a Swedish immigrant, Ellen Peterson, who was twenty-five years old. Al had just turned twenty-seven. Wasting no time, during the next decade they had seven children.

In 1901, they moved back to the Basin. Beyond blacksmithing, Al continued to hunt and trap, and they added three more children to make an even ten. During this time he was the first white man to discover Granite Hot Springs that lies up Granite Creek—north and east of the Basin. The warmth of the hot springs melted the snow cover, provided winter grass, and offered easy and bountiful hunting during the winter months. Today, Granite Hot Springs is a popular summer and winter destination which was enhanced by the Civilian Conservation Corps during the Depression. In the winter, it is only accessible by dogsled or snow machine.

Al and his two older sons, Lin and Nate, began timbering the area above the river approaching the South Rim. Later Nate would cut and haul timber in the area and further south. Eventually that swath of clear cuts became known as the Sanford Trail and replaced the Noble Trail as the primary route into and out of the Basin for the ranchers from Daniel and Big Piney.

But once again in 1905, when Albert Einstein published his four papers that revolutionized physics and the understanding of the universe, Al Sanford felt the draw of another adventure and took his family, including all ten children, on a covered wagon tour of Alberta, Canada. From there they stopped again in Miles City, Montana and bought a ranch. After an uncharacteristically long stay that lasted seven years, they sold the ranch and in 1912 headed to Thermopolis,

Wyoming—more than thirty years after he first rode into the town that is known for the world's largest hot springs. Perhaps the springs provided relief from the Wyoming winters. But as another remedy, Al learned to play an unusual combination of instruments that included the violin, guitar and accordion.

In 1921, Al and Ellen decided to return to Sublette County and settled in Daniel. In 1924, at the age of fifty-eight, Ellen died. Al moved to Merna and lived on the ranch owned by his daughter, Deal, and her husband, Ed Todd. On July 4, 1929, ready to hunt, Al rode over Beaver Ridge to the Clarkson place—not far from the South Rim of the Fall River Basin. On July 5, he rode up the creek, but that evening his horse returned without him. Later the next day he was found dead, with his rifle still in his hands. A dead moose lay a short distance away. He was sixty-five years old and had died of an apparent heart attack.

Sandy Marshall

Walking in snowshoes, Sandy Marshall and Bill Roy set their trap lines along North Beaver Creek. That year, 1889, had been a good one for mink, muskrats and wolverines. During the same year, it is likely that the two trapped in the Fall River Basin. Roy, who had emigrated from Canada, was smitten with the Beaver Ridge country and in 1891 he settled near that ridge.

As young men, Alexander "Sandy" Marshall, and his partner, Woodberry Moore, came into the Kendall Valley from Nova Scotia. Kendall Valley sits on the northern end of today's Sublette County. He homesteaded on what today is the O Bar Y Ranch. He received his patent in 1904. In 1906, Sandy Marshall and Moore sold their homestead to Art Doyle, a one legged cowboy, bronc rider, and soon-to-be successful rancher.

At that time everybody had to rely on skis or snowshoes for winter travel and Sandy stood out as accomplished with both. His handmade skis were ten feet long and four inches wide. He used one long pole and covered up to sixty miles in a day. He also built and operated the first sawmill in what is now Sublette County. The water-powered mill sat at the mouth of Mill Creek, near the Green River Lakes. At different times, brothers Vint and Art Faler, operated the mill for him. In 1911, Marshall sold the mill to Bill Bowlsby of the Fall River country, who moved it and sited it on Upper Dell Creek.

During the late 1890s and early 1900s, Sandy and others built overnight cabins along their trap lines. Those lines extended to the Gros Ventre on the eastern edge of the Fall River Basin then along the Fall River, finally reaching north to Cliff Creek. Those "cabins" were really no more than log lean-tos that measured four feet by six feet inside.

Sandy Marshall was an early entrepreneur and frontiersman who flourished at a time when the Basin was reserved for only the toughest pioneers. Later—the exact year has never been reported—he died next to his trap lines on Little Spring Creek, a tributary of Cliff Creek. Sandy Marshall Creek in the Cliff Creek drainage is named in his honor.

Others

Characters like Alex "Deadshot" Swenson and Jim Williams, a former Butterfield stage driver out of Los Angeles, settled along the Upper Fall River no later than 1900, but together they will reappear in the next chapter, *The Originals*.

Although he settled at the upper end of Dell Creek, Charlie Bellon (also sometimes spelled Bellin) knew everyone in the Basin and particularly enjoyed Deadshot's company. As a very big man, he dwarfed Alex. He worked as a tie hack and carpenter, and his size earned him the moniker "Moose." His ability to handle logs and his carpentry skills also earned him a reputation as a first class log home builder.

Although barely shadows in the early light of the Basin's history, two trappers and prospectors staked claims in the Basin. Nels Bartlett allegedly had a platinum claim along Jack Creek, and even though he never disclosed its location, it is unlikely that it was a paying or valuable claim. He lived with his brother, Wilson, up Dell Creek and their homestead was later acquired by Shel E. Baker.

Similarly, Jack Davis panned for gold and did discover a fine gold dust, but it was so fine that he could never pan enough to make it a rewarding claim.

Two other similarly fleeting characters arrived sometime near the turn of the century and after that filed their homestead entries. In 1902, Henry Schloser homesteaded on the Upper Fall River, just down river from Charlie Noble's place. He was Charlie's first nextdoor neighbor. In 1901, Josephus McDonald settled on the other side of the river beyond Dry Island. Although coming a little later in 1907, a year after the Kellogg brothers founded a company that made the first ready-to-eat cereal, Kellogg's Corn Flakes, Frank Clark homesteaded on the west side of the river near today's highway. Clark's Butte and Clark's Draw near his homestead were named after him, and he completes the picture of those earliest pioneers.

The Next Wave of Homesteaders

The Falers

It wasn't a memorable wedding ceremony, but then Clarabelle Cook was only seventeen and her husband Daniel, eighteen. In the late 1870s, they were married near Cowley, Kansas. Foretelling a life of mishaps and hardship, a tornado blew down their first home in 1879. They moved to Julesburg, Colorado, and less than a year later moved again to Meeker, Colorado. In both places hunting may have been the primary source of income. Reflecting another itinerant life, the Falers moved again in 1881 to Fort McKinney in Wyoming Territory. Dan cut and hauled wood for the fort. As if hardship offered its own reward, in 1882, they traveled by covered wagon to Oakland, California. This time Dan had a short term contract to plow and sow wheat. On their way back, they stopped for a short time in Willow Springs, Wyoming, just beyond Rawlins, and then in 1884 they settled and ranched in Baggs, Wyoming. Still not a big town today, in the 1880s, Baggs then consisted of a store, a saloon, post office and a school.

In the summer of 1889 and after seven moves in ten years, the Falers and their eight children—five boys and three girls—settled near Daniel. A little later they moved to a ranch at the mouth of Pole Creek. Aside from two four-horse teams, they brought seventy head of cattle—enough to support a family or to start a new business. In 1892, after two years in the Daniel and Pinedale area, the family (except for Vint, the oldest boy) moved on again, this time to the Fall River Basin.

Vint homesteaded on Pole Creek and worked in Kendall. Later he ran a bar and started a freight business. His son, Harold, and his wife, Beulah, began a successful merchandising business, first in Boulder and then later in Pinedale. The store, Falers, which they started in Pinedale, serves today as the grocery, pharmacy, housewares supplier, camping outfitter, fishing and hunting store, gift shop, local deli, and hardware store.

Once settled in the Basin on what is now part of the Pfisterer Ranch, the Falers established an Indian trading post that traded goods for furs and hides to the Bannocks and Shoshones. As Daniel trapped and hunted, day to day management of the trading post fell to Clarabelle. A little later, their son, Arthur, homesteaded in the Basin along the Hoback River where even later Link Shidleler established his place.

Generally, the Indians were good neighbors and customers. But in 1895, a spirited uprising among the Bannocks occurred. Historically and under an 1868 treaty between the U.S government and the Shoshones and Bannocks, the Indians could use the Fall River Basin and the Canyon as hunting grounds and summer camp. The white trappers and hunting guides in Jackson, as well as some in Daniel and the Hoback Basin, wanted the Indians forced onto their reservation, thereby leaving the country for the exclusive use of the guides and their customers from the eastern United States and Europe.

Initially, the Indians refused to abide by any such request by the area whites. The governor of Wyoming, W. A. Richards, sided with the whites and requested federal troops. After several confrontations and a few Indian arrests, tensions rose. Of course, the newspapers made the most of this "Indian outbreak." As the Indians continued using their hunting privileges, a Jackson Hole posse was formed, including men from Bondurant. But as they approached the Canyon above the Basin, the Bannocks made a break for it, and after a few shots, two Indian deaths, and some injuries, the "battle" was over. The whole episode lasted just a few days and then life returned to normal. However, it did account for the name of Battle Mountain, a prominent red rock cliff between Bondurant and Jackson, and the conflict acquired the status of a special historical event often discussed or written about in the subsequent years.

During the uprising, many women and children in the Basin, including the Falers, fled their homes. In the hills above the trading post, Dan, Vint and Arthur had built a primitive fort under a protective rock ledge based on an earlier concern for their safety. With supplies in hand, Clarabelle and the younger children fled to this fort, only to return a few days later and continue their trading business.

If the Indian "battle" provided more drama in the Basin's history, the next act in the Faler family's life proved more tragic. After the 1895 confrontation between the Bannocks and white settlers, the residents of the Basin began to suspect what the Faler children knew all along—namely that Daniel had been abusing his wife and alcohol was very likely a co-conspirator. As a mountain man and as they said then an "old rounder," Daniel must have been brutal.

On the night of June 7, 1898, Daniel became more violent, and Clarabelle took her baby and walked to her son Arthur's place. The next morning Dan came riding over the hill to Arthur's homestead on the Upper Fall River. Arthur saw him coming and laid his gun in his wagon box and kept his hand on it. As the "old man" pulled up, he shouted, "I come to get your mother. She is going home with me."

Arthur replied, "No she ain't." Dan reached for his rifle in the scabbard on his saddle and Art grabbed his gun and opened fire. He shot his father dead and knocked him off his horse. Some reports say he shot him five times.

Art and his mother buried Daniel further down Stubb Creek from Arthur's homestead where the gravesite can be seen today. Daniel was thirty-eight.

Since Sublette County did not then have a newspaper, the *Evanston Wyoming Press* on June 25, 1898, wrote a short four-line story on the shooting under the headline, "Another Tragedy in Uinta County." Charlie Noble, who lived not far from Arthur Faler's place, said he witnessed the shooting and evidently first told Perry Pfisterer. Since then the story has been retold and then told again. However, over the past fifty years the fundamentals of the story have remained the same. Only two differences in the reports of this killing have emerged. The newspaper reported that Arthur "gave himself up, stood trial and was acquitted on the grounds of self-defense." The oral histories say that there never was an inquest. Next, the Evanston paper stated that Arthur used "a six shooter." The oral tradition simply cites "a gun" and does not specify whether it was a pistol or a rifle. However, a rifle was the firearm for hunting, and it was more accurate and powerful.

As the first known and reported murder in the Basin, it captured the community's imagination and has now become part of its folklore.

After Daniel's death, Arthur moved back to the original homestead. Clarabelle and the other children then lived with Vint on his Pole Creek ranch. She married Ed Miller in 1900, and in 1910 she owned the Pinedale Hotel. In 1911, Arthur and his mother sold the original homestead to Perry Pfisterer. In 1940, at the age of eighty-eight, Clarabelle died.

The Bowlsbys

The Bowlsby family's life in America began in Pennsylvania. During the1830s they moved to Ohio, but steadily traveled further west. First, in the late 1840s they farmed in Wisconsin and then resettled in Nebraska. Finally, in 1899, they headed to Wyoming and the Fall River or Hoback Basin.

By the time Emmanuel and Lydia Bowlsby settled in Wyoming, they had seven grown children. However, only two boys homesteaded and stuck it out in the Basin. The first and oldest, William "Bill" Crandell, was twenty-seven and married with two children when they arrived in the Basin. His wife was Amelia Miller Boomar and their two children were Arthur William, born in 1897, and Sylvia, born in 1899.

Perry, Bill's younger brother, was the other Bowlsby who settled in the Basin. He, too, was born in Nebraska in 1877.

In 1902, their father, Emmanuel, died in Pearl, Wyoming, and four years later their mother, Lydia, died in Alcova, Wyoming. Their new life in Wyoming was short-lived.

Bill Bowlsby homesteaded on Jack Creek Flats and Perry on Upper Dell Creek. Perry started a successful freighting business and even though they lived in the Fall River Basin, he and his wife owned the old Daniel Hotel from 1919 until 1929. One of their daughters, Stella, who helped them manage the hotel, was briefly married to Charlie Bellon, who the reader met earlier in Part Three. He was a big man and an accomplished carpenter, who was well liked by Basin residents.

Just after their arrival, Bill and Millie had their third and last child, Della. Realizing the need for immediate employment to support his young family, Bill, similar to other Basin pioneers, worked as a tie hack at the Kendall camp. As he and the family became more settled, Bill gained a reputation for his humor. No one enjoyed a good joke more than Bill. He developed a deep appreciation for flowers, but the short growing season did not support a wide variety of annuals or perennials. So Bill solved that problem by staging his own death and receiving nearly a lifetime's worth of condolence flowers grown in warmer climates.

Jokingly, but with a piercing accuracy, Bill once said that if a person lived in the Basin for twenty years he or she could be called a chokecherry. It is a shrub that produces an edible but yet very bitter or pungent berry. His comment lampooned the conflict, rumors and envy that often could plague a small rural community, particularly during winter or early spring. That label stuck and even the Pinedale newspaper, the *Roundup*, often referred to the residents of Bondurant as Choke Cherries—perhaps not fully appreciating its origin.

In 1911, Bill bought the Sandy Marshall sawmill at Kendall and in 1912 moved it to Upper Dell Creek where he operated it until 1945. Throughout this time he managed his ranch and ran his cattle on the Jack Creek Allotment, and later on the Hoback Allotment. After his first wife, Millie, died, in 1928, he married a Hoback Basin schoolteacher, Alma Allendar, who, like the Bowlsby family, was short in stature. Basin residents said the Bowlsbys—now including Alma—were "shorter than a minute." Since they were shorter than average, the Bowlsbys built their kitchen cabinets and door frames noticeably lower than average.

Although Arthur, Bill's only son, was born in Haysprings, Nebraska, he homesteaded in the Basin next to his father. Later he moved across the road and bought the Jesse Budd place on the Upper Fall River and joined the Hoback Stock Association. Originally, the property had been the Kilgore Ranch. His father leased Arthur's homestead which had been adjacent to his place.

At eighty-two, Bill Bowlsby died on December 31, 1954, in Jackson, Wyoming, where he was buried. Later his wife, Alma, moved to Arizona and lived well into her 90s.

Arthur said the vows at his "first" wedding in 1928 when he married Evelyn Ruth Beasely. They had three children. He was thirty-one and rumor suggested that before Evelyn he had been married and divorced three times. After another divorce, he married again in 1938. With Virginia Burns, he had three more children— William, Raymond and Dewey—and the two lived together until their respective deaths.

Growing up and taking his place in the community, Arthur Bowlsby acquired the nickname, "Banty." He was short in stature standing only five-foot-four—just a bit taller than Napoleon Bonaparte. He was feisty and fought like a bantam rooster. His nickname, Banty, fit him like a chicken in a chicken coop. Every one in the Basin knew him as Banty.

As a boy and younger man, he was an excellent, but daredevil skier. It was rumored that he had at least five wives. When these were combined with his *nom de guerre*, Banty, they produced grist for the Basin's character and rumor mill. Adding to that grist was Banty's penchant for telling stories that were at best minor exaggerations and, at worst ,simply invented.

Whatever the combination of ingredients and their preparation, it led to longevity. At ninety-seven, in1993, Banty died in Bondurant and was buried in that cemetery.

The Pfisterers

The name didn't sing like Carson, Cody or Horn and most guessed that the family came from some place in Germany. But in 1897-1898, John "Perry" Pfisterer rode over the Tetons from Idaho and up the Canyon into the Fall River Basin. One story has him riding in on a stolen horse chased by lawmen, but since he owned a ranch in Idaho and had registered his first brand there, that story seems far-fetched.

The West attracted all kinds—the hustler, the adventurer, the itinerant, the stickers and builders. Perry Pfisterer was a sticker and a builder. Near the turn of the century, he homesteaded the KC Ranch that later became the V-V. He sold that ranch to the Van Flecks in 1911 and purchased the original Faler homesteads from Clarabelle and Arthur. He homesteaded about sixty acres just south of the V-V and added acreage adjacent to his new ranch by buying the Matheson homestead and eighty acres from Eugene Robinson. Also during those early years, he served as one of the first mail carriers bringing mail from Merna to Bondurant.

He made 1911 an even more memorable year when he married Georgia. For the first year they lived in the original Faler buildings, but during the next year they moved Arthur Faler's house to their chosen building site and for the next twenty years lived there. They had two sons. Eugene was born in 1912 and Jake was born the next year. In 1931, they built a modern, ten room home with new conveniences, such as running water and electricity generated on site. Not long after that Perry died and his wife, Georgia, and two sons managed the ranch.

Despite their well established reputation in the Basin, during World War II, the family's German origins engendered hostility among some county residents. Ironically, having had two sons, Georgia's hobby was making doll dresses, and she enjoyed the company of her sons' wives and other women visitors. Later in life she became severely diabetic and required frequent medical care.

Save for a year of school in Los Angeles, Jake lived his entire life ranching in the Basin. And he was devoted to the business. Jake enjoyed a good story and a drink. His wife, Mary, came from Nebraska and was regarded by other Basin residents as well educated and cultured. She taught school at the Noble ranch and the Fish Creek School, two of several elementary schools in the Basin. Despite her desire to travel and see more of the world, Mary joined Jake in that life long commitment to the ranch.

His son, Harmon, and Harmon's wife, Sandy, now own and manage the ranch. Sandy grew up in Swan Valley, Idaho. They have three children: Stephanie, the oldest and in her late twenties, Crystal, who is a college student, and the last, Jake, who lives in Oregon, but often comes home for roundup.

In some respects, and even though opposites, Gene and Jake, the Pfisterer brothers, were builders like their father. They acquired more acreage in the Basin and operated a successful ranching business. In 1941, Gene purchased the L. W. Sargent ranch near Daniel. Then in 1947 Gene added the Conwell place, also near Daniel, where he lived with his first wife, Ida Mae McKenzie, who came from California. Fulfilling the Hollywood stereotype, in California she had acted and sung. She continued her "stage" career in Sublette County by helping to write and produce the annual Rendezvous Pageants, the County's reenactments of the area's mountain men gatherings. She branched out into oil painting and became a member of the Sublette County Artists Guild. But she and Gene would not spend the rest of their lives in matrimonial harmony. His brother, Jake, often said that Gene changed women as often as he, Jake, changed shirts.

Aside from his gentleman ranching, Gene enjoyed a good party and thought of himself as a ladies' man. Earlier, he and his friends worked the bars and dances in Jackson and Pinedale. In 1953, he sold the Daniel ranch and bought the Stockman's Club Bar in Pinedale. By that time he had married Kay Buston, but they divorced, too. Today, Kay still owns and manages Stockman's.

During the Stockman years, Gene always kept a Colt .45 under the bar. When he tended bar, he constantly advertised his shooting skills. Late one afternoon, a good customer of Stockman's Club Bar looked across the street to Stockman's competitor, the Cowboy Bar. That customer told Gene, that there was "no way in hell" that he could shoot across the street into the Cowboy Bar's cigarette vending machine and frighten away the customer struggling with the machine. Always up for this type of challenge, Gene took out his Colt and shot right through his own plate glass window. The bullet instantly pierced the Cowboy's entry door and the cigarette vending machine. The potential customer dropped to the floor and then ran out of the Cowboy Bar.

Gene owned Stockman's until 1967 when he bought a ranch along Forty Rod Road just north of Daniel. Change came in 1967 when he married Ellanora Estill, formerly Ellanora Lemire. She was born in Helena, Montana, in 1920, and Ellanora had married Joe Lemire in 1938. They moved to Daniel in 1950 and until their divorce, they worked on a local ranch, the Quarter Circle Five.

Gene sponsored an annual steer roping event and owned a prized quarter horse stallion, Tippo. During his days at Stockman's, Gene also sponsored "cutter races" down Pine Street, the main street of Pinedale. In a cutter race, a driver standing in a chariot with sled-like runners is pulled by a two horse team. They are run during the winter and the race is against time. It was no coincidence that the cutter races ran right by Stockman's, and Gene happily welcomed all the competitors and spectators.

Despite his image as the life of the party, when he rode and worked his cows he was deadly serious. He died in 1977, and a year later his third wife, Ellanora, died.

Shel E. Baker and the Campbells

The drier air and altitude caused the wagon wheels to creak as the horses pulled them up the Rim. But getting down into the Basin took more time and patience—switchback after switchback and all the while dragging a huge log chained to the back of the wagon that worked like a brake.

At last they reached the floor of the Basin. Happily climbing down, Shel unloaded the wagon containing their supplies and prospecting equipment. Shel's father and his father's friend pitched the tent and set up the kitchen fly.

That summer, 1895, had been hot and dry in Salt Lake and their first trip to the Basin had taken longer than expected. The sound of a slow moving river and a late afternoon breeze made them forget the parched lips, dust and stiff legs. The folks who had told them about the Basin and urged that they visit, certainly knew what they were talking about.

Sightseeing and fishing had their place, but the three men had gold on their minds, too. The next few days they worked their way up

Jack Creek, panning at every bend. After a week they still had not found gold or any other mineral of value. Reluctantly, they drove the wagon back to Salt Lake.

Shortly after returning, Shel married Beulah Campbell. They first settled in Clear Creek, Utah, but later moved to Logan. In the early 1900s, they had two children, Josephine and Theodore. However, even after fifteen years, the memories of the Fall River Basin had the drawing power of a strong magnet. In 1910, Shel and his wife's two brothers, Lorenzo "Lennie" and Arthur Campbell, hitched up the horses and drove them to the Basin. They staked out homesteads on Jack Creek Flat. Shel settled near the upper end of Jack Creek, and Arthur homesteaded next to him. Later in 1917-1918, Hearly Fronk, a coal miner from Superior, Wyoming, and his family settled next to Shel Baker along Jack Creek. Lennie settled below all of them on Jack Creek Flat and just above the Bowlsby homestead. Arthur also homesteaded another 158 acres next to his brother. However, Arthur and Lennie Campbell returned to Idaho. Reluctantly, Shel agreed to spend the winter in an old cabin on his future homestead. If the Basin winter proved too harsh, all three had decided to homestead in a more hospitable climate.

In the spring of 1911, after surviving the winter, Shel returned to Logan, and he brought his wife and two children to their new home, where they lived and ranched for the next thirty-six years. Shel's brother-in-law, Arthur Campbell, also filed his homestead claim in 1911, and his brother, Lennie, filed in 1912.

In 1919, Shel and Beulah had their third child, Ruth Louise. In 1924, another child, Howard John, was born. Later, Theodore, the Bakers' first son, would file his own homestead entry near his father's place. In 1933, he married Muriel Loveridge, a school teacher from Salt Lake, and ranched with his father until Ted's death in 1945.

In 1923, Josephine Baker married Eugene Holt, a rancher, who also homesteaded near the Bakers. They ranched in the Basin for many years, and they ran their cattle on the Jack Creek Allotment.

Eventually, they moved to Jackson, but continued to ranch.

In 1939, Ruth Baker married Grover Snyder, and they ranched in the Basin as well. In 1944, Howard married Pauline Hansen, the granddaughter of Benjamin "Bondy" Bondurant.

In 1947, Shel, his son, Howard, and another homesteader, John Wertz, sold their Basin ranches and moved to Montana. Together, they moved over a thousand head of cattle and fifty horses from the Hoback Basin to Jackson, Wyoming. From Jackson they drove the cattle and horses over Teton Pass into Victor, Idaho, and loaded them on a train. Finally, they unloaded the stock at their destination, Divide, Montana.

In 1953, at age eighty-eight, Shel died and was buried in Jackson, Wyoming.

Shel Baker's story has special import as it introduces the Campbell family who will re-emerge in clearer focus in *Part Five: The Cowboys.*

Frank Van Fleck and the V-V Ranch

The 1913 coin toss was a high-stakes flip to divide two jointly owned properties. Neither Roy nor Frank could decide which one of the two properties had the greatest value. If the coin came up heads, Frank would win the V-V Ranch at the mouth of the Hoback Canyon and his brother, Roy, would win the store, the Jackson Mercantile. If Frank came up with tails, he would have won the store and Roy the ranch. The coin came up heads, and Frank took over the V-V that he and Roy bought in 1911 from John "Perry" Pfisterer. Perry Pfisterer had homesteaded the V-V, but when he owned it, the ranch was called the KC Ranch.

Primarily, Frank and his wife, the former Pearl Nelson from Jackson, ran the V-V as a dude ranch and fall hunting lodge. During the winter storms when the Hoback Canyon was closed, the ranch also served as a warm and safe harbor for those who were traveling to Jackson and stranded. The guest ranch consisted of a large rustic lodge that also served as the ranch headquarters and a number of small log cabins. Frank built a successful business and developed it into an attractive "destination" resort during those years when dude ranching was still a major adventure for those from the East and Europe. Later, he and Pearl divorced. They had one son, Clinton Van Fleck, who later lived in Jackson, Wyoming.

Reflecting the popularity of the "Dude" experience in those early days, three other dude ranches operated in the Basin. In 1919, Noah Booker, whose family homesteaded at the turn of the century on Cottonwood Creek just south of Daniel, launched his dude ranch business. In 1922, Wallace Hiatt from Chicago started the Triangle F. Later Paul Frazier purchased the old George Parody place on upper Dell Creek and operated a dude and hunting camp with four log cabins that was known as the K-O. Later the lodge, a few cabins and the business were moved by the Fraziers across the highway and below the V-V. Of course, the Bondurants had the original Basin dude ranch.

Roy and Frank Van Fleck's parents were born, raised and married in upstate New York. They moved briefly to Nebraska then turned back east to settle in Paw Paw, Michigan, where Roy was born in 1879.

In 1899 Roy, traveling by wagon, moved to Pearl, in North Park, Colorado, a gold mining boom town. He built and managed a merchandise or general store there. Back in Michigan, Frank fell forty feet from a windmill tower and luckily survived with no permanent disability. However, he contracted tuberculosis or "consumption." Roy returned to Michigan and persuaded Frank and their parents that the dry mountain air would improve his health. And it did.

Together the brothers returned to Pearl, and when the boom went bust, Frank traveled to Casper, Wyoming, and worked on a sheep ranch. Roy disposed of the store. In 1906, Roy packed up the remaining merchandise in his wagon and headed north to Lander, Wyoming, where he met Frank. Like many before them, they planned to move to Oregon. But on their way, they stopped in Cody, Wyoming, and met Buffalo Bill Cody, who, Roy reported, was "tying one on" in a local saloon. Sober the next day, Cody invited them to his lodge, Pahaska Teepee, on the eastern edge of Yellowstone National Park. Made from logs, Pahaska served as a hunting lodge, drinking establishment and entertainment center for Cody's friends and acquaintances. During the heyday of his Wild West Show, the lodge was a popular recreation spot appointed with some of the first draft beer spigots in the West.

Roy and Frank stayed several days, and before they left, Buffalo Bill convinced them to visit Jackson Hole and lay in some elk meat for the trip to Oregon. By the time they arrived, it was already late September. Soon snow would cover the passes and mountains, so they stayed in Jackson, helping to build the first Mormon church in that area.

Liking Jackson, the brothers started the Jackson Mercantile that was located on the ground floor of the "clubhouse," the first building on the town square which had been built in 1896. Achieving nearly overnight success, the brothers could afford to buy the V-V.

Frank ran the ranch until his death in August, 1938. He had just returned from a nearby steak fry with his ranch guests when he was stricken by a fatal heart attack. His former wife, Pearl, sold the ranch to Albert and Margaret Feuz in 1944. They operated it until 1966-1967 when Roy and Caroline Fisk bought part of it. Around that time it was renamed the Black Powder Ranch. The Fisks purchased the rest ofthe property in 1972. Dr. and Mrs. Paul Cornell bought it in 1996, and completely renovated it. The Cornells put the ranch on the market in 2003, and it was finally sold to Sam Coutts of Jackson, Wyoming, in fall, 2005. Mr. Coutts had previously owned Camp Creek Inn south of Hoback Junction. Not only does Sam now own a hunting guide business but plans to reopen the "Black Powder Ranch" as a summer guest ranch.

Jake Query

In 1907, Lionel " Jake" Query and his wife, Minnie, and their children moved to Sublette County from Seattle, Washington. They first leased the Roy place near Beaver Creek, but in that same year they homesteaded one hundred and sixty acres in the Basin and proved up in 1914. Jake built a six-room house, and they lived in the Basin for almost thirty years.

Considered a very accomplished "old time" cowboy, Jake rode for Charlie Noble.

Around 1915, he received the contract to carry the mail from Daniel to Bondurant. Jake and Minnie bought a house in Daniel, and their children attended school there. They sold the property in 1919 and settled again in the Basin. During his stay in Daniel, Jake joined a few others who together formed the Green River Valley Good Roads Club. They were boosters and lobbyists for improved roads, an essential ingredient for economic growth and convenience.

By 1920, and after much trouble, a "first class road" through the Hoback Canyon was completed and that opened up the first direct

auto route from Rock Springs to Yellowstone Park—about twelve
years after Henry Ford brought out his Model T and six years after he
pioneered the assembly line production of his car. Not surprisingly,
Jake began to supplement his income with road construction and
maintenance. At that time he owned the Basin's only road grader.

Eventually they sold their property to Helen Revett and two
of her friends from Chicago, who spent their summers in the Basin. In
1940, Helen briefly joined the Hoback Stock Association and
attempted to run forty-five head of cattle on the Allotment. Since the
old Query place apparently did not come with a grazing permit, the
Forest Service disapproved her application.

Dave Hicks

Dave Hicks was born in Spanish Fork, Utah, on May 5, 1883. He was the son of Samuel Moroni Hicks and Caroline Jarvis, who spent most summers in Kendall Valley with their daughter, Florence, and her husband, Spencer Hecox. Coming from Evanston or Mountain View, Wyoming, at age twenty-five, Dave filed his Basin homestead entry in 1908. That same year he married Molly Allen of Pinedale. Eight years later he proved up on the 160 acres. Still on the Upper Fall River, his property lay just across the river from what would later become Bill Stong's homestead.

Two of his brothers, Ralph and William Arthur or "Art" Hicks from Mountain View, Wyoming, followed their brother to the Basin. After his marriage to Anna May Myrick in 1913, Art homesteaded near his brother in 1916 and proved up in 1921. Much later, their more flamboyant brother, Ralph, showed up. He filed his claim in 1940 and received his patent in 1947.

Dave Hicks died in Evanston, Wyoming, in 1958, and his brother, Art died in 1942.

Ralph was born in 1893 and married Daisy Dean Hatch in 1915. In their middle years Ralph and "Miss Daisy" moved to the Basin, and they quickly gained some notoriety. Ralph often wore a cowboy hat with a wide brim and a pistol in a holster or tucked into the waist band of his jeans. He was a forceful, if not a demanding man. He always seemed to have a feud with someone.

On the other hand, Daisy was striking in appearance. Her brown eyes complemented her darker complexion that silently spoke of her Cherokee heritage. She wore her hair pulled back and high heels. Both carried themselves as if they were people of means, but no one knew if it was just style or real wealth.

They were not, as some say in the Basin, "cattle people," but made their living running a hunting camp and a gas station. Ralph also trapped. His hunting business catered to people like Erle Stanley Gardner, then a famous author and creator of the Perry Mason series.

Although they had seven children, including Lois, Ralph and Daisy liked to party and gamble at the Wort Hotel in Jackson Hole. Ralph often went by himself to the Wort and gained a reputation as a "man about town." Ralph died of a heart attack in the winter of 1952. He was fifty-nine years old. Ralph's parting gift to Daisy was a pile of debt. She later remarried, and is still kindly remembered in the Hoback Basin.

Aside from starting a "settlement" of the Hicks in the Basin, Dave's homestead had achieved some historical distinction by virtue of its earlier residents. First, Arthur Faler settled on it, and that is where he shot and killed his father. Arthur never proved up on it, but the Sanford family occupied it during one of their brief stays in the Basin.

After the Sanfords, the Reaser family leased it, and they had their own special story. In 1898, around the Brown's Park area of Utah, Charlie Reaser shot and killed Cleophas J. Dowd, one of Utah's most puzzling lawmen. Charlie claimed self-defense and was acquitted. Fearing retribution from Dowd's friends, he hurriedly made his way to the Fall River Basin. He and his wife, Minnie, (a seemingly popular name at the time) had seven children. Charlie acquired a new measure of respectability by working as the game warden between Merna and Bondurant. Sometime before 1908 they settled near the Daniel. It has been reported that later Reaser and his wife moved to Jackson Hole and started a church then known as the "Brothers Church."

Apparently with a nose for shooting, just after Charlie had escaped Utah with his life, he intervened on behalf of Frank Wilhelm, a rancher along Horse Creek west of Daniel. In a land dispute with his neighbor, Truman Andrus, Frank shot him. Truman Andrus was severely wounded, but lived. In any event, a jury convicted Frank of felonious assault, and he was sentenced to four years in the State Penitentiary in Rawlins, Wyoming. Charlie Reaser circulated a petition on his behalf, and Frank was released after serving two years of his sentence. Later Frank sold his ranch to Austin Richardson, and Truman Andrus, Frank's nemesis, sold his ranch to Austin's good friend, Clarence Webb. Frank's daughter, Helen Wilhelm, homesteaded in Fall River Basin. In 1916, she filed on one hundred and sixty acres a little below the V-V Ranch. Her patent was awarded in 1920.

After David Hicks proved up on the homestead, Link Shideler bought it from him, and ever since it has been known as the Shideler place.

Cleophas J. Dowd

In an article, *Cleophas J. Dowd, Utah's Most Enigmatic Lawman*, Utah historian and author, Kerry Ross Boren, wrote:

Cleophas J. Dowd remains one of the most controversial and mysterious characters of the Old West, yet few people recognize his name today or are aware of who he was, although he was not only Utah's greatest lawman, but probably the greatest gunman of his era.

While Boren's article strikes me as an exaggeration of Dowd's life, it accurately placed him in the center of outlaw history.

Born in 1856, Cleophas was the oldest son of Irish immigrants, who had recently moved from Boston to San Francisco, California. Despite a young life of delinquency, he studied for the priesthood, and when twenty-one years old he took his vows. But celebrating that occasion, he shot and killed a man in a saloon brawl, and that episode revealed Dowd's violent temper.

Having heard about this hideaway, he fled to Brown's Park in northeastern Utah. Brown's Park was home to outlaws including Butch Cassidy and the Wild Bunch, Tom Horn, and Ann Basset better known as the "Queen of Rustlers"—later all were reported to be friends of Cleophas J. Dowd. Even Kit Carson, John Wesley Powell, and mountain man, Jim Baker, left their footprints on Brown's Park. The Park straddles the Green River, and on the southwest it was protected from bad weather and lawmen by the Unita Mountains.

Just after arriving at Brown's Park, Dowd lived at the James Warren ranch, home to horse and cattle thieves. Shortly, in a fight with another outlaw, he shot and killed his second man. Wearing his priest's robe, Dowd even presided over the man's burial. Later Dowd allegedly met Frank and Jesse James, who were staying with Jim Baker in Brown's Park. It was also reported that Cleophas won a shooting contest with Jesse James. Then Dowd made his livelihood by selling horses to outlaw gangs.

Eventually he married Ella, the daughter of Mormon Bishop, Charles E. Colton. One story holds that earlier he had married an Indian woman. Around 1885 and still selling horses to outlaws, Dowd was appointed deputy sheriff of Utah's Unita County by Ella's uncle, who was a lawman. In the late 1880s Cleophas became a railroad detective and then a Pinkerton detective. By then he owned a ranch in Brown's Park where his wife and children lived. But his marriage fell victim to his violence and frequent absence.

Also, around the late 1880s and in a covered wagon, Charlie Reaser and his family drove near Brown's Park and met Dowd. Dowd, who in a fight with his own brother was shot in the groin, was looking for help on his ranch. He made a fatal mistake and hired Reaser. On April 11, 1898, Charlie Reaser shot Dowd in the ranch's harness shop. The motives for the killing ranged from an intense dislike for Dowd and his abusive behavior to being hired to kill him. After claiming self-defense, a Justice of the Peace found Reaser innocent.

However, fearing for his life, Reaser took his family and fled to the Hoback Basin. It is alleged that the Sundance Kid chased him to the Utah and Wyoming border.

Dowd was buried on his ranch. And today Brown's Park is part of the 13,455 acre Brown's Park National Wildlife Refuge that borders the northern end of Dinosaur National Monument in far northwest Colorado.

The Latecomers

The earliest Basin pioneers settled or ranched in the early to late 1890s. The next wave of homesteaders, who began to build the community and stabilize it, washed into the Basin between the late 1890s and the early 1900s. The reader has already been introduced to these pioneers and homesteaders.

Although not too distant from the Basin's "founding fathers and mothers," the latecomers began to arrive well after 1915, and many did not migrate until the 1920s and some even later. By the time many settled, the Prohibition Amendment to the Constitution had been passed (1920) and repealed (1933) and Babe Ruth had already had his sixty home run season (1927).

Many latecomers took up homesteads along the Upper Fall River and others settled on Jack Creek Flats. A few settled on Dell Creek. Following the deaths of the early pioneers and ranchers, a few of their children, like the Pfisterers, Campbells, and Bowlsbys, chose to stay, and together with the latecomers, they defined life in the Basin during the 1930s, 1940s, and early 1950s. Many of those pioneers' children and the latecomers have now died, as well.

In another history some of these latecomers could play a major role, but in this one, most of them will receive just a nod or two of acknowledgement. A few will reappear as best supporting actors or actresses in Parts Four and Five.

One main reason accounts for the latecomers' more modest character development. This history focuses on the earliest pioneers and ranchers who helped build the community and define its social life. They also built the Fall River and later the Hoback Stock Association that gave the Basin much of its identity. They were the same people who created the ranching and cowboy tradition of the Basin and the early twentieth century West. Since each of these latecomers was connected to the Stock Association, they earned an "honorable mention." But they simply were not "present at the creation," nor did they substantially define the early cowboy tradition.

Julius "Albert" Miller

The Miller homestead and ranch were tucked between Shorty Burnitt's place on the Upper Hoback and the Kilgore ranches that later became the Jesse Budd place and then the Arthur Bowlsby home. He was born in 1906 and arrived in the Basin around 1927. He filed his homestead entry in 1928, and was awarded his patent in 1935. Albert and his wife, Randy, lived in a neat three room log house. Placed by family and friends on the Upper Hoback Road, a boulder with a bronze plaque marks the location of the Miller homestead and sawmill.

He joined the Hoback Stock Association and ran about thirty to forty head of cattle and ten head of horses on the Allotment. He enjoyed trapping and hunting, but earned most of his income from harvesting and sawing timber. He also helped build the log library next to the Bondurant Church. In 1982, Albert died in a snowmobile accident. However, it was fitting that he died doing what he had come to enjoy the most.

Two Women Homesteaders:
Mary Dempsey and Jessie Hathaway

Both of these women homesteaded along the Upper Hoback as a means to expand the adjacent ranches of their husbands or relatives—a very common practice in Wyoming and the rest of the West.

Immediately down river from Jesse Budd's ranch, his wife, Mary Dempsey, homesteaded. They had been married in 1906. She applied for her patent in 1917 and proved up in 1921, and not surprisingly, the Dempsey homestead worked as an integral part of Jesse Budd's ranch.

Down river, next to the Budd and Dempsey place, sat Jessie Hathaway's homestead. Jessie, the sister of Charlie Noble's first wife, Grace Hathaway, filed her claim in 1915 and received her patent in 1919. Again, her place supported the Noble's Basin ranch. The Noble ranch included a small log home, barns and corrals. Later Charlie Noble's son, Kenneth and his wife, Alice Jewett, lived at the ranch. Like his father, Kenneth also became a member of the Hoback Stock Association and ran about eighty head of cattle on the Allotment.

Elmer Nutting

The Nutting homestead rested just below Charlie Noble's ranch. He filed his entry in 1925 and proved up in late 1931. Even though Nutting Draw took its name from Elmer, he ran just a few head of cattle on the Hoback Horse and Cattle Allotment. During the late 1930s he worked as a tie hack at Lead Creek camp. Still later, he and his wife, Madageine, helped manage the cow camp and Charlie Noble's ranch. The cowboys reported that his wife, a stout no nonsense woman, found little use for the niceties of hospitality when it came to cowboys. Charlie Noble told Elmer he could stay, but unless Elmer's wife treated Charlie's cowboy with the respect they deserved, Madageine had to go. Although Elmer's wife chose silence over words of courtesy, the cowboys' life on the ranch quickly improved.

Bill Stong

Next to the Nuttings and toward the highway lay Bill Stong's one hundred and sixty acre homestead. Born in 1898 in McCoysville, Juanita County, Pennsylvania, he spent his early life at home. When his first and only marriage failed, he moved to Sheridan, Wyoming, where his cousin, Rex, owned and operated a ranch and farm. From Sheridan he headed to the oil fields of Casper, Wyoming, and finally in 1921, at the age of twenty-three, he drove his team of horses and wagon to the Basin and the Upper Hoback

He filed in 1921 and won his patent in 1927. He lived in a small rectangular log cabin that he built. Later he added a log tool shed next to his cabin and a log barn and corrals. He earned a reputation for hard work, and even though he kept to himself, Bill enjoyed occasional company. A pipe seemed like a near permanent fixture in his mouth, and with a twinkle in his eye, he could still tell entertaining stories. Somehow he seemed always to have local news or other developments to report. Of course, Bill joined the Hoback Stock Association and put about fifteen to thirty head of cattle and eight horses on the Allotment. His Hereford cattle won praise as some of the best in the Basin.

He died in 1980 and was buried in the Daniel Cemetery. His last will and testament gave his ranch and belongings to his friend and neighbor, Bob McNeel, who bought Charlie Noble's Basin ranch in the mid-1950s. In 2006, the original Stong homestead and outbuildings still stand as one of the best preserved and picturesque homesteads in the area.

John Wertz

Originally John homesteaded on the Jack Creek Flats next to the Bowlsbys. He filed in 1917 and proved up in 1922. Near that homestead, a draw that drops into Jack Creek would later be named Wertz Draw—well deserved recognition for a man who rode his horse from Texas to the Hoback Basin. While he may have ranched, he developed into a first class craftsman, who specialized in using elk horns for furniture art, who cut them into knife handles, candle holders, letter openers, lamps and a wide variety of other items. By about thirty years, he predated a stunningly expensive market for those same items that thrives today in Jackson, Wyoming, and other western resort communities. Less by design and more by circumstance, his skill transformed him into something of a social institution in the Basin. More of that story will soon unfold.

In 1933, either through a sale or trade, Wertz acquired the John "Daddy" Linn homestead from Frank Hansen, the Bondurant's son-in-law. Linn, born on a plantation in Georgia, moved his family to Big Piney in 1910 when he was already forty-nine. The original Linn homestead sat south of the V-V and just off the river. In 1934, Frank Hansen repurchased all but four acres of that homestead from John Wertz. On those four remaining acres John built a three-room log sided house, a garage and workshop. Here and about one hundred yards off the highway, in 1939, John opened the Wertz Novelty Shop. The travelers, who were heading to Jackson or Yellowstone, became its main patrons, and the shop proved successful. Later John sold the shop, and soon the reader will discover that the shop became the nucleus for a Hoback Basin social institution.

Noah Booker

In 1919, Noah bought the old John Rogers homestead and built a dude ranch business that operated through the 1930s. Not surprisingly it was called the Booker Ranch and specialized in pack trips. Having been born in Missouri in 1882, Noah was thirty-seven when he started this new venture.

Noah and his parents moved to Wyoming in the late 1890s. When they hitched up their wagons for the trip, his father, William "Pappy" Booker, had turned fifty-five and his mother, Mary was forty-seven. Noah was twenty-one. In 1900, all three filed homestead entries on North Cottonwood Creek south of Daniel.

Aside from ranching, Pappy Booker served as Special Constable for the emerging justice court in Daniel. That court adjudicated civil claims and criminal matters, including murder and thereby establishing the first law and judicial system in the area.

Using his homestead as collateral, Noah bought and sold property in the early days of Daniel. During those visits he must have met Grace Van Winkle, a school teacher. She lived in Daniel and taught first at the Charlie Ball ranch. Then she taught at the Merna School and next at the Bronx school. Finally she taught at the Bondurant school.

Noah found beauty in Bondurant beyond that of nature. He married Grace in 1923. Noah was forty-one and Grace forty. Perhaps too set in their ways, they were divorced in 1934. However, Noah operated the dude ranch until 1938 when he first leased and then sold it to Roy Nealeigh and his family. For several years both the Bookers and Nealeighs ran cattle together on the Hoback Allotment.

Beyond his dude ranch and dabbling in cattle, Noah played the violin. He did not play just an ordinary instrument, but a Stradivarius. Also during the thirties, Noah began to enjoy his drink a little too much and liked to party with his friends. His last party took place in a log cabin south of Pinedale near Boulder, Wyoming, and Boulder Lake. They drank and played music. Noah coaxed beautiful notes from his Stradivarius—both classical and bluegrass. When he finished, he put the violin back in the cabin, and then Noah and his friends sat around a campfire. Before they knew it, the cabin started to smolder and then broke into flames. Noah rushed into the cabin frantically searching for his violin but the cabin collapsed. Both Noah and his rare violin perished. It was May 21, 1954, and Noah was seventy-two years old.

His decision to risk his life for his Stradivarius was not the act of someone who was just drunk. In the 1950s and nearly two hundred and twenty years after Antonio Stradivari's death, only about 650 of his violins had survived. Today, they sell for between $1.25 million and $2 million.

Noah's former wife, Grace, continued a long life of community service in Bondurant and deeded the land for the present Bondurant elementary school. In January, 1978 she died at age ninety-five.

Wallace Hiatt

After his 1910 discharge from the Navy and instead of returning home to Chicago, young Wallace found a job as an Idaho cowboy. Occasionally, the owner of the Idaho ranch asked him and other cowboys to drive recently purchased horses down from Cody, Wyoming, through Jackson, and over Teton Pass into Idaho. During those horse drives, Wallace heard about the Fall River Basin that sat just south of Jackson and the rough and tumble cowboy life there. Back in Chicago, Hiatt learned that the Bondurant homestead might be for sale. Certainly not familiar with Basin winters, Wallace made his trip to the Basin in the winter of 1919. He came by train to Opal and by mail truck to south of Big Piney where the truck broke down. From there he took a dogsled to Daniel where Frank Hansen met him with a pair of skis. Wallace was at best a novice cross country skier. Since the temperature hovered near fifty below zero, that last twenty miles must have been unforgettable and seemed like an almost neverending trip.

In the end, the Bondurants chose not to sell, but after

surviving the ordeal of his winter trip, in 1922, Hiatt homesteaded one hundred and sixty acres that lay a mile south of the Bondurants and east of the old highway. Wallace and his two daughters moved from Chicago, and they must have marveled at the transition from life in a big city to life in the Basin. Either his first wife died or they were divorced. He built two small cabins and set up a store in a large canvas tent. The cabin logs came from Bill Bowlsby's sawmill. Those modest cabins marked the beginning of the Triangle F Ranch. They received the patent on their homestead filing in 1926.

Around this time Hiatt's uncle, Charles Bronnenberg, homesteaded in the Basin across the highway from Noah Booker's ranch. He helped build the Triangle F guest ranch and run the store. With his uncle "minding the store," Wallace accepted an invitation to travel to California and manage the horse transportation business in Yosemite National Park. The job paid well, and he needed the extra cash to further build the Triangle F Ranch. At the Park, he met Alice, who soon became his second wife. Later it was reported in the Jackson weekly newspaper that she was the first woman to receive a college degree in forestry. They moved back to the Basin and operated the dude ranch and store. In the 1930s the highway was relocated, and they rebuilt and enhanced the Triangle F at its current location on the west side of the highway. Newspaper accounts state that a fire at the old location made this transition more a necessity than a convenience. However, a service station, grocery store and "confectionery" store remained on the east side of the highway.

The ranch consisted of a main lodge with two large river rock fireplaces, six guest cabins, four out buildings and a corral. Although not in use, it still stands today.

In 1939, as a winter recreation complement to the Triangle F, the Hiatts bought twenty acres at the junction of Granite Creek and the Hoback River—several miles from Bondurant into the Hoback Canyon. They built log ranch buildings and a "filling" station. That lodge sat south of Battle Mountain and was called Battle Mountain

Lodge. That land is now in the Bridger-Teton National Forest and the buildings were standing intact until a few years ago when they were sold and relocated.

Sometime in the 1940s, the Hiatts sold both the Triangle F and Battle Mountain Lodge and purchased land on Bryan Flats located much closer to Hoback Junction and Jackson. The property lay at the far northern edge of the Hoback Canyon. On that location they built another dude ranch, the Broken Arrow, and operated it until the 1950s when they sold it to Buster and Lois Leeks, who continued it until 1962. John L. Lewis, the prize fighter, was one of the Hiatts more notable guests. The Jackson newspaper also reported a fire at the Broken Arrow. Sometime after the sale in 1954, the Hiatts moved to New Mexico where Wallace served as the business manager for the Apache Tribe of the Mescalero Reservation. Wallace also worked for the Navajos' Industrial Development Agency. Later he became a trader of Indian art and artifacts

Not only did Hiatt contribute much to the dude ranch business in the Basin and its early reputation as a "frontier" destination resort, but since the Bondurant post office was located at the Triangle F for many years, many Hoback Association members listed the Triangle F as their official address. Wallace Hiatt died at Veterans Hospital, in Grand Junction, Colorado, on July 10, 1976. He was survived by his wife, Alice, four daughters, and three sons.

In the 1970s, the Triangle F was purchased by Jim Kelson, who lives south of Park City, Utah, and near Heber City. Although the ranch is "mothballed," it remains in excellent condition which is a tribute to the quality of its original construction.

The Others

Some prominent Basin families or just interesting individuals, who settled as early as 1915 and as late as the 1940s and 1950s, now deserve recognition. By virtue of their connection to the Hoback Stock Association and its tradition, a few, like the Farris and the Mack families, will be much better illuminated later. Some others are worth an honorable mention now.

First in line is the Fronk family. Shortly after their arrival in 1919, Hearly Fronk, his wife, Jennie, and their older children, became established and respected Hoback Basin settlers. Since they homesteaded on Jack Creek, their immediate neighbors and friends were the Bakers, the Campbells, and the Bowlsbys. Consequently, they ran their cattle on Jack Creek and later became members of the Jack Creek Association. However they soon branched out and met many other Basin homesteaders.

Later, the children of Hearly and Jennie Fronk, particularly the fifth child and daughter, Eileen, became prominent Basin citizens. Eileen, who eventually married Billy Dockham in 1940, became an artist, historian, writer, and a unique link from the Basin's past to its more current times. She dutifully and gleefully educated many newcomers.

Leaving the hard life and primitive conditions of a coal miner in the early 1900s, Hearly Fronk drove a wagon and a borrowed team of horses to the Hoback Basin in 1917. He explored Jack Creek Flats and immediately filed his homestead claim near the upper end of Jack Creek, then returned to Superior, Wyoming, and his life as a coal miner. In 1919, with his wife, two teenage boys, Vince and Dan, daughter, Dorothy, and a one year old baby girl, Lillian, the Fronks moved to upper Jack Creek. They first lived in a two room log cabin with a dirt floor. The cabin had been built by an earlier settler.

Eileen was born in 1921 just as the new house and furniture had been finished, and she had the distinction of being the only Fronk child born in the Hoback Basin. The Fronks, like others in the Basin, struggled to make a living. They helped other ranchers hay and that small income allowed them to improve their own land. When Vince and Dan turned twenty-one, they homesteaded next to their parents and greatly expanded the Fronk ranch property.

Later, Eileen and Billy bought part of Fronk ranch and ran the Quarter Circle XL Ranch for the next eleven years. They sold that property and moved to a few acres on the south side of Highway 191 and just north of the Upper Hoback Road. Changing careers, Billy built custom log homes and Eileen taught art classes and emerged as one of Wyoming's most talented wildlife artists. Eileen was a member of the Ladies Guild that was created to care-take the Episcopal Church, St. Hubert the Hunter. Billy and Eileen played important roles in creating the annual Bondurant BBQ at the church, which supported the Ladies Guild. Billy's specialty was the baked beans, and even today they are known as "Billy beans."

Billy died in 1992, and Eileen at eighty-two survived open-heart surgery, but did not recover from another surgery to fix an aneurysm. With many images of future paintings in her head, she died

on November 21, 2003, survived by a son, Hearly, and his
family and a daughter, Sharon, and her family

Next in line is James "Levi" Hill. In 1915, at age twenty-nine,
Levi filed his homestead claim on lower Dell Creek. He proved up on
his entry in 1923, but was never considered a Basin resident.
Although he worked for Daniel area ranchers, Levi was afflicted with
gold fever. In late September, 1954, Levi and three companions rode
off on another gold crusade near Dell Creek. All rode black horses, and
later their color was considered an omen of death. In steep rocky
terrain Levi's horse fell over backward, crushing his chest and his head
on impact.

Help was summoned and several Basin residents rode to the
accident. The hole in his head showed his brain tissue. They built a
stretcher and carried him down the mountain. Other Basin residents
rode or walked up the mountain to help with the stretcher and the
horses. Miraculously still alive when they reached the Basin floor,
Levi died on a gurney in the Jackson hospital.

Orin Robinson homesteaded near Fisherman's Creek in 1915.
Paid by the ranchers, he started out in predator control, trapping
wolves and bears, including grizzlies. He ended up as a thirty year
supervisor for the U.S. Fish and Wildlife Service, and a butte near his
homestead is called Robinson Butte.

Moving towards Bondurant, Fred Miller homesteaded in 1916
and proved up in 1920. Miller Draw is his legacy today.

Others like Fred Watts, Lee Koontz, Eugene Robinson, Andy
Erickson and Willie Jones ranched and ran their cattle on the Jack
Creek Allotment. The Parodys, Green Beeman, Rollie Ottenberg,
Dave Riling, Oliver Robinson and Charles Barrett, settling along Dell
Creek, all contributed to the Basin's history. For example, two draws

toward upper Dell Creek are named after two Dell Creek homesteaders —the first is called Parody Draw and one just west of it is known as Riling Draw.

In 1924, Carroll Noble, the son of James Noble, who settled in Cora, homesteaded in the Basin. Also his sister, Freida, homesteaded there. His family ranched in Cora, and he used the Basin property as summer pasture and hayfields. In 1944, they sold those properties to buy another ranch in Cora. As Zach and James Noble were brothers, Carroll would have been Charlie Noble's cousin. But as noted earlier, these latecomers' distance from this history's purpose is too great. Perhaps another day will give them their due in the court of history. Some like Carroll Noble have already appeared in that court.

Social Life

In the earliest days, dances, cards, picnics, berry picking and rodeos composed the mainstays of entertainment. They were interspersed with conversation, jokes, stories and often more than a drink or two. Dancing was the highlight, particularly during winter and among the single men and women. And pinochle was the card game of choice.

Until the church and community center were completed in the early 1940s and automobiles were more common, the residents' homes served as the centers for social life, particularly during the winters. Since a mile was the meter measuring the distance between homes, during the winter only those who lived closest to each other would gather together. For example, those who lived near one another on Dell Creek, Jack Creek or the Upper Fall River formed "neighborhoods" and separate social clusters.

Skis and snowshoes or "webs" afforded the only means of winter transportation. Skis called "rancher skis" were handmade wooden skis standing seven feet tall. They were secured to the foot by simple leather bindings or knee-high leather boots attached to the ski that the skier slipped into with stocking feet or moccasins and then laced up the boot binding.

Traveling any distance by this means took time, particularly if a traveler pulled a sled full of kids. But if the homesteader traveled in the late afternoon or early morning when the lower temperatures created a snow crust that could support them, it took less time. Not surprisingly the winter social events lasted from evening until the next morning. One neighbor would stay home and feed the livestock of those who partied. The children would spend the nights and sleep near the woodstoves.

When the snow melted and traveling became easier, the ranch work became harder. Calving, branding, fixing fences, cutting or castrating calves and horses, riding the rough string, turning out cattle, checking the range, doctoring calves, irrigating, and finally haying, filled most late spring and summer days to the brim. But occasional weekend picnics, particularly the Fourth of July celebration, offered a respite from the long summer days.

Many of the early amateur rodeos started around the community picnic. Wild horses from the Little Colorado Desert or the most ornery from the rough string made up the rodeo stock. With no fences or corrals, if a pick up man missed the bronc rider, he and his bucking horse would disappear together over the rims of the sagebrush hills. Later for the benefit of the community and his dudes, Wallace Hiatt and the Triangle F hosted the Fourth of July rodeo.

Beyond the more organized social events, the post office offered a more routine place to chat and socialize. Mail was delivered twice a week in the summer and once a week in the winter. Not only did the post office provide essential mail and package service, but the postmaster or mistress operated it like a clearing house for community events, accidents, news, and most delicious of all—rumors.

These elements of frontier social life underscore again the somewhat contradictory nature of early ranching and cowboy life. The impulse for independence gave way to the need to help each other and cooperate.

However, lest anyone believe that the Basin forged the hardy and idyllic social life, like smaller communities and large families, the Basin had its ups and downs. And its downs revealed such intense rivalries and occasional animosity that the Basin acquired the name "Battle Valley" and "Smokey Row." During one period a rivalry between the Campbell family and the Hicks triggered these disputes.

In the earlier days the log schoolhouse could be taken apart log by log, moved, and reassembled. One summer and fall it might be located on Jack Creek, the next school term on Dell Creek and the following summer on Fisherman's Creek. Not only did the location of the school offer convenience to those closest, but it was a sign of prestige. Every year the school's location became a matter of womanly warfare. In a typical dispute, one combatant took off her shoe and pounded her opponent. Some bystanders, just watching the fight, were injured.

At one spring dance all of the attendees—both men and women—broke into a fight, over what, no one can remember. Since most men had guns, it was a miracle that no one was shot. They would fight over irrigation ditches and disputed water rights. Out of pure spite one rancher cut another's barbwire fence. And that victim knocked out the rancher who cut his fence, with a fencepost.

In a dispute over water rights, a truly huge woman named Lisa stood and blocked the road where Paul, the other party in the disagreement, had planned to access his irrigation ditch. Paul grabbed her by her hair and said, "Well, Lisa, if you'll just stand still, I'll go around you."

By the late 1930s and early 1940s, social life and protocol began to change. Separate schools had been built on Jack, Dell and Fisherman's Creeks and eventually they were consolidated into a single more modern school. Cars, trucks and better roads gave residents more mobility and access to larger towns. Next, the

Bondurant Episcopal Church, St. Hubert the Hunter, and its companion community center were completed. Together they created a more central gathering spot, and in 1941, the annual Bondurant BBQ made its debut. As we know, in 1939 John Wertz opened his novelty shop and operated it for about ten years. During this period he made an elk horn chair for the church.

In 1947-1948, one of the Basin's most distinctive and popular social institutions made its entrance. Arriving from Chicago with his wife, Marge, and two children, Walter Floerke bought John Wertz's "elk horn" novelty shop. The family was Jewish, and during the 1920s and 1930s, Floerke had worked as an accountant for undisclosed clients in Chicago. Whether it was fact, speculation, or imagination, many locals assumed that he had worked for the mobster, Al Capone. This story further suggested that in order to keep him out of the reach of the law and grand juries, the Capone organization sent him to Bondurant, Wyoming. Why else would a successful Chicago accountant land in such an isolated place?

Initially, Floerke operated the novelty shop selling Wertz's inventory of elk handled knives and forks, candle holders, furniture, and postcards. Then he transformed it into a bar and added a store. Beyond the log building housing the bar, the property included a barn and chicken coop. Walter used the barn for storage, but shortly after his arrival it burned down.

Although officially known as the Elkhorn, a living memorial to John Wertz, every one called it Floerke's, the first and still only bar and store in the Basin. Eventually about one hundred yards off the road, Walter designed and built a metal building and triangular Texaco station. Texaco bought the rights to the station design. He powered the building complex with two windmills. The wind power was stored in large glass tanks that worked like wet cell batteries. The windmills stayed in place until the late 1970s.

Later in the same complex, he opened a general store that became known for its ice cream and fishing lures, which were sold for use in the trout pond near the store. As a talented entrepreneur, Walter Floerke built a successful business and much more.

Floerke's became an institution, particularly among cowboys, roundup riders, ranchers and hunting guides. In fact, it offered the first "drive through" liquor store. If a cowboy rode by pushing cows, his friends would run out and give him a "go cup" full of whiskey.

Walter worked as both the bartender and gas station attendant. When a car or truck pulled up to the pump, it would trip a wire, and a bell would ring in the bar. Floerke would quickly pull on his Texaco jacket and put on his Texaco cap and rush out and pump gas.

Sometime in the 1970s, Kirk Ramsey from Cleveland Heights, Ohio, bought the Elkhorn and started some renovation, moving the bar and store closer to the road.

During the late 1980s, it was purchased by Gloria and Richard Thomas. They added guest cabins and built a restaurant between the bar and store. It still fills a genuine community need, but the cowboy tradition may not be as strong today as it was during Floerke's time.

In 2003, Richard and Gloria put the Elkhorn up for sale. After seventeen years as proprietors, they sold the Elkhorn to Jim and Hazel Malmin in late 2005. The Malmins were from Daniel, Wyoming, via California.

Now our story can begin to dig deeper into the original characters, who animated the Basin at the beginning of the twentieth century and beyond.

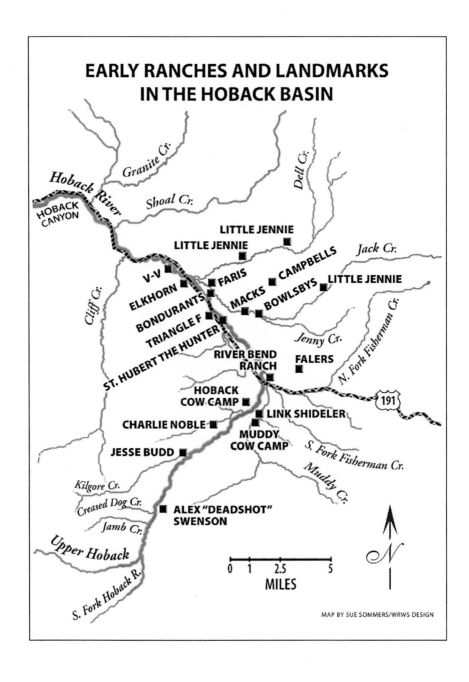

EARLY RANCHES AND LANDMARKS
IN THE HOBACK BASIN

MAP BY SUE SOMMERS/WRWS DESIGN

Part Four

The Originals

This Part features individual narrative histories of those characters who contributed most to the tradition, identity and folklore of the Basin. Even if these folks had settled in another place, the strength of their personalities, distinctiveness, and determination would have given that place its identity. While remaining historically accurate, the purpose of this Part is to make them come alive. Earlier, all of the Originals have been introduced and although each is the prime-time player in their respective time slots, the stories of a few friends and the development of related characters will add more texture and depth to these "movers and shapers."

Charlie Noble.
Photo courtesy of the Green River Valley Museum, circa 1930s.

Charlie Noble

If you arrived late that warm first day of August, 1955, all of the pews in Big Piney's St. Anne's Catholic Church would have been full. Latecomers had to stand in the back or outside. Reverend Charles Bartlett presided over Charlie Noble's memorial service. Noble's second wife and four grandchildren were the only immediate family left, and they sat in the front pew. Some of his later friends who were still alive served as pall bearers. They were Dan Budd, Phil Marincic, Jr., Clarence Davis, Sr., Bob McNeel, and Gene Pfisterer.

Reflecting Charlie's community recognition, the editor of the local weekly, *The Big Piney Examiner* placed Charlie's obituary on the center of the front page above the fold. The story to its immediate right covered Gene Pfisterer's upcoming annual steer roping in which Gene offered a one thousand dollar purse for first place. Since very few rodeos at that time offered any amount approaching that, this event drew cowboys from all over Wyoming. The adjacency of his obituary to the steer roping event would have amused Charlie.

During the previous fifty years, Charlie had epitomized the pioneer rancher, who through unrelenting hard work and innate business acumen, had become well-known and respected. He'd become a community institution. Some would say a legend. Any good cowboy who worked and rode for him claimed it as a rite of passage. Also, each could tell a Charlie Noble story or two. Old timers still do.

Charlie Noble died on July 29, 1955, in Ogden, Utah. His second wife, Fannie Tarter, was at his side when he died at their Ogden home—a place where they'd spent more time when Charlie's health deteriorated. At age seventy-six, he finally succumbed to diabetes and colon cancer. Both illnesses were compounded by decades' worth of hard drinking, chewing tobacco, and smoking. These three habits or addictions were common among that era's ranchers and cowboys.

His end was as hard as his life's beginning and even his middle years were filled with pain and loss. He ate a steady diet of tragedy and loneliness. In his case, "the fault was in the stars, not in himself." If he felt alone at the end, nobody knew but him. And Charlie wasn't talking. He never did talk much, anyway.

While he could not change the stars in his life's constellation, not only did he overcome adversity, but that feat molded a determined and resilient character, which could digest most tragedies. Charlie's first and lifelong affliction was a clubfoot—a birth defect where the foot, including the bone, joints, muscles and blood vessels, is misshapen and twisted out of position. Usually, the foot turns inward and down and cannot step flat on the floor. With age and no corrective action, the condition becomes very painful. When walking, a twisted foot and crippled gait are the most visible symptoms.

For that reason, Charlie never wore cowboy boots, and he rode more often than he walked. Not surprisingly, many photos show him sitting. Despite his clubfoot, Charlie stood six feet and three inches tall. He was lean and sinewy with a light complexion and expressive eyes under bushy eyebrows.

No one could claim that Charlie was talky or gabby. In at least one sense, his few words were considereded as a virtue. He could not be accused of spreading gossip or rumors.

When he did speak, the words were direct and to the point and were delivered in an almost staccato cadence. He wasted none of them. For example, when introducing himself to someone, Charlie would say, "Charlie Noble and you?" Yet the attentive listener knew he possessed a dry and understated sense of humor. He couldn't have been called a bellylaugher, but he enjoyed drinking with his friends, practical jokes and the sound of laughter.

Beyond the purchase of his foster father's Big Piney ranch and Fall River homestead in 1913, around 1920 Charlie bought another ranch on North Piney. That acquisition meant Charlie was improving and managing three ranches. He ran as many as three thousand head of cattle and more than a few horses. All ranchers work long hours, but even his contemporaries admitted that Charlie set records for hours and days worked. For him, ranching was not a way of life, it *was* his life.

Charlie treated his cowboys well. He never asked a cowboy to do anything that he had not done, and most of the time, he worked right alongside them. He even ate and drank with them. Unlike today, in the early 1900s machinery represented only a small part of the cost of the ranching business. Good men and horses were the ingredients for success. Since cowboy wages started at thirty dollars a month, Charlie could hire all the cowboys he needed, particularly for calving, branding, driving cattle, and haying.

Charlie's brand was a simple oval lying on its side. As it looked like a chain link, it was called the "link" brand. Due to its elegant simplicity, ease of application and visibility, many ranchers considered it the finest brand in Wyoming.

Beyond his ranches and family, Charlie had four passions: his shaggy black and white dog, Handsome, his bottle of whiskey, his chewing tobacco, and his pipe. Every day as a treat, he cut a steak for Handsome and usually the dog buried it. Of course, at the end of every day Charlie treated himself to a drink and a smoke on his pipe.

A Biographical Sketch

Charlie's birth name was Charles Powers. He was born March 28, 1879, in Joplin, Missouri. His mother died during his birth. Somewhat later his father, a railroad engineer, was killed in a train wreck. Little is known about Charlie's life between his father's death and his encounter with the Zach Nobles. He either stayed with relatives, his parents' friends or in a foster home.

Sometime in the mid to late 1880s, at the age of six or seven, Charlie met the Noble family, most likely when Zach was working near the North Platte in Nebraska. Without a trace of doubt, two separate oral histories say Charlie came west with a wagon train, following the Oregon Trail. As the Zach Noble family lived near the Trail segment that cut through western Nebraska, this version of their meeting gains credibility. One story even suggested that his wagon train had been attacked by Indians.

The Nobles adopted Charlie, and in 1888, with nine year old Charles Powers Noble in tow, the Zach Nobles arrived in Big Piney. His foster father's early days in Big Piney; Charlie's introduction to the Fall River Basin; and his first ranching years, have already been covered in Part Two.

In 1905, Grace Hathaway, a schoolteacher, arrived in the Daniel area from Buffalo, Wyoming. She taught at the Merna School and boarded with William "Pop" Snider and his wife, also named Grace. Around 1898, the Sniders settled near Merna, some of the first settlers in the Horse Creek area. Both Graces had lived in Nebraska, and Grace Snider, the postmistress, named the post office Merna after a Nebraska town near where she had lived.

Soon Charlie started visiting the Sniders—a not so subtle excuse to see Grace Hathaway. In a similar gambit, he brought the Sniders a Christmas turkey. The turkey must have been tasty and left fond memories, because in 1906, Charlie and Grace were married.

She moved to the Big Piney ranch.

The exact chemistry and initial attraction between them will remain a mystery, although Grace's beauty obviously played a role. Whatever the basis for the initial appeal, the deeper differences between them soon became apparent. The new husband and wife were opposites, particularly in character and lifestyle. Better educated, refined and delicate, Grace could not make the transition to the life of a ranch woman—cooking for robust but less than civilized crews, cleaning up after them, splitting wood, washing clothes, churning butter, and if needed, helping with the calving, branding and haying. Eventually they reached an accommodation, allowing each to lead independent lives.

Their first child, Kenneth, was born December 14, 1909. Following his birth, Charlie bought a house in Big Piney where Grace and young Kenneth lived. Two years later their second child, Thelma, was born. She contracted pneumonia and died as an infant. The loss of her daughter crushed Grace.

Their third child, Gene, was born January 19, 1918, in Omaha, Nebraska, close to her family. When Grace returned to Big Piney, she and the two boys stayed in town. However, a few years later they began to spend part of their summers in the Fall River Basin. These visits pleased Charlie and soon life in the Basin became the highlight of the boys' summers.

As the next decade passed and the boys started school, Grace's illness became more apparent. She began to spend more and more time with her family in Nebraska. Finally, cancer won the battle, and she died March 28, 1936. Her death ended thirty years of marriage. She was buried in the Big Piney Cemetery next to her infant daughter, Thelma.

Grace and Charlie's youngest son, Gene Hathaway Noble, married Ruby Wilson of Big Piney on September 7, 1938. They lived on the Big Piney ranch. But one year after his marriage, at age twenty-one Gene suddenly died from diabetes.

Gene's older brother, Kenneth, married Alice Jewett in 1930. They had four children—Kenneth Jr., Robert, Sally, and Donald. After the ranch house or cabin in the Basin had been expanded and remodeled, the family moved to that ranch. Charlie Bellon, the tie hack, who lived in the Basin, completed that renovation. Then on January 22, 1941, Kenneth and Alice were both killed in a car accident near Rock Springs, Wyoming, leaving their four children orphans. Kenneth was only thirty-two.

As child rearing was not Charlie's strongest suit, Alice's parents, who were early members of the Fall River and later Hoback Stock Association, raised the children. Alice's brother, Don, was the children's legal guardian.

Charlie willed his Hoback ranch to his grandchildren, and after his death they sold it to Charlie's friend, Bob McNeel, and his wife, Lois who was the daughter of Ralph and Daisy Hicks. Two years before his death, Charlie put his home ranch on the market and started a bidding war. Eventually, the Miller Land and Livestock Company won the war. Charlie then sold his North Piney ranch to Joe Budd, another son of the original Dan Budd.

Charlie's clubfoot, hard living, and the early and tragic death of his entire immediate family, began to exact an emotional and physical cost. His health faltered. A few months later he entered a hospital in Soda Springs, Idaho. A nurse, Fannie Tarter, helped in his recovery. Aside from that care, she and her family had spent much of her earlier life in Big Piney and Daniel. Also Charlie must have known about the exploits of her mother, Mamie, and father, Bob. With such connections between the two, on May 5, 1941, they were married. And so began another unexpected chapter in the life of Charlie Noble.

The Tarters

Fannie Tarter came from an infamous lineage. Her father, Bob, and mother, Mamie, were married July 30, 1880, in Oneida, Idaho. It was her second marriage. They settled near the Snake River in Idaho and Fannie, their first child, was born June 11, 1883. Her birth marked the beginning of her father's long career as a horse thief and scoundrel. Their Idaho neighbors called him a "notorious cutthroat."

After joining his brother, Dan, and three friends in the theft of four horses, Bob turned state's evidence to the territorial law officers, and his brother was convicted and sentenced to seven years in the Idaho Territorial Prison. Unrepentant, Bob soon graduated to professional horsethief. He and his gang moved around Idaho, Wyoming, and Montana. Usually, they stole horse in Idaho and ran them over Teton Pass into Wyoming. Sometimes they sold them as far north as Montana. During these years on the run, Mamie, whose full name was Frances Miriam Tarter, traveled with the gang and acquired practical, though not licensed, nursing skills. Later she served as midwife to many expectant mothers.

After saving some of their ill-gotten gain and continuing to stay out of the sheriff's reach, in 1887, they bought a ranch and settled in Big Piney. Within two years they achieved the status of "respectable ranchers," but in 1891, the Tarters moved to Bob's family ranch in Oregon. Evidently his mother was sick, and Bob wanted to be present so eventually he could inherit the ranch.

That same year his brother, Dan, won an early release from prison—where, of course, Bob's testimony had sent him—and began contesting Bob's plans to take over the family ranch. Although the two brothers pursued independent lives, in 1896, after a heated argument, Dan shot and killed his brother, Bob. Then ten years old, Fannie witnessed her father's death and later wrote about it. Mamie, who was then thirty-four, was not at home when Bob died.

Bob's death begins an extended period in which Mamie, originally a Mormon, reinvents herself numerous times. After returning to the Big Piney ranch, in 1897 she married a third time. The lucky groom was Henry Edmonson, another horsethief and Bob's friend, who had just been released from the Montana Penitentiary. Within a few months, Henry shot and killed one of young Fannie's suitors and was convicted of murder and sentenced to life in prison.

Mamie and Fannie filed two additional homestead claims near the Big Piney ranch and then bought, restored and managed the Emerald Hotel in Evanston, Wyoming. Later it was renamed the Elk Hotel. Unable to help herself, Mamie married John Dolan. This was her fourth wedding.

In 1900, Mamie sold the Big Piney ranch and about that same time entered into a business partnership with Rudolph Swartz, a Swiss immigrant. She put the hotel under new management and with Rudolph opened up a saloon in Kendall near the tie hack camp that made railroad ties for the regional railroad. Saloon management offered her new opportunities—dealing poker and smoking cigars. In 1903 she opened up her own saloon, the Fremont, which was near what one year later would become the town of Pinedale. In 1904, she and Rudolph were among the first to purchase a few lots in Pinedale, and that same year she divorced John Dolan. Fannie, Mamie's oldest daughter, then a grown woman, married Phil Burch from Colorado and they ranched near Cora, Wyoming. Fannie developed into an accomplished horsewoman.

In 1906, Mamie and Rudy—just business partners—bought the Sarah Dodge ranch in Daniel and built a ten room log roadhouse that provided rooms, meals and alcoholic beverages. Mamie owned or co-owned the Evanston Hotel, the Fremont Saloon and the Daniel roadhouse and ranch.

Starting in 1910 and over the next two years, she and Rudy began to divest themselves of their properties. Mamie traveled to California. Her daughter, Fannie, who by then was herself a divorcee, completed a nursing degree and accepted her first nursing position in Denver, Colorado.

In 1915, Mamie married a fifth time, and the groom was a Montana rancher. Two years later it ended in divorce. In 1920 at the age of sixty-one, she married a sixth time, and this marriage, her last, may have set a new standard for quirky relationships. Remember her earlier husband, Henry Edmonson, the horse thief and murderer, who was sentenced to life in prison? Well, he received a pardon and reunited with Mamie. They settled in Lava Hot Springs, Idaho, where she died at age seventy-six in 1935.

Following in her mother's footsteps, before her marriage to Charlie Noble, Fannie was married and divorced twice. After Charlie's death, she married three more times. Perhaps she was seeking to match her mother's record of six marriages.

Although the history of the Tarter family is well documented, little is known about Charlie and Fannie's fourteen years of marriage. Yet its longevity, her concern about his health, and her willingness to give him nursing care later in life all say something about the quality of their relationship. For example, once they were married and with the misplaced hope that it might persuade him to quit, she did not allow Charlie to drink in the house. In some respects they were similar: both had faced and survived adversity and that made them a more sympathetic and compatible couple.

Having had no children and finding little solace in the later marriages, in 1969, at eighty-six, Fannie died.

Phil Marincic, Sr., with a friend in the Hoback Basin.
Photo courtesy of Helena Linn.

The Friends

Most of Charlie's friends were other ranchers or cowboys, who rode for him. His better friendships were forged with those who worked with him early in his ranching career. They included Link Shideler, Johnnie Curtis, Guy Carr, Guy's brother, Bill, Ned George, and Phil Marincic, Sr.

Phil occupied a special place in Charlie's life and deserves his own short history. His life reflects the common experiences of early immigrants whose backgrounds, names, and languages were a far cultural distance from the earlier English, Scottish, Scandinavian and even German settlers.

Part Two introduced Phil and noted that from 1911—1927 he worked as Charlie's foreman in the Basin. During those sixteen years he spent his summers, falls and early winters living at Charlie's cow camp. Usually, he did not finish back riding until near Christmas. In 1920, Phil filed a homesteading claim on six hundred and forty acres just below the South Rim. In early 1926 he received his patent. Most likely using his Basin property as collateral, in 1927, Phil bought the Muleshoe Ranch in Big Piney and with it the permit to run his cattle on the Fisherman's Creek Allotment in the Fall River Basin. By the 1930s Phil knew the Basin as well as anyone—maybe better.

In 1889, Phil Morgan Marincic was born in the town of Zagorje in Slovenia, then part of Austria. In 1929, the Slovenes joined the Serbs and Croats and formed Yugoslavia. In 1991, Slovenia became an independent state. After a bitter dispute with his father, in 1903, when he turned fourteen, Filip (later changed to Philip) left home— never to see his parents again. He headed to Bremen, a port city in northern Germany, where he became friends with Peter Kinnick, a Dutch runaway. Soon they joined other poorly paid crew members on a freighter. After two years, they disembarked and left the ship at Newport News, Virginia.

From Newport News Phil traveled west, picking up English and odd jobs along the way. He stopped in Pueblo, Colorado, but soon traveled to Cumberland, Wyoming, where relatives lived. Phil started his ranch work herding and trailing sheep from Cumberland to Kemmerer. Eventually, in his late teens, he found his way to Big Piney and Charlie Noble's ranch, and a lifelong friendship began. In Big Piney, a few ranchers and others had difficulty pronouncing and spelling his last name—a challenge, if not an affront, faced by many eastern and southern European immigrants. That problem prompted many to change the spelling of their names. Phil's first employers just declared that they would call him Phil Morgan. For a number of years, many thought that Morgan was his last name.

Phil met his future wife, Elva, at a dance in the Charlie Clyde Hall located in Big Piney. They were married on September 11, 1929, and had seven children. Keeping the Basin tradition alive for the next generation, when the children reached six or so they each joined their father on the cattle drives to the Basin from Big Piney. Later the oldest, Phil Jr., worked for Charlie Noble, too. Finally, the Marincics sold the Muleshoe and then bought the Luce place on the Green River. The Luce place became the home ranch.

In 1969, the same year Fannie Tarter died, Phil at eighty years old was fatally felled by a heart attack in Thermopolis, Wyoming. His death signaled the end of a special generation that had opened up the Basin and rode tough and hard. Only a few like them would follow.

Despite his clubfoot, Charlie could ride and rope with the best of the cowboys. After a fall roundup, Charlie and his cowboys had just hit the stockyards in Opal, Wyoming. They were working the cattle in the yards when a steer broke out of the corral and started running. Charlie jumped on his horse and made a loop in his rope. A bystander and dude sitting on the fence asked Charlie what he was going to do. Charlie replied, "Bring that steer back at the end of my rope." The dude then said, "Not on that little horse." Charlie quickly replied,

"Twenty-five bucks I can."

The bet was on and soon Charlie came back, dragging and jerking the steer at the end of his rope. Riding by the dude to collect his twenty-five dollars, Charlie jibed, "What could I do, if I had my spurs?" That night Charlie took the cowboys to the saloon and put the twenty-five dollars on the bar and bought drinks all night long.

When cutting or gelding young stallions, a rider would rope the horse's front feet and then drop him to the ground. Another would tie, cut and brand. "Front footing" a horse takes strength, skill and endurance. The roper has to drop the horse hard enough and stun him so that the cowboy on the ground can tie up the feet without getting kicked. If dropped too hard, the horse will break its neck. Charlie could front foot horses all day long and almost never missed or killed a horse.

During a teachers' ride in the Basin, one of Charlie's cowboys, Bill Pope, was really working to help an extra heavy set teacher get into the saddle. He started to sweat when Charlie spit out his tobacco and said, "Look at Bill Pope! Look at him! If I'd asked him to work that hard, he'd want his wages raised."

When Charlie ate with his men, he expected some manners, not a free-for-all. A young boy from New York, who had just joined the hay crew, was reaching way across the table rather than asking for a dish. When he made an extra long grab, Charlie caught him by the back of the neck in mid-air and said, "Here, here! One foot on the floor please."

One summer Charlie had a ranch cook who spent more time opening cans than actually cooking. Seated at the table so everyone could hear, Charlie observed, "If she ever loses that can opener, you boys will starve to death, as sure as hell."

Through the bunkhouse window Bob McNeel and Grant Beck could see Charlie coming their way from the house. That determined walk was immediately recognizable. No longer allowed to drink in the house, Charlie was looking for whiskey and knew where he might find it.

With practiced speed and agility, Grant and Bob poured all but a swallow of their whiskey into a cup. That cup went under the bed. When Charlie knocked and swung open the door, Grant passed the near empty bottle to Bob, who then gave it to Charlie. This scheme not only saved the cowboys their whiskey and money, but with no ill will, it kept Charlie sober—until he started storing his whiskey in the barn.

These stories would not be complete without one about Phil Marincic, Sr. During a roundup in the Basin, all the cowboys were mounted and ready to ride, but they waited. Before starting out, Phil's horse, Ol' Cherry, always bucked like a saddle bronc in a rodeo. The cowboys were waiting to watch Phil get bucked off. He strolled out of the cabin, picked up Ol' Cherry's reins and threw them at the horse. The horse performed like real rodeo stock, but Phil wasn't in the saddle. When Ol' Cherry had gotten that initial buck out of his system, Phil picked up the reins, mounted and rode off. Embarrassed, the cowboys realized that they didn't know Phil's horse as well as he did.

When the stories are over, what remains are the vivid memories of youthful freedom, late nights at the bar and early mornings at cow camp, and riding the rugged beauty of the Basin.

Dead Shot circa 1930s. *Photo courtesy of C.C. Feltner.*

Alex "Dead Shot" Swenson

He stood just a few inches over five feet in height, but he made up for his short stature with a sizable imagination. Some said that Alex's tall tales made him taller—at least in his own mind. He wore a white, well-worn, even battered cowboy hat. He had a prominent nose made less apparent by a bushy handlebar moustache and slightly sloped shoulders draped with a pair of wide suspenders. And he always wore a pistol and told anyone who would listen, that he was a dead shot with that revolver. Despite that braggadocio, he had a gentle and generous disposition.

In 1901, Dead Shot filed his homestead claim at the end of the settled portion of the Upper Fall River. At that time no one had settled farther up stream. He built and lived in a one room log home with a low ceiling. Since the Basin residents didn't pay for the entertainment he provided, Dead Shot trapped and hunted for a living. To pay for his initial homestead improvements, he helped build a few log cabins in the Upper Green River near Kendall. That may have been where he first met Charlie Bellon and another friend, Jim Williams.

Jim Williams.
Photo courtesy of the Paul Allen Collection, Sublette County Library.

Those two worked at the Kendall tie hack camp.

In addition to his trigger finger, Alex had a very green thumb. Although he had a fine garden, he was best known for his strawberries and oats—crops that were only dreams to those who lived in the Basin, where the growing season is sixty to ninety days. And he happily shared his horticultural wonders.

Besides Charlie Bellon, who helped the few early settlers on the Upper Fall River, Dead Shot's closest neighbor and friend was Jim Williams, who had earlier driven the Butterfield Stage. Since the homesteading records show no claim filed under Jim's name, it is likely that he squatted on land just above Dead Shot's place. Moving down river, Dead Shot's next closest neighbors were the Kilgore brothers, and after the Kilgores' homesteads was Charlie Noble's parcel.

The Butterfield Overland Mail

John Butterfield, an Albany, New York, businessman specializing in early transportation, saw the growing demand for Pacific Coast mail delivery. In March, 1857 Congress authorized the first overland mail service stipulating that the semi-weekly service take no more than twenty-five days. While Butterfield was the force and energy behind the service, he formed a partnership with other express companies, including Wells Fargo and Company. That partnership became known as the Overland Mail Company, but the more familiar name, Butterfield Overland Mail, prevailed during the first few years. It was awarded a $600,000 government contract to launch the service.

The founders had one year to survey and improve the route, build the stage stations, purchase the stagecoaches, hire the drivers and stock the line which ran a somewhat circuitous route from

St. Louis and Memphis through Arkansas, Texas, Arizona, and on to Los Angeles and San Francisco. That route ran almost twenty-eight hundred miles

On September 15, 1858, the first stagecoaches left from opposite ends of the route and made the trip in twenty-one days. The company's founders had already spent a million dollars. While the efficiency of its mail service was never questioned, at best the company's passenger service made for an arduous and uncomfortable journey. For two hundred dollars in cash and a luggage limit of forty pounds, a passenger could take the cross-country ride enduring sleepless days and nights, bad food, drunken travelers and drivers, and even at the stage stations inadequate toilets and bathing facilities.

By 1860, Wells Fargo chose to use the Pony Express to carry mail on a direct central route from Missouri to Denver and Salt Lake and on to California. After more management disputes, Butterfield left the company and Wells Fargo consolidated its position. By 1862, the Pony Express was out of business, and by 1866, Wells Fargo ran all of the overland express companies. When the transcontinental railroad was completed in 1869, all overland mail contracts were cancelled.

Years before, Jim Williams had driven the Butterfield stages out of Los Angeles to the Arizona stage station. Born in 1842, when he drove those stages he was about twenty-six years old. His goatee stood out as his most enduring and distinctive feature. Although he worked at the Kendall tie hack camp along with Charlie "Moose" Bellon, Jim mainly drove freight wagons for the owners of the Daniel store.

Not only did Jim Williams possess a special touch with a team of horses, but he could compete with anyone in toughness. Once when he drove a team from the Basin to Daniel, his horses spooked, and he had a runaway team on his hands. Jim was thrown from the wagon and broke his leg. As the horses kept running, Jim crawled five miles back to his cabin and set his own leg. Even though the leg healed, he had set it a little off center, and after that he walked with a slight crook and limp.

In 1929, Jim staggered into Dead Shot's cabin injured or seriously ill. Dead Shot began to hitch up his four horses in order to make the trip to the Jackson hospital. But Jim, who was eighty-seven, never made it out the door alive. He was buried in the Bondurant Cemetery about twenty-five paces southeast of Dead Shot's grave.

Dead Shot's best story and the one that solidified his moniker began when he hitched up his horses and drove them off towards Pinedale. He planned to re-supply his provisions. On the way he claimed a black bear rambled out from an aspen grove, and before the bear could spook his horses, Dead Shot pulled out his pistol and killed the bear with a single shot. Later and with a straight face, Dead Shot said, "Well suh, I loaded up that bear on my wagon and took it to Pinedale so I could weigh it. And guess what? That bear weighed just five hundred pounds."

When locals and others heard the story, they smiled, but out of courtesy, never asked how a small, slight man could pick up and load five hundred pounds of dead weight—even when Dead Shot tried to suggest it was a small bear.

One of the landmarks above Dead Shot's homestead is Creased Dog Creek, a name bestowed by another Dead Shot story. As he told it, "Well, suh, there was a dog that kept howlin' up on this little creek close to my cabin. So I thought I would just crease him with my pistol and scare him off. Well, you know what? I creased him a little low, but it sure stopped the howlin."

Incidentally, the Creek that is just west of Creased Dog Creek is named Jamb Creek. But no one knows the origins of its name. Many children who grew up in the Basin initially thought that the name was

"Jam" Creek and that sounded sweeter to them than the real name. However, the creek is tightly wedged or "jambed " into the drainage. Others believe that a rider jerked or jambed his bit into his horse's mouth, and the horse bucked him off into the creek bed. But these explanations are just speculation.

Alexander Swenson arrived in this world November 23, 1867. His part of the world was Randers, Denmark, located in the west central Juland, the peninsula that sticks up from northern Germany and extends into the North Sea. This peninsula is known to English speakers as Jutland. Two islands make up the balance of Denmark: next to Juland is Fyn, home to Hans Christian Andersen, and just beyond Fyn is Sjaelland, where Copenhagen is located.

Generally, life in Juland and specifically in Randers was based on agriculture and farming. Alex's mother's maiden name was Pernilla Presdotter and his father, Anders Svendsson. He was one of five children, and his brother Fritz was three years older than Alex. Undoubtedly, his parents were farmhands with little education, and they worked for very low wages. It is also likely that their children had very little formal education. Most farmers who employed these workers offered them one quarter acre gardens to enhance their livelihood.

During the 1860s and 1870s, Denmark was the only Scandinavian country that allowed Mormon missionaries into the country. Looking for new recruits to expand their membership, the Mormons targeted the poorer agricultural workers and poor or unemployed industrial workers who, hoping for a better life, had recently moved from the farm to the city. Since they were poor and poorly educated, the Mormon offer of free passage and train travel to Utah and a guaranteed job was an offer that many could not refuse. Joining twenty thousand other Danes, Alex's family converted to The Church of Jesus Christ of Latter Day Saints in 1871.

About ten percent of these Danish converts accepted the free transportation, but ignored the call of the Church and stopped and settled in western Iowa or eastern Nebraska. Alex's oldest sister, Hilda, and her fiancé were the first of the family to immigrate to Salt Lake City, Utah. Then Alex's mother and two sisters arrived. Not long after, Fritz and Alex arrived in Spring City, Utah, a Danish community ninety miles south of Salt Lake. Unable to speak English or perform an adult job, at first the boys had great difficulty. It was even reported that they became rowdy troublemakers. Soon their father arrived, a move that the family would profoundly regret.

During the winter of 1878, their father was gathering firewood when he got lost in the snow. When found, both of his legs had frozen. They had to be amputated, and within a short time their father died of blood loss and shock. Alex would soon be twelve and his brother fifteen.

Fritz returned to his mother and sisters in Salt Lake City, but sometime when he was still a teenager, Alex joined a circus traveling through Mt. Pleasant, a small town near Spring City. The circus made its way to Wyoming, and during one of its performances, Alex was walking the tight rope and fell. He was seriously injured and the circus chose to leave him behind. His age at the time of the accident has not been recorded, but he still must have been a teenager. During the next decade or more, his whereabouts are simply unknown. But sometime before the turn of the century, he arrived in the Basin.

Around July 26, 1942, at the age of seventy-five, Alex "Dead Shot" Swenson died in his bed from a heart attack. Since he lived by himself and was somewhat isolated, it was common for him to be out of circulation for a day or two. As a result, a few days had passed before he was missed and found. By then the mice had gnawed off his ears. He was buried in the Bondurant Cemetery.

The Daniel Ranchers

Although Clarence Webb was eight years older, he and Austin Richardson arrived in Daniel area within a year of each other. A few years later, they became ranchers, neighbors on Horse Creek west of Daniel, and very good friends. The community school, the Merna School which their children attended, was first located in Clarence's bunkhouse, but later a one room log school was built on Austin's ranch. Both Webb and Richardson were members of the Fall River Association and the Horse Creek-Beaver Cattle and Horse Association. They were captivated by the Basin country, and they both firmly believed in giving back to the community that supported them. Even though for decades they ran cattle with Charlie Noble, in terms of education, family life, community service, and lifestyle, they were Charlie's opposites.

Austin Richardson

In 1849 Austin's father, Etheal, was born in Eagle, Wyoming County, New York. In 1872 he moved to Grand Island, Nebraska, and became a pharmacist. In 1859, his mother, Adna Caroline Durkee, was born in McHenry County, Illinois, but spent the next eighteen years in the Chicago area. In 1877, the same year that her future husband moved to Clarks, Nebraska, Caroline moved near the same town, taught school, and lived with her married sister.

Two years later, Etheal and Caroline were married. During the next decade three children were born—Marion in 1881, Austin in 1886 and Ida Laura in 1888. In 1900, Etheal developed a malignant tumor in his arm. Following its amputation and an infection, he died. In 1905, Caroline moved her family to Omaha, Nebraska, where more opportunities expanded her children's horizons.

In 1906, Caroline and Austin traveled to Daniel, Wyoming, and visited a close friend from Clarks, Nebraska, Lola Tomblin Chamberlin. After Lola's husband died in Clarks, she met and then married John "Van" Vandervort, a Civil War veteran and widower.

Austin Richardson
Photo courtesy of Dianne Boroff.

They owned and lived on the Flying V Ranch a mile outside Daniel. The Green River Valley's early fall color, sun and crisper mountain air captured Austin and his mother. Later, remembering his early days on the windy plains of Nebraska, Austin observed with a slight smile that the Nebraska wind blew so hard he had to hold on to his eyebrows.

In 1907, Austin, his mother, Caroline, and his sister, Laura, moved to Daniel. His oldest sister, Marion, stayed in Nebraska, later moved to Denver, Colorado, and died in 1918. The three bought and operated the Daniel store until 1912 when they sold it to the Barbers and George Pixley. During this time, Caroline also served as the third Daniel postmistress and in the mid-1920s Austin accepted the appointment as the seventh postmaster. Before the store was sold, Laura married Harry Thompson, a local cowboy and later a successful rancher.

With the proceeds from the store sale, Austin and his mother bought the Frank Wilhelm place a few miles up Horse Creek from Daniel. This is the same Frank Wilhelm who shot his neighbor, Truman Andrus, in a land dispute. Around 1915, Austin also worked with an H. H. Nelson, a representative of International Life of St. Louis. In other words, he sidelined as an insurance salesman. Soon Austin and his mother filed homestead claims near their ranch and further expanded the ranch's acreage. In 1923, Austin bought part of the Odle place from Fritz Coyte, and in 1929, he bought the rest of the Wilhelm ranch. Over the next fifteen years they added four more pastures.

Although he was Secretary of the Horse Creek-Beaver Association, Austin's first love was the Fall River Basin, where he ran cattle, too. He used any excuse to camp, fish and hunt in the Basin. He may also have served as one of the first Secretaries of the Fall River Association. In late summer 1932, at the mature age of forty-six, Austin married Mary Elizabeth "Beth" Mayre. She was forty-two. They were married in Bondurant by Reverend Best.

Beth was born in Galveston, Texas, but her family soon moved to Denver and then Chicago. She received a teaching degree, and in 1913, when she was eighteen, she started teaching at the Boulder school, south of Pinedale. Later she would teach in the Fall River Basin, Daniel, and Pinedale. Like Austin, she adored the Basin.

After returning to Chicago to teach literature and English at Sterling Morton College, Beth and two friends from Chicago purchased the Jake Query place and spent summers in the Basin. Prior to her marriage, she also collaborated with a few others to write and publish a series of popular English textbooks. Beth and Austin lived on the Horse Creek ranch with Austin's mother until her death in 1944. Austin and Beth adopted two children—first a boy, Austin Mayre, and then a girl, Mary Caroline, who, on a winter day when she was just over two, wandered over to Horse Creek and fell through the ice and drowned.

Austin was a civic-minded member of the county and first served as land commissioner and then as a county commissioner from 1933-1939. But he was also known to ride through Daniel whooping it up with his friends. He was a well-respected stockman and rancher. As the *Pinedale Roundup* noted after his wedding, he "needs little introduction as he has made his home here for the past twenty-six years where he has gained the respect and admiration of his sterling silver qualities of character."

Austin also maintained a lifelong friendship with Clarence Webb. Based on his romance with the Basin, it was fitting that during a fall hunting trip in the Basin, when Austin was remarking about the mountain views, he fell off his horse—dead of a heart attack. It was September 10, 1948 and he was sixty-two.

Clarence Webb

Clarence Webb was born November 1, 1878 in Franklin County, Indiana. He grew up on a small ranch near Cowdrey, Colorado, that his father, Willis, and mother, Angie, homesteaded. He attended the University of Wyoming, and as an undergraduate studied veterinary medicine. Clarence also played football for the Wyoming Cowboys. But most of all, he broke horses and rode the rough string for the Big Creek Ranch and others in Colorado. During that time, he held the title of All Around Cowboy and Bucking Horse Champion at Steamboat Springs, Colorado.

He married Lillian Gertrude McCasland in 1906. When they married, Clarence was twenty-eight, and Lillian had turned nineteen. Lillian was born in Illinois in 1887, but her family soon moved to Colorado, where she met Clarence. In 1908, the Webbs sold the Colorado ranch and bought the Truman Andrus ranch on Horse Creek, about eight miles west of Daniel—now known as the Webb place. Truman was Frank Wilhelm's neighbor that Frank shot. Shortly after they bought the old Andrus place, Clarence, his

Clarence Webb
Photo courtesy of Gordon Bray.

wife, Lillian, and his mother filed homestead claims adjoining the original ranch holdings.

Later Clarence and Lillian had three daughters—Irene, Helen, and Mildred or "Mickey"—and a son, Willis or Bud. When old enough, the children also homesteaded adjacent to the current ranch holdings, thereby greatly increasing the Webb ranch acreage.

As noted, Clarence was a member of the Horse Creek-Beaver Association and the Fall River Association. And he would spend as much time as ranch life allowed whittling and talking with his neighbor and friend, Austin Richardson.

To supply the ranch in those days, it took two trips a year to Opal with a six horse team, a wagon and a trailer wagon. Since Opal was about 115 miles from Horse Creek near Daniel, the round trip took about ten days. They bought in quantity: a thousand pounds of flour, five hundred pounds of sugar, cereal, oatmeal, cracked wheat, and graham meal in twenty-five pound wooden boxes; dried fruit in twenty pound boxes, and cheese in five or ten pound boxes. It took a whole day to unpack the wagons and store the provisions.

Aside from building the ranch and his cattle herd, Clarence lent a helping financial hand to many homesteaders, trappers and small ranchers. He served on the school board for thirty years, but could also dance the night away. Just after the Webbs bought the Andrus ranch, they hosted a dance for Horse Creek residents. The local Pinedale weekly, the *Roundup* reported, "one of the largest and jolliest crowds that has ever gathered in this locality to enjoy a lively Wyoming dance.... It was a dandy, you ought to have been there."

After forty-three years, in 1951 the Webb family sold the ranch to Boyd Kelly and moved to Ogden, Utah. At seventy-four Clarence died in Denver, Colorado, on January 31, 1952.

Lora and Gordon Jewett, 1947.
Photo courtesy of Robert Noble.

Gordon Jewett

Although Johnnie Curtis probably didn't know it, Gordon Jewett could also claim membership in that very small club of Sublette County ranchers who grew up in New England. Gordon even attended a private school, South Berwick Academy, located, of course, in South Berwick, Maine. But let's get back to the beginning of Gordon's story.

Many generations ago, the Jewetts had emigrated from York, England. Gordon's grandfather, Elisha Jewett, settled in South Berwick, Maine around the 1840s. He became a prominent citizen and businessman. However, later in life, his propensity to aid the poor nearly bankrupted him.

He had a brother, Captain John Woodman, who died at sea on his first voyage as a ship commander. Elisha was intent on naming his first son after his brother, but the first two boys died as infants and finally the third survived. The surviving son, John Woodman Jewett, would become Gordon's father.

Young John, who drove that day's equivalent of a Mustang or

convertible—a smart buggy with a spirited team of horses—fashioned himself as a "man about town" in South Berwick. Over her father's objections, in 1880, John courted and married Mary Elizabeth Yeaton in South Berwick.

Like many in any younger generation, the new couple planned to break away from familiar territory and family tradition. They traveled to Maxwell, Nebraska where, with no experience or credentials, John started a ranch. In 1881, their first child, Charles "Gordon" Jewett, was born. Two years later, baby sister, Jessie, came along. Not surprisingly, John proved inept as a rancher and financial manager. Mary Elizabeth had inherited a substantial sum from her father, and that provided a much-needed financial cushion. Also Mary Elizabeth began to assert more financial control over their lives.

In 1892, at thirty-seven, John died of pneumonia, and he was buried in Maxwell, Nebraska. With her two children, Mary Elizabeth returned to South Berwick, where Gordon completed school. But at seventeen Gordon traveled back to Nebraska and began a fifteen-year association with the Milldale Cattle Company, a large stock company near Stapleton and Arthur, Nebraska. Gordon traded lobster for steak.

Within a few years, Gordon became the company's foreman, inherited ten thousand dollars from his mother's brother and bought over twelve hundred acres in the Nebraska Sand Hills and six hundred head of cattle. To top that off, in 1908, he married Lora Ella Neal, an Iowa native, who was teaching in Ogallalah, Nebraska.

Ogallalah is located on the western edge of Nebraska near the eastern border of Wyoming. It was named after the band of Sioux Indians who populated western Nebraska. Originally, Ogallalah developed as a famous "cow town" and served as a station along the earlier Texas to Wyoming and Montana cattle drives.

Within a year of their marriage, Gordon and Lora had their first child, Donald, and by 1911, they had added three more: Frances, Jessie Alice and Dean. One year old Frances died in 1912.

By 1913, Gordon sensed that it was time to move on and

become his own boss and a full-time rancher. Unlike his father, he certainly knew the business. His friend from Nebraska, Cy Kelly, had settled near Daniel, Wyoming, and encouraged Gordon to buy the Harrison ranch, that was located along South Horse Creek and south of Merna Butte. It sat in sight of Prospect Peak, and although a few others settled near the Harrison ranch, no one had settled farther west.

With the proceeds from the sale of their Nebraska ranch, the Jewetts bought the Harrison ranch, and in September 1914, Gordon and two friends boarded a freight train with the Jewetts' possessions, ranch gear and four hundred head of cattle. For 115 miles from Opal to Horse Creek, they drove wagons and trailed the cattle. Arriving at the Harrison ranch, they immediately built additional corrals, sheds and finished a two story log home started by the Harrisons. By late fall, the rest of the family joined Gordon and they settled in for the winter.

Perry Bowlsby freighted in their winter supplies that year. After much work by the early homesteaders, that summer brought a telephone line installed for those living on Horse Creek—a real luxury for that time. The telephone helped ease the isolation of those early years.

Around 1914 or 1915, Gordon's mother and his sister, Jessie Alice, came to Wyoming and filed homestead claims adjacent to the old Harrison ranch. By spring, 1915, Gordon joined the Horse Creek-Beaver Association that was occasionally called the Mumble Peg. Like fellow Horse Creek ranchers, Austin Richardson and Clarence Webb, but a little later, the Jewetts would join the Fall River or Hoback Stock Association. As a practical matter, the Hobacks were not that much farther north of the northern boundary of the Beaver Creeks.

After five years on the Harrison ranch enduring harsh winters, Gordon and Lora started looking for a modestly more hospitable ranch location. In 1919, they bought the Gilbert Hayden ranch on Cottonwood Creek—just south of Daniel and miles north of Big

Piney. The Jewetts' new ranch was known as the lower ranch and the other one on South Horse Creek was known as the upper ranch. After the Jewetts moved to the lower ranch, the Baines helped out on the upper ranch, but by the 1920s, Clure Smith and his wife, Lola, managed the old Harrison ranch. As noted in Part Two, later Clure would ride for the Fall River and then Hoback Stock Association.

In 1927, when the Smiths still managed the upper ranch, an out-of-control cookstove fire burned the ranch house. Two old cabins were moved to the ranch and they served as the Smith's home. Adding to the bad news, Gordon's mother died that year, and he buried her next to her husband in Maxwell, Nebraska.

On brighter notes, in the summer of 1928, Lora Jewett hosted the organizational meeting that established the Sublette County Artists' Guild. Subsequently, the Guild wrote and published the first histories of the area.

In 1929, on the eve of the Depression, Gordon bought another ranch. Over the years, Gordon had succeeded as a rancher and was the last Jewett who deserved the status of an original. When Kenneth Noble and the Jewetts' daughter, Alice, were killed in a car accident, even though their son, Don, was legal guardian, Gordon and Lora raised their grandchildren, further testimony to their strength. Oddly enough in 1946 and 1951, the Jewetts had two more fires at their lower or home ranch on Cottonwood.

In 1948, Gordon and his two sons, Don and Dean, formed the Jewett Land and Livestock Company. In 1953, Gordon had a stroke, and at age seventy-two during the shipping of his cattle, he died. Lora, who moved to a house in Pinedale, died eight years later.

A Snapshot of a Cowboy

Clure Smith's father came from Michigan, his mother from Illinois. Apart from a search for new opportunity, no one can remember their exact reason for settling in LaBarge, Wyoming. But many Big Piney and Daniel ranchers started in LaBarge, including James Mickelson and Niels Miller—both Danes. LaBarge also afforded Clure Smith the chance to grow up as a cowboy.

Clure was born in LaBarge in 1898. He had a sister two years older and four younger brothers. All of the children were born roughly two years apart. The 1910 Census suggests that sometime between 1907 and 1909, the family moved closer to Daniel. Their address or post office, named Halfway, sat just south and west of Daniel near Cottonwood Creek. At the turn of the century, the six day a week stagecoach brought the mail and passengers from Opal to Daniel and the rest of the upper country.

In his early to mid-teens, Clure started his life as a cowboy, and he became a very good one. At first, he rode for a few Big Piney outfits, including Frank Fear's ranch. In 1917, when Clure turned nineteen, President Woodrow Wilson declared war on Germany and Congress passed the military draft. Soon after, Clure received his draft notice. By the time he finished basic training in 1918, Germany and Austria-Hungary showed signs of fatigue. Clure was stationed state-side and toward the end of 1918, the war had wound down and then ended.

Like many romances before the war, Clure and Lola's bond grew stronger, and sometime before his discharge, they married. When Clure returned to Sublette County, he and Lola started working for Gordon Jewett, and soon they managed the Harrison ranch. That assignment began a long association between Clure Smith and the Jewetts.

Clure stood at a medium height. He looked thin but muscular. He wore a wide brim cowboy hat tilted back on his head and a slightly joking smile. He had the discernible bowlegs of a cowboy who'd started riding in his teens.

As Gordon ran his cattle on both the Horse Creek-Beaver and Hoback Allotments, Clure rode with ranchers and cowboys in both Associations. Although at first he just rode during turn-out and roundup, he began to "know" the country in both allotments. Also those days allowed him to refine his reputation as a practical joker.

In the late 1920s, Lola and Clure separated and divorced. Somewhat later each remarried and ironically their spouses were both residents of the Hoback Basin. Clure married Jessie Harris, a cook at the Triangle F Ranch, and Lola married John Haley, Lot Haley's son. Jessie was also known as "Cookie."

By the late 1930s, at Gordon Jewett's urging, Clure signed up as the Hoback Association's main rider. For the next thirteen years, until the mid-1950s, he rode for the Association. During his tenure the name "Coyote Allotment" mistakenly gained currency. Fred Turner, whom the reader met earlier in Part Two, rode with Clure in the early 1930s. Later Fred rode for Jake and then Gene Pfisterer, and while in the Basin, he married Betty Frazier, the daughter of the

Fraziers, who ran the K-O Dude Ranch. Fred and Betty were married for fifty-eight years.

During the mid-1950s, Clure and Jessie went to work for Tom Kearns of Salt Lake City, who had just assembled and built the Little Jennie Ranch. Clure may well have been the first cowboy and ranch manager hired by the Little Jennie. To show his appreciation during those first years at the Little Jennie, Tom Kearns gave Clure a registered quarter horse mare, Miss Huzzy. Clure waited twelve years to breed the mare. Finally she threw two colts, and after their births, the women of the Basin gave a baby shower for Clure complete with baby blankets and bottles.

After a few more years at the Little Jennie, Clure and Jessie were gathering steers along Shoal Creek. Jessie had recently been complaining about a pain in her left arm. As she rode to the cow camp and opened the corral gate for the steers, she fell to the ground unable to catch her breath. By the time Clure rode towards the corrals, she was barely breathing. Soon she died—a dislodged blood clot had stuck in her lung.

By the early 1960s, Clure's own breathing became more difficult and labored. Lung cancer explained that constriction. Until his death at sixty-seven in 1965, he stayed with his daughter, Margie Thurston, who lived with her husband in Helena, Montana. Clure was buried in the Pinedale Cemetery.

Mother Williams, far right. *Photo courtesy of Tara Miller.*

Mother Williams

The cigarette smoke hung heavy around Clyde Hall's poker tables and bar. Just about every customer had a cigarette hanging from his mouth or wedged between his fingers. The last rays of sunlight could barely penetrate the fog of smoke. The music and clatter of feet from the dance hall upstairs reminded the bar patrons, who had arrived earlier in the day, that the afternoon had turned into early evening. Although the drugstore on the main floor of the Hall was closed, Doc's cafe next to the bar was still serving dinner.

Most nights during the late fall, winter, and early spring, "Mother" dealt poker and Black Jack. He only dealt stud or draw poker. Everyone who played knew Mother Williams was the "house man." His friend, drinking companion and fellow gambler, Charlie Clyde, built Clyde Hall. Charlie tended bar and managed the gambling and drinking business. He leased the upstairs dance hall, where the Big Piney high school boys played basketball, high school seniors celebrated their graduation, and younger children performed plays and concerts. Until the Depression hit, Charlie owned and managed the Hall that also included a billiard parlor and barber shop. During its time, Clyde Hall served as the center of Big Piney social life, and often stayed open all night long and well into the next morning.

Mother Williams was short and thin. Although he had a rough look about him, he had a mellow disposition, a happy-go-lucky attitude and many friends. Those who rode with him called him that "old breed of cowboy." When most cowboys rolled their own cigarettes, Mother gained distinction by smoking only "manufactured" cigarettes. He smoked constantly while enjoying his whiskey and water—but not too much water, please— and throughout a good night of gambling, he drank more than a few glasses of whiskey.

In 1912, Wilbur D. Williams arrived in the Green River Valley. He was then twenty-six years old. Mother Williams was born in Newman, Illinois, however, when twelve years old he moved with his family to Kansas. Just after he arrived in Big Piney country he worked for the Cottonwood Land and Development Company that build the large canal that flowed out of the Green River and into Cottonwood Creek. He also worked for the company that built the reservoir on the 67 Ranch and a few other ranch stock ponds. During his first years Mother planned to homestead near Cora. However, he settled in Big Piney and started riding for the Budd family. Mother and the Budd family forged an association that spanned almost ten years.

Explaining how Williams acquired the nickname, "Mother," one story has been tied directly to the days when he worked for the Budd family. The Budd nieces and nephews liked to explore the delights of Big Piney's toy and candy stores. Williams kept his eye on them and would shepherd them back home. A similar story holds that when Charlie Clyde's wife of just three years, Mae Whitman from Big Piney, died just after childbirth at the age of twenty-four, Williams helped Charlie raise his son. Since Mother and Charlie shared the night life of a gambler and bar owner, as an infant, Charlie's son, who was also named Charlie, spent some of his evenings in a wooden box under the bar.

Belying the circumstances of his upbringing, yet confirming the devotion of his father, Charlie's son went to the University of Wyoming and received a degree in vocational education. He eventually worked for the Wyoming Department of Transportation as a surveyor and then a highway engineer. Later he and his wife first moved to San Jose, California, where he received his Masters degree in Industrial Technology. They then moved to Sonora, California, where he taught at Sonora High School for the next twenty-five years and served as an adjunct instructor at Columbia Community College.

However, getting back to the origin of William's name, these stories, at a minimum, reveal Mother's special talent with children.

In the early 1920s, and after a stint in Europe during World War I, Mother started riding for Phil Marincic, Sr., who was then riding for Charlie Noble in the Fall River Basin. Until the mid-1930s Mother continued to ride for other ranchers in the Basin, but after those years he rode again for Phil Marincic, Sr., who then owned the Muleshoe Ranch, and summered his cattle on the Fisherman Creek Allotment at the Hoback Basin. In 1926 Mother also homesteaded on 160 acres below the South Rim and near Phil's original homestead. For the balance of his cowboy life, Mother maintained a close relationship with Phil Marincic, Sr., and also worked for him during the winters and helped feed his cattle. But ranch work always ended just in time for Mother to start his night job at Clyde Hall.

Mother had as soft a hand with horses as he did with children, but he also had a special ability to "mother up" a cow and her calf. Many of the early ranchers believe that his nickname reflected that ability.

Mother also became an accomplished camp cook and was well known for his sourdough pancakes and biscuits.

While Mother liked to cowboy, he liked the gambling and bar life, too. Those last two passions he shared with Charlie Clyde. About the same time that Mother Williams started his life in the Green River Valley, Charlie discovered the Big Piney country. Although he

Charlie and Mae Clyde, circa 1930.
Photo courtesy of Charlie Clyde, Jr.

came to Big Piney from Kemmerer, Charlie was born in Fort Stanton, New Mexico, in 1891. As a young man in the southwest, Charlie played minor league baseball and even tried out as a pitcher for the then Washington Senators. He stayed in the southwest until he moved to California where he worked for Taft Oil. That assignment brought him to Kemmerer, and in the early 1920s, he left Taft, moved to Big Piney, and built Clyde Hall. Aside from the energy business, the entertainment business, and cards, he continued to play amateur baseball and excelled at the sport. In Big Piney he enhanced his reputation as an accomplished ball player. Charlie Clyde owned and managed Clyde Hall for almost fifteen years.

Ironically, gambling was illegal during the whole forty year period in which it flourished wide-open in Wyoming. In 1901, the Wyoming Legislature passed a law that prohibited gambling. Since it had become the favorite pasttime among Wyoming's men and more liberated women, only a few counties dared to enforce the law, and most cities licensed gambling and drinking establishments. Wyoming citizens gambled on anything from poker and dice to horse and foot races. Large sums of money or property changed hands. Those days are in sharp contrast to 2005 when the state differs from most of its neighbors by not permitting a lottery like Power Ball and even outlawing electronic bingo.

Adding another measure to Wyoming's standards of hypocrisy, in 1918, Wyoming citizens voted three-to-one in favor of Prohibition. Similar to other towns across the country, Prohibition did not stop drinking or the saloon business. Indeed, it fostered small ranchers and other entrepreneurs, who built stills and made "a pretty good drinking whiskey" and the extra income from its sale. The Roaring Twenties did roar through Wyoming.

Finally, federal raids and better county enforcement depressed the saloon business. Unfortunately, by 1935, when Prohibition was repealed, Charlie and his creation, Clyde Hall, had fallen victim to the Depression. With money tight, particularly in the ranching and farming business, gambling, drinking and eating out went out of fashion—for long enough to drive him out of business.

Charlie was also so generous with his money that he was known as a "soft touch." Some said that he gave away more money than some men earn in a lifetime.

When Charlie Clyde's business evaporated, he opened up Clyde Hall as a very low-cost or free residential center for the "rail riders" or Depression era "hobos," who traveled across the country on the freight trains looking for work—any work. That act of generosity earned him the community's praise and loyalty. With many rail riders staying at Clyde Hall, the building served as an early day hiring hall for local businesses and ranchers. Usually the workers were hired for day work or temporary jobs, but during haying season the ranchers found their crews at the Hall. The itinerant workers were paid a dollar a day as regular members of the hay crew. If a crew member stacked loose hay, he earned $1.50 per day. Most of their earnings were sent home to their families.

Sometime later Mother Williams and Charlie Clyde renewed an informal partnership and worked at Farrell's bar and restaurant. Mother resumed his position as dealer and Charlie his post as manager and bartender. When a cook threw the cookstove coals out the back door, a wind ignited them, and the fire burned Farrell's to the ground. The fire burned so hot that no one could touch the gas station pumps across the street. It was surprising that the garage did not go up in flames, too.

Charlie Clyde moved to Pinedale in 1941 and did regain his footing. He tended bar and ran card games for Chuck Woods at the Club Bar. Later the Club Bar became Stockman's Bar and Restaurant, one of the most popular drinking establishments in Sublette County, and owned by Gene Pfisterer. Charlie worked for Gene, too. During the winters, he "babysat" the GP Bar Guest Ranch, a bar and restaurant with guest cabins on the Green River Lakes on the northern end of the Upper Green River Valley. It was then owned by Stan Decker. Charlie would shovel snow off the roof, put up firewood, and otherwise ensure that the ranch survived the winter.

While Charlie worked at Stockman's and the GP Bar, Mother continued to work as a cowboy, but later in life he became very ill. Mother eventually spent his last years at Kimberly Manor, a retirement home in Rock Springs, where it was reported that he still played poker with the other residents. On August 22, 1975 and at the age of eighty-nine Mother Williams died. He was buried in Big Piney.

Charlie died in 1959 at the age of 68 and was buried in Kemmerer.

Everett "Buffalo Bill" Curtis

It ran in the family. Like other Big Piney ranchers at the turn of the century, his father, Johnnie Curtis, drove the mess wagon and worked as a cowboy in the Hoback Basin. Growing up in Big Piney, Everett first rode for the Greenwoods and then the Thompsons.

Since both families summered their cattle in the Ryegrass Allotment, Everett was also a regular rider for the Ryegrass Association. That Allotment of rolling sagebrush hills ran south and west of Daniel and encompassed open range between South Cottonwood and Horse Creek. Also, two other members of the Ryegrass Association, Carroll James and Gordon Jewett, ran cattle in the Basin. Some of the Big Piney ranchers who summered their cattle in the Hoback Basin trailed them through the Ryegrass. That is how Everett made or acquired his reputation with others ranchers and cowboys, particularly those from the Basin.

When asked about Everett, the eyes of the cowboys lit up and a smile crossed their faces. Whether he made them laugh or was the perfect subject of cowboy humor and practical jokes, no one said.

He was not a tall man, but wore boots with extra high heels to boost his height. Everett had a handlebar moustache and also grew a long goatee. He dressed the part, and when he had the goatee, the other cowboys would call him "Buffalo Bill" Curtis.

He rolled his own cigarettes with Bull Durham and smoked day and night. His bedroll was checkered with cigarette burns, and once he even burned down the Thompson ranch bunkhouse in Big Piney. He had a sixth grade education, but discussed the characters of *Gone with the Wind* and on occasion even turned philosopher.

One day when he was helping the Basin cowboys move their cows through the Ryegrass, Everett got off his horse to open a gate. As he closed the gate, his goatee got stuck in the gate loop. Laughing at that predicament, the others just rode off leaving Everett to trim up his goatee with his pocket knife.

Not too long after that and without his goatee, Everett and Bob Thompson were riding home for lunch. Afraid that they would be late and miss the meal, they cut across a field holding Bob's big American Saddlebred stud horse and his mares. Everett, wearing his batwing chaps, was riding Croppie, his one-eared horse. Bob was riding a young horse behind Everett when, with no warning, that stud horse walked over to Everett and grabbed him by those batwings, shook him a few times and dropped him on the ground. With all of that excitement, Bob's horse started bucking so he could not help Everett. When Bob's horse settled down, Everett was still shaking. Never before or since had that stud horse done anything like that.

In the late 1960s, Everett became afflicted with heart disease and bouts of pneumonia. In a letter to the Greenwoods, Everett profoundly regretted how his illness had ravaged his body and spirit and then robbed him of his friends and the way of life he loved. As Everett would have said, he hit the "end of the trail" in a veterans hospital in Salt Lake City.

Courtesy of Tharon and Bob Thompson
with some memories from
Bob McNeeland and Grant Beck

Harve Stone.
Photo courtesy of Cheryl Stone Johnston.

Harve Stone

Just about every Friday and Saturday night, the familiar chords of Hank Williams' song, *Heh, Good Lookin'*, and Patsy Cline's recording, *I Fall to Pieces*, floated off Harve's guitar strings. His voice pushed the melodies deeper into the bar and animated those dancing. Harve's friend, Paul Hansen from Pinedale, played the saxophone and other back up instruments, and although the Pack Saddle Trio often had to pick up a drummer, its favorite was Jack Spanky, who earlier had played with Lawrence Welk.

The Trio played Pinedale's Stockman's and the Cowboy Bar, but just as often, it played dances at the Bondurant Community Center and other similar local venues. However, since Gene Pfisterer then owned Stockman's and was Harve's friend, the Pack Saddle boys did enjoy playing Stockman's. Similarly, when Jack Spanky moved to Dubois, Wyoming, the Trio spent more time playing around the bend of Towgotee Pass.

Like many Americans in the 1940s and 1950s, the Pack Saddle Trio liked country-style dancing music, and, of course, their audiences shared their musical taste. The Trio's repertoire ranged from Hank Williams' fast paced songs like *I Saw the Light* to the more plaintive song, *Crazy* by Patsy Cline. Jim Reeves and his big hit *He Will Have to Go* became the slow dance favorite.

As the weekend performances pushed towards midnight and Harve sipped a few more VO and waters, the music and evening lightened up and usually ended with the more fast paced Hank Williams' *Jambalaya (On the Bayou)*. Everybody who could walk was dancing the two-step. At the end of the evening. Harve would take out his can of Velvet tobacco, roll a cigarette and take a deep relaxing drag.

After those summer and early fall weekend nights, Harve, his wife, Lois, and their three daughters and adopted son would return to the Basin and the Hoback Stock Association's cow camps.

Even though quiet, Harve stood out as a handsome and nearly quintessential cowboy and bronc rider. Until toward the end of his life, Harve's most visible signs of age were the more noticeable wrinkles around his eyes and mouth and the slower more painful movements of a bronc buster. Those facial wrinkles were etched by almost forty years of riding in Wyoming's sun and wind. When friends and acquaintances spoke and even now speak about Harve, their words convey a respect, even reverence for him. Although some of that may stem from his recent death and still vivid memories, most of that sentiment comes from a genuine recognition of just how good a cowboy, horseman, and neighbor he was. Also, even if not effusive, he still felt a deep, albeit understated love and affection, for his wife, Lois, and their four children, and particularly the life they shared riding the Basin.

When his friends became ill or died, Harve was the first to step in and comfort and to help. He was not a complicated man. He was straightforward and never seemed confused about what was right or wrong—a trait valued by his friends and a stark warning to those who were not.

A Biography

Born on May 16, 1919, near Burke, South Dakota, Harvey Hubert Stone arrived as the fourth child of Oscar and Sophena Stone. In 1935, when Harve turned sixteen years old, his family moved near Wiggins, Colorado. Until he was nineteen, Harve worked in his father's fields and picked up odd jobs. He also started riding saddle broncs in local rodeos. Although little is known about his parents, Harve did gain his appreciation for music from his father, and he was the only family member who later owned his own ranch—a dream his father kept pursuing, but never achieved.

In 1938, Harve moved to the Hoback Basin and first stacked hay for Shel Baker and then started working for the Campbell Ranch which had been homesteaded by Lorenzo or "Lennie" Campbell. After Lennie's death, his son, Walden, ran the ranch, and Walden and Harve, who were about the same age, became close friends. About a year later, Harve met his future wife, Lois Faris, at a dance hosted by the Campbell family.

Since Harve was strong but thin and sinewy, during his early years in the Basin, many called him "Slim." Later, Harve preferred his given name but a few, like Kevin Campbell, just called him "Stone."

In September 1940, Harve and Lois married. Even though under construction and only three logs high at the time, they chose the Church of St. Hubert the Hunter for their wedding. Lois was the daughter of Jessie and Will Faris, early Basin homesteaders. She was barely nineteen and Harve was twenty-one.

In October, 1941, their first child, Brenda Colleen, was born, but she died about three weeks later. Then Harve and Lois traveled to Colorado and returned the next year with Larry Lee, an adopted son. For the next four years, Harve and Lois worked on a number of ranches in Sublette County including the Circle Ranch in Big Piney. During that time, Harve met Gordon Mickelson, a Big Piney rancher.

Later Harve, his best friend, Walden Campbell, and Gordon Mickelson enlisted in the Army, and after the war, Harve and Gordon became good friends, too.

In December, 1944, the Germans launched their last major counteroffensive against Allied troops in Europe. The Allies were pushed back to Belgium, and although their line never broke, the center line bent, creating a bulge. Accordingly, that engagement became known as the Battle of the Bulge. Fearing a prolonged fight even though very late in the war, the U.S. Army hurriedly drafted more infantry soldiers, and that sent Harve and Gordon to Fort Hood, Texas, for basic training. Walden was sent first to Colorado Springs and then to Fort Benning, Georgia. All three ended up in different infantry divisions

The immediate need for more troops in Europe cut short their training, and Harve and Gordon boarded a train traveling to their port of departure. They sailed to England and then crossed the Channel to France. By then the Allied troops had stopped the German advance at the Battle of the Bulge and American aircraft rained bombs on Germany. Although separated and serving in two different infantry divisions, Gordon and Harve arrived at the European theater in time to cross the Rhine at Remagen and push the Germans back into their homeland. By May 1945, the Germans surrendered, and although returning separately, by late summer Harve, Walden, and Gordon were back in Sublette County. Harve and Gordon soon met again and began a long friendship. Later the reader will learn about an unusual chance meeting in Europe between the best friends, Harve Stone and Walden Campbell.

Harve reunited with Lois and they continued working at local ranches. By now Lois' passion for the history of the Rocky Mountain fur trade began to develop. Later, she would begin to paint those landscapes. But a passion for history was not the only passion they shared. On June 12, 1947, Cheryl Lynn was born and she was followed by her sister, Glenda Elizabeth (better known as Libby), who was born February 12, 1951.

In 1954 and thirty-five years old, Harve took the job as cow boss for the Hoback Stock Association. Harve's immediate predecessor, Clure Smith, had just moved over to the Little Jennie. Cheryl was then seven and Libby only three. A year later their third daughter and last child, Katrinka or "Trinket" was born.

Life in the Basin

As soon as they moved to cow camp, Cheryl started riding with her father. When old enough, the two other girls saddled up, too, and Lois cooked for the cow camp, particularly in early June when the cows were turned out on the Allotment and during the October roundup.

Harve's reputation as a rodeo cowboy preceded him in the Basin. For the next decade, the members of the Association would send him their rankest or most difficult horses so he could ride them out and train them. Rarely did any one of those renegades buck him off. But one young white gelding threw him, and he hit the ground of the round pen with an audible thud. Surprisingly, Harve let the horse go that day, but the next morning he mounted him again and rode him until the gelding calmly walked around the pen. Years later Harve complained about a stiff neck. After x-rays, the doctor told him that some time ago he had broken his neck. Harve knew the culprit—that four year old white gelding.

Harve taught his daughters the talent of understanding and riding horses. His pride in their ability grew. When he had not completely finished training a horse, and it was still a little rough, he proudly told his friends that those horses were good enough for his daughters.

Harve rode for almost twenty years in the Basin, but so the children could attend school, he built a house in Pinedale where they spent their winters. In 1959, Harve and Lois homesteaded on Forty Rod Flats about twenty miles north of Pinedale and established their own ranch.

In his own words, Harve described life in the Basin:

The first place we moved into was called 'the Muddy Cow Camp.' It had a dirt floor, wood cookstove, two rooms, no electricity, an outdoor toilet and the water had to be hauled a mile. We stayed at Muddy for a month in the spring, scattering salt and cows over the range. Through the years of having this job, we saw some amazing things. Cheryl and I watched a cow moose have her calf. The way the hair was standing up on the back of her neck, I knew she was ready to defend it.

One spring day we rode up on a ridge and found ourselves surrounded by two hundred elk. To this day I get chills when I think of it. The calves had no idea what we were, so they came right in between our horses. We actually touched them, and, of course, no one had a camera.

I don't recommend anyone doing this, but we did chase a bear cub up a tree while its mother ran off over the hill. We sat and watched him for awhile until he finally got tired, and climbed back down the tree and ran after his mother. I am surprised that she didn't come back and chase us up the tree.

About the middle of every summer we moved to the Cliff Creek Cow Camp, where we stayed for about six weeks. It was probably about the nicest of the three camps. It had a big creek running behind the cabin, but still no electricity or indoor plumbing. The cabin was one room with a lean-to attached for the kids to sleep in.

One night a porcupine got into the cabin. Having no lights, I had to climb from the bed to the table, then onto the stove to get to the wood box. There I kept a small hatchet for splitting kindling. When we got up the next morning, there was porcupine blood and quills all over the place, but I won the battle.

Cliff Creek is the only place I've ever heard a mountain lion scream. Hearing that in the dead of night sends chills up and down your spine.

Our next camp was Shoal Creek. Most years we just camped out in the open, as we only stayed there a few weeks. There was a little cabin, but it made us ride so far. I remember coming back to that camp one day and could see something white flapping in the breeze in the trees we were camped under. When we reached camp we saw that a squirrel had taken Cheryl's nightgown up a tree.

One day Cheryl and Libby were moving some cows. Trinket was about three and she was riding with Cheryl. Some of the bulls got to fighting so they had to put Trinket up in a tree until they got the cows lined out. When they went back for her, she was still hanging on.

Because Trinket was so little and we were always camping around creeks, we told her that there were Indians in the willows. That kept her pretty close to camp. In 1960, the Association built a new cow camp. On Trinket's first trip to the outhouse tucked above some willows, she found an arrowhead. Needless to say, that really spooked her.

When we moved into the new camp, we thought we were living high. We had electricity and a well with a hand pump. Of course, that ended our having to move to the other camps and made it easier to care for the three thousand head of cows we moved every summer.

In 1983, about ten years after Harve finished riding for the Hoback Stock Association, Lois succumbed to cancer. She was sixty-two years old. Harve missed her but continued to ranch. As he said, "Since that time, life on the old homestead hasn't been the same."

As the years passed, Harve raised a solid herd of cattle, kept up with his friends and family and helped his grandson, Boone Snidecor, get into the horse business. After a time of failing health, on February 10, 2004, Harve Stone died at St. John's Hospital in Jackson, Wyoming. He was eighty-five and had been a living legend.

The Faris Family

On March 19, 1892, Lois Stone's' father, Will or William Tecumseh Sherman Faris, was born in Pricetown, Ohio. Eight years after his father died, Will, his brother, two sisters and mother, Sara, loaded up the wagon and headed west. They sold the wagon and horses in Missouri and took a train to Clayton, New Mexico, where they homesteaded and settled for a few years. Will learned to speak Spanish and rode and trained horses with Mexican cowboys or *vaqueros*. Also, he worked for a tailor and local sheriff.

In 1913, after his brother married and his sisters went their own ways, Will and his mother decided to explore more of the West. They traveled to Taos, New Mexico, and ambled through Colorado into southeastern Wyoming. After they arrived in Pinedale, the first oasis along the southern edge of the state, Benjamin Bondurant recommended they homestead in the Fall River Basin, and they did. In 1913, Will filed his homestead claim on Dell Creek just below a bench where fire pots and tipi rings were found and where six Indians allegedly were buried.

Will's mother, Sara, did not embrace the Basin winters and when her son, Blaine, came she returned to Clayton, New Mexico. During those first years, Will trapped and worked for the U.S. Geologic Survey. His great uncle, Jim Baker, was a somewhat renowned mountain man and Indian scout. Baker trapped with Jim Bridger for a number of years and scouted with Kit Carson.

In 1901, Lois Stone's mother, Jessie McMaster, was born in Buffalo, New York. By 1917, the family ended up in Rock Springs, Wyoming, via Alberta, Canada. Her father failed at ranching in Canada, and his brother encouraged them to come to his home in Rock Springs where he worked as an undertaker. Jessie worked for the Rock Springs daily newspaper, the *Miner*, and in a flower shop.

Since Will's sister, Celeste, was then staying in Rock Springs, she asked Jessie to hold a door key for her brother. That is how Will and Jessie met, and in 1921 they married in Green River, Wyoming. Fighting a late snowstorm and mud, Will and Jessie finally made their way to Will's homestead in the Basin—a one room cabin sitting on one hundred and sixty acres. Their immediate neighbors were the Bondurants. Later Celeste married Walt McPherson, and they, too, moved to the Basin.

Over the years they bought another one hundred and twenty acres and built a sizable and comfortable ranch with a water wheel that generated electricity for their home. Until the mid-1950s, the Basin did not have electricity, and until 1961 residents did not have home telephone service that reached beyond the Basin.

Will and Jessie also ran a sawmill on Dell Creek. They had three children, Donald, Lois and Wilma, and everybody helped milk cows, hay, cook, feed cattle in the winter and snake logs for the mill.

Despite the isolation and hard work, Jessie and Will enjoyed the ranch life and the outdoors. In fact, Jessie became an accomplished fisherman. They sold the ranch to Pete Cameron in 1973. Will died in Pinedale in 1982 and at ninety-four Jessie died in Sonoma, California. Pete Cameron sold the ranch to its current owner, Paul Ellwood, and aside from the Campbell Ranch and the Pfisterer place, the Faris ranch is the only early homestead still intact and functional.

Norm Pape.
Photo courtesy of Norm and Barbara Pape.

Norm Pape

Sunday night finally gave way to the early light of a mid-April Monday morning. Although an unusually warm March had melted the snow around Norm and Barbara Pape's ranch house, in Wyoming snow, sleet, rain, and high water can come in April, May, or as late as June. But that spring the birds, elk, mule deer, and pronghorns had already started their annual migration north to their summer homes.

Norm rises just before daylight. He knows that in an hour or so his two sons, Fred and Dave, will start feeding eighteen hundred head of cattle. Soon another 850 calves will join the herd. In an hour Norm himself will join his sons, but at seventy-six, he knows he can savor the quiet and new light of the spring morning.

Norm enjoys hunting, fishing, friends and good conversation. But most of all and from the comfortable perch of his log ranch house, Norm became captivated by the birds and wildlife and their seasonal wanderings and habits. They play against an ever-changing backdrop of white snow, fall and spring browns, and finally the green of early summer. And every moment or two the sunlight or even the gray light of an an overcast day, alters the scene. The surrounding snowcapped mountains—the Wyoming Range on the west and the Wind Rivers on the east—add special color and majesty to nature's comings and goings around the Pape Ranch.

Norm keeps a pair of binoculars at each end of the house, and in that way he can observe life outside at close range. Adding to this panorama is the smell of morning coffee and toast, those topped off by a subtle, but deep-seated sense of place—a place that holds over a century of Pape history in Wyoming.

While described in common terms, Norm's observations of the natural world convey a genuine, if not nearly religious, appreciation of life's colors and rhythm. At a minimum, Norm's eavesdropping on nature's sights and sounds rewards him with relaxation and simple enjoyment.

No matter how rewarding nature's reverie, above all Norm is a rancher and now the oldest member of a very successful ranching family. Yet Norm's life demonstrates that people who ranch or cowboy are more complicated than conventional thinkers may believe.

The life of a rancher revolves exclusively around cattle and, in all kinds of weather, the attendant demands of calving, branding, caring for sick cattle, haying, shipping cattle, and winter feeding. But while one rancher might train and sell quarter horse colts, another might serve his or her church. The next might play sports, fish or hunt with their children. Others might travel abroad or be members of a singing group. In these senses, they are no different than similarly engaged and interested people who might happen to live elsewhere.

Of course, one of Norm's most notable traits and the one that gives him the greatest satisfaction is that he is living—the only member of the "Originals" cast who is alive today.

Although the Pape's ten thousand acres allow them to pasture most of their nearly three thousand head of cattle on the home ranch, Norm followed the lead of his grandfather and father, who during the summer and fall ran some of their cattle in the Hoback Basin and were members of the Hoback Stock Association. Together his grandfather, Fred, and father, Lester, ran about two hundred head of cattle in the Basin. Today, Norm and his sons run 269 heifers and twelve to fourteen bulls—one bull for about twenty-five heifers.

Until recently, the Papes drove their cattle early each June from their ranch up to the Rim and then down the highway into the Basin. Now they drive them about halfway to the Basin and then truck the last half of the trip. In mid-October they still drive their cattle up the highway, over the Rim and into the driveway leading back to their ranch. In the fall after the cattle hit the driveway, all those who helped with the drive get to enjoy a remarkably ample and tasty tailgate lunch.

Today, with more cars and trucks driving at high speed and often bad weather, the fall drive carries some risk for riders and cattle. On October 12, 1983, the Papes, Jim McKinney, the Association's rider, and John Ross, the second rider, were pushing cattle up the highway towards the Rim. It was cold and snowy. The lead and rear trucks that warn drivers to slow down for cattle were in place. Seemingly out of nowhere, a semi-trailer truck loaded with flagstone slammed into the string of cattle. The truck had lost its brakes, and the driver control. Five head of cattle were killed instantly. Two more were so badly injured they were shot. Blood was all over the road. The remaining cattle were returned to their pasture in the Basin. The next morning the riders nervously trailed them out again, but this time with no accidents. However, six head could not walk and were trucked home. Luckily, no rider was hurt or killed.

Eight years later, the Papes added more to the history of the Basin. In summer 1990, the Papes ran steers on their Hoback permit. At the end of the fall and even after two weeks of back riding, they ended up thirty steers short. Every rancher expects to lose a calf or two and maybe a cow or bull, but the loss of thirty steers was extraordinary and expensive. No explanation was ever offered, but rustlers were suspected. The next year, the Papes took non-use in the Basin and used private pasture, but by 1994 they were back in the Basin.

As noted in Part Two, Norm's father, Lester, served as Secretary of the Hoback Stock Association until his death in 1975—a term of service that lasted nearly forty years. Norm's thirty year tenure in that same job rivals his father's term. The two managed the Association's finances by collecting dues, paying the bills, and managing cash flow. The invoices or bills included the salary for the riders, salt for the cattle, fuel and truck and trailer maintenance. They kept the minutes of each meeting and thereby recorded its history. As long as anyone can remember, the Papes have hosted the Association's spring and fall meetings where Barbara served and serves coffee and dessert. Every attendee leaves his cowboy hat in the entrance hall, but brings his sense of humor to the meeting.

And thinking of that sense of humor, one more Pape story can fall into place. Norm and his sons were some of the first Sublette County ranchers to use All Terrain Vehicles or "four wheelers" to move and manage their cattle. Compared to a horse, an ATV is quick and efficient, particularly on flat land. The terrain of the Basin requires working horseback including fixing fence, salting and moving cattle. Since Norm's first-year heifers have been a little unruly to move or cut out of a herd, the Basin ranchers and cowboys often joke that only by making the sound of an ATV while on horseback will the Pape heifers take a cowboy seriously.

Rock Solid

In the British Commonwealth only a person who has the attributes and skills that can make him an all around citizen, businessman, or athlete can win the accolade or description, "rock solid." In Australian tennis camps, such an award is often given to the best all-around player and competitor—the highest possible compliment.

Norm Pape is rock solid. Not only has he built upon and refined his father's and mother's land and ranch legacy, but he has also gained a reputation for breeding and raising some of the finest cattle in the Sublette County and in Wyoming. He has managed a partnership with his sons, and together they have made the ranch a financial success.

Norm has served as a member of the local school board and the Wyoming Game and Fish Commission. He was president of the Sublette County Farm Bureau and for many years served as a member of the Soil Conservation Service. He cares about his community and its ranching heritage. Norm knows that ranching, conservation, open space and wildlife habitat all go together. During the last twenty-five years he has witnessed the change in land ownership and values. Norm's sanctuary will remain intact for another twenty-five years, even as the sons and daughters of other ranchers leave their family ranches. Attracting his well-educated sons and giving them the responsibility for the ranch stands out as an uncommon achievement.

Norm and Barbara are both active members and lay leaders of Pinedale's Saint Andrews Episcopal Church, and in every respect they have given generously to the church. A few years ago Norm was diagnosed with prostate cancer. Not only did Norm survive; he joined a few other Sublette County cancer survivors, and they started "Kickin Cancer," a nonprofit devoted to giving financial support to cancer patients or their families.

The comments of other ranchers stand out as the most telling. They can be summarized by a single phrase—*when Norm talks, it is worth listening.* Others might call it wisdom. At a time when the currency of decency has been dramatically depreciated, Norm is simply a decent man.

A Family Tradition

Norm is devoted to his family and family tradition. Although the family tradition is ranching, a rancher cannot succeed without hard work and a spirit of generosity that encompasses his neighbors and friends. Norm's grandfather, Frederick Herman Pape, started the tradition, but his great uncle Will, Fred's brother, was the catalyst.

On January 26, 1872, Fred Pape was born in Bloomington, Illinois. The family moved to Kansas, and later Fred followed Will to North Park, Colorado, where Fred worked on some cattle ranches and started his education in the cattle business. He returned to Kansas, and in 1896 married Lena Johnson, who Fred had known as a child.

In 1904, meager farm income and drought prompted a move to Bronx, Wyoming, where again Will Pape then lived. That Wyoming community was named after one of the five New York City boroughs. Norm Pape's father, Lester, who was born in 1897, had turned nine when the family moved to Wyoming.

Initially, Fred bought one hundred and sixty acres from Gibson Blackwell, including a one room log cabin, a corral, and small stable. He paid eighteen hundred dollars. The next year Fred and Lena built a relatively spacious twenty-four foot square cabin and three years later built a much larger home. During this time Fred began to build the Pape Ranches by acquiring other homesteads, such as Fred Harrison's, and Mason Philip's properties. Those homesteaders, who sold, usually did so because of the death of a spouse or the inability to make an economic go of the homestead. Sometimes it was homesickness for the place they'd left. They sold to the neighbor they liked the best or who had helped them the most. Fred even bought his brother Will's homestead and the property of Lena's brothers, Clarence and Court Johnson.

That land allowed him to improve and expand his herd, and he began another Pape tradition; raising high quality Hereford cattle.

Fred's brand, the "W," is now owned by his grandson, Norm. Old Fred, who laid the foundation for the Pape Ranches, died on March 10, 1950. He was seventy-eight years old. Making room for his son and his family, a year earlier Fred and Lena had moved to Pinedale.

Although born in Kansas, Lester Pape was raised and attended school in Bronx, Wyoming. However, he took two out of state detours. First, he attended high school at a "prep" school in Corvallis, Oregon, and served in the army during World War I. After his duty tour, he returned home and started ranching on the Johnson place that his father had acquired.

At any time, breaking into the ranching business requires courage and a willingness to take substantial financial risks. In the early 1920s, it was even riskier. Since buying sheep was significantly less costly than starting a cattle herd, Lester started ranching with some old Columbia ewes. As the demand for wool continued after the war, his herd grew to eight hundred. He sold both lambs and wool.

During the lean years, Lester trapped beaver, muskrat, and coyote, and the sale of the furs allowed the Pape family to survive and then thrive. However, more than once when deer and other game animals were scarce, the family dined on porcupine. Later, Lester became a trophy game hunter and continued his passion for collecting antlers shed by elk and mule deer. He also collected antiques and made home movies.

Over the next years, he picked up on his father's tradition and acquired more nearby homesteads and started raising Hereford cattle. He built his commercial grade herd to over one thousand head. His brand, the " ME ," is still used by the Pape Ranches today, and all the cattle they run in the Hoback Basin have the "ME" brand which is very easy to see.

One of Lester's finest days was November 1, 1925. On that date he married Mary Hillier in Green River, Wyoming. Lester was twenty-eight, Mary only two days shy of twenty-three. He was a handsome cowboy in his hat and angora chaps, and Mary was a pristine beauty from Kansas.

Bringing the Basin back into focus, in the early 1920s at eighteen years old, Mary, a schoolteacher, left Kansas with her mother, Dora Alice, to finish teaching summer school in the Fall River Basin. She took over in August and finished the term in November. They lived with her sister, Ethel, whose husband, Grover Dressler, owned a small ranch near the Rim. Later she taught at the Beaver School up Horse Creek. Shortly after their marriage, Mary gave up teaching and helped run the ranch and raised their children, and that brings the story and tradition back to Norm.

On August 8, 1930 just at the onset of the Depression, Norman Frederick Pape made his appearance with his twin sister, Nadine Francis. They were the first twins born in the Jackson Hospital. If they could have, they should have taken a bow. Ironically, a year earlier Mary gave birth to their first twins, Karmen and Kenneth. However, Kenneth died as an infant. Their last child, Miriam Lesta, was born in 1935.

Continuing their father's tradition, until seventh grade Norm and his sisters attended the Bronx school. They attended eighth and ninth grade in Pinedale. Placing a premium on education, Norm and his sisters graduated from Wasatch Academy in Mt. Pleasant, Utah. At that time Sublette County schools in Pinedale did not provide ranch children with transportation. As a result, a number of those kids went to Wasatch Academy.

In 1948, all three Pape children continued their education at the University of Wyoming. Norm majored in agribusiness and left the University in 1952 and joined the army. In 1952, the Korean War had reached a high pitch and included some of the war's most famous battles—Heartbreak Ridge, Bloody Ridge and Punchbowl. Until 1954, Norm was stationed at Fort Benning, Georgia—its high temperatures and humidity marked a dramatic contrast to Wyoming weather.

After a six month adventure in Nicaragua as an exchange student and then approaching twenty-five, Norm returned home and continued to enhance the family's ranching tradition. Like his father, on September 27, 1959, Norm had one his better days when he married Barbara Jean Bower. That date would mark the beginning of a lifetime partnership.

Barbara grew up on the family farm and attended school in Worland, Wyoming. She enrolled in Casper College, a community college, and then graduated from the University of Wyoming. She majored in home economics. Until she married Norm, Barbara worked as a home demonstration agent in Carbon County. Like Norm's mother, Mary Hillier, Barbara plays a central role in the ranch, its record keeping and financial management.

Norm and Barbara have three children. The first, Jane Ann, born in 1960, lives with her husband, daughter, and son in California. The two boys, Fred born in 1962 and David born in 1964, both live on the ranch with their families. Not only have the boys continued the ranching tradition, they have also sustained a cross-generational tradition of sound management and good working relationships between father and sons.

These traditions that span four generations can only evolve from the power of place combined with the strength and appeal of family. That combination has worked like a magnet, attracting generation after generation. But since Fred and his wife, Michelle, have two daughters, and Dave and his wife, Naomi, have a daughter, a question remains—will any of the granddaughters or their future spouses feel the pull of that magnet and then as the fifth generation further nurture that ranching tradition?

New Horizons

Early in his life, Norm Pape naturally excelled in his ranch education, but just as important, he embraced a good formal education, including higher education. He served in the army and then went to Nicaragua as an exchange student. He chose to expand his horizons, but always returned home. In 1971, Norm and Barbara took their first trip and hunting safari to Kenya and east Africa. Three years later, Norm and a few friends returned to east Africa. He has traveled the world to fish, hunt, and gain insight into other cultures. Yet he enjoys his home and his family. About every February, Norm and Barbara fly to Arizona and then travel to visit his daughter and her family in California.

Norm could well have succeeded in any profession. But he chose ranching, and this small part of the world is forever thankful. During the early summer in 2003, Norm and his family hosted the St. Andrew's annual ranch Mass. Norm delivered the sermon. At the end of that sermon, he said:

We move through vast fields of opportunity on a road built by our own choices, interests and talents. It is the gift of the journey and how you choose to travel that forms the essence and purpose of life.

Norm has enjoyed the journey and has given that gift to others.

John "Peck" May

Forty-seven years. Usually a number like that brings to mind a couple in their seventies approaching their golden anniversary or the age of someone moving well past middle age. But in this case the number refers to the length of time John A. "Peck" May worked for the Pape family. Considering that today many change jobs every five years or more often, twenty-five years of service to one employer is rare, forty-seven years is simply remarkable.

Peck was treated like a member of the family and at mealtimes joined the family table. He came from Kansas and never married. Those two factors may explain his affinity for the Papes. While Peck had five brothers and a sister, they lived in other states. The Papes became Peck's Wyoming family.

In 1936, when he was twenty-three, Peck and his friend, George Blincoe, left Kansas and headed to Bronx, Wyoming. Almost immediately George started teaching at the Bronx school. The nine students in his first class included Karmen, Norm and Nadine Pape. Around the same time, Peck bought some land from old Fred Pape and began his near lifelong tenure with the Pape family. That tenure was briefly interrupted when Peck and George joined the armed forces in 1941.

Although a capable and reliable hand, Peck was never considered a top-flight cowboy. But the other cowboys and ranchers liked Peck and enjoyed his company. The Basin's fall roundup stood out as the highlight of Peck's year. For thirty-two years, he set up his tipi near the main cow camp and renewed old friendships. A bottle of whiskey helped take the chill off the evening air. When he finally retired, the Stock Association gave him an engraved silver belt buckle, an event still remembered by those who attended. Peck was touched by the gesture.

Although Peck enjoyed his adult beverage, he was not a frequent drinker. But every so often, he went to the Green River Bar in Daniel. He had a few drinks and picked up a bottle. On one of these occasions, with a good buzz and healthy appetite, he pulled up his chair to the Pape dinner table. The entrée that night was porcupine stew served on a bed of noodles—often the way the Papes served chicken. Also porcupine looks like white chicken meat, but doesn't taste remotely like it. Most at the table could only manage small tentative bites, but thinking that he was feasting on chicken, one of his favorite dishes, Peck ate three helpings.

When he retired, he sold his property and then moved into the Sublette County Retirement Center. Dick Brewer, who worked with Peck, took over. Before he retired, Dick had worked thirty-eight years for the Papes.

Kevin Campbell, left, and Tom Filkins.
Photo by Sherrill Hudson.

Part Five

The Cowboys

In Parts Two and Three, each of these cowboys made cameo appearances, and when they were mentioned, I promised the reader that later they would take center stage. Their time has now arrived. Kevin, Gerry, Tom, and Vic are all accomplished cowboys, and through life's rearview mirror, they can easily see their predecessors. They are united by ranching, their devotion to the Hoback Basin, its history, and their connection to the Hoback Stock Association. Yet, they are very different. Their portraits reflect some of those similarities, but mainly reveal their differences. Although each of their profiles reaches back in time, this story begins for all of us on June 10, 2005.

My alarm rang at 3:45 a.m. No stars. No moon. Just dark black. I briefly thought that I should still be asleep, but I swung out of bed, stepped into the bathroom, walked downstairs, and started the coffeemaker. I looked at the thermometer. It read fifteen degrees. It was Friday, June 10, 2005, and the first day of turnout—the day that cattle can start grazing on the Hoback Allotment. But I thought *snow*. That day, I wore long underwear and my flannel-lined jean jacket.

After dressing, drinking my coffee, and gazing at the *Casper Star Tribune*, Wyoming's only statewide newspaper, I walked to the garage. I opened the garage door and started my truck. My truck clock read 4:45 a.m.

My drive to the cow camp took fifty to fifty-five minutes. After we got our horses out of the corral and saddled up, at 6:00 a.m. Tom Filkins, the cow boss, his wife, Marilyn, and I "trailered" from the Upper Hoback cow camp to the Little Jennie Ranch. On the way up the Dell Creek Road, we hit the first real light of morning. It was overcast with drizzling rain and spitting snow. At 6:30 a.m. we met the other riders just west of the Little Jennie.

That day we would drive three hundred head of Little Jennie's Black Angus cattle down the Dell Creek Road to the Elkhorn and then push them south on the highway until we reached the lower entrance to the Reseed Pasture.

By the time we unloaded our horses and put on our slickers and headstalls, Gerry Endecott, the Little Jennie's Ranch manager, and his four man crew were moving the cattle from the upper pasture down through an open gate that immediately led to the Dell Creek Road. Aside from Tom, Marilyn and me, riding that morning were third generation Jack Creek ranchers Kevin and Lennie Campbell. Joining them was Heidi Campbell, Kevin's daughter and only child. Aside from helping the Little Jennie that day, Heidi rides for the Jack Creek and Fisherman's Creek Associations.

Whether it is the tradition, the rough country, or way of life, those who ride and compose the Hoback Stock Association share an unspoken kinship—a special fraternity where humor punctuates their conversations. That fraternity especially characterizes the relationship between Tom Filkins, Kevin Campbell and Gerry Endecott. That friendship has been bred over a decade of riding together, respect for each other, and the need for a good laugh.

Gerry's wife, Rusty, and Bud, an old time cowboy who rode for the Little Jennie, drove the flag or warning trucks. One truck stayed ahead of the cattle and another behind. They warned and slowed traffic in both directions and lanes.

As we started down the Dell Creek Road, Gerry turned towards us and said, "Every year it seems to snow or rain on turnout day. We won't break that tradition today."

Gerry had his two cow dogs, Katie and Gypsy. Tom had his dogs, Doc and Skeeter. Kevin's older dog, Spade, was left at home. Even with these well trained dogs, cowboys still whistle, talk, and shout at the cattle. Those exhortations will get the cows' momentary attention, particularly when starting to drive grazing cows. But every cowboy knows that when he talks to the cattle, none are really listening. However, the cattle talk reassures the cowboy of his dominant role, and when the cows just won't go anywhere, it offers him therapeutic benefits. A hundred years ago when trailing cattle for days, the cowboy's own voice may have been the only human voice he heard. Like today, cattle talk helped break the monotony of long days in the saddle.

The more difficult or slow the cattle, the higher the voice's volume and the more profane the cowboy's messages. Many of these messages are nearly universal among American cowboys. Aside from a soft whistle or the ubiquitous shout of "heh" or "heh cattle." The more apt phrases are: "Go somewhere." "Be a leader." "Get up, get up." "Get up the hill." "Line out." (go in single file so the cows and calves can stay together.) "Find the hole." (Meaning an open gate that the cattle should go through.)

When cowboys move cow-calf pairs, the slow walking or wandering mother cows may first be called, "you biddies," "ladies" or "girls," then, "you bitches," and finally, "you stalling sons of bitches."

Inevitably, due to their small size, the calves will end up at the back of the moving herd, and they are more gently called, "little ones" or "kids"—at least until they start a run back when they think that their mothers are behind them rather than ahead of them.

In uttering these phrases, a serious or I-really-mean-it tone is essential. Most of these phrases are used in a variety of combinations. For example, "Heh cattle, go somewhere," "Ladies, find the hole." "Get up there girls," or "Move it kids."

If a rancher's grazing allotment is in grizzly bear country, by growling like a bear, the rancher can really get his cows' attention.

Fortunately, the first part of our ride into the rain and snow lasted only two hours. That day I rode "drag" or behind the herd—not the most rewarding experience. After an hour or so, all the slow-moving cattle fall to the rear, as well as the calves. Today, everyone wore their yellow rain slickers. As they trotted ahead of me, they looked like yellow bobbers dancing on the water.

After pushing the cows through the Reseed gate and up the hill to a grassy but now muddy meadow, all the riders circled the herd. Shortly, Gerry and Kevin began to cut out the pairs and the spayed heifers. The riders' job in the circle is to ensure that cows without their calves stay in the herd. Just after beginning the cut, a heavy and near horizontal snow blew through the meadow. More than an hour later we finished and headed back to the horse trailers near the Little Jennie. From start to finish, we rode only four hours, a long enough ride on a cold, wet, and windy day.

The next day, Saturday, June 11, we attended the third annual Sublette County gelding sale. It offered over fifty horses for sale. Most came from Wyoming, but others traveled from Utah, Idaho, Montana, and Minnesota. Last year Kevin Campbell's gray four year old gelding commanded the highest bid of the sale, sixty-five hundred dollars. In 2005, he entered a black four year old. He sold him for thirty-eight hundred dollars, and at the 2006 sale Kevin sold a four year old red roan for five thousand—again the top price of the sale.

Over Saturday night the weather cleared and under Sunday's partly cloudy skies near their ranch, we gathered the Campbells' cows. We drove them down the Jack Creek Road and then "pointed them north" to Shoal Creek that sits at the lower end of the Hoback Canyon. That ride took over six hours—an average day of riding in the Basin.

Later in June we turned out more cattle. Steve Robertson and Victor Mack Jr., both Association members, joined us during those days. But another summer had begun for those who keep the Hoback

Basin's cowboy and ranching tradition alive. Today's cowboys are close relatives of their predecessors who lived over one hundred years ago. For them, who they are and what they do are the same. They are cowboys, and their livelihood is ranching. In contrast, a New York investment banker's real passion may be wildlife photography, but what he does for a living has no connection to what he likes or who he is underneath the shell of his wealthy profession.

It has been my privilege to ride with these cowboys and give them a voice and history. A poem, *Epitaph*, by Margot Liberty included in *Graining the Mare, The Poetry of Ranch Women* captures an elemental dimension of their lives. My slight rephrasing reads:

> *They may never shake the stars*
> *From their appointed courses,*
> *But they love good women,*
> *And they ride good horses.*

The four cowboys, who best represent that spirit and the Basin's cowboy tradition, will now finally appear in full color.

Kevin Campbell, 1995.
Photo by Katherine Campbell Bond.

Kevin Campbell
and the Campbell Family

The calendar read mid-September, 1974. In August, Kevin had just turned twenty. Like his father, Walden, at that age, the Basin's younger women clamored for his attention. After all he was a cowboy and a third generation Campbell at that.

But that morning it was all business. At 8:00 a.m., just beyond the cattleguard on the road leading into Cliff Creek, he met Rodney Pearson who then rode for Jake Pfisterer. Elsewhere the sky had a bright blue hue and the sun had started to warm the day. But the steep hills and high red rock cliffs surrounding that stretch of Cliff Creek kept the valley floor dark and cold.

They unloaded their horses and put on their headstalls. Although by that fall Kevin had spent five years training and riding other ranchers' horses, this morning he rode his seven year old brown mare. His father, Walden, found her on the Wind River Indian Reservation near Pavillion, Wyoming. When purchased, the mare had just turned three years old. Like many horses in the 1970s and earlier, the brown mare had a rough and wild temperament. No one expressed any surprise when she bucked, but neither Kevin nor anyone else knew that morning was that she would buck and buck hard for the rest of her life.

Their first job required gathering cattle off the steep eastern slope of Cliff Creek. That hillside had at least a forty-five-degree angle, and its vegetative cover was mainly sagebrush dotted with spruce and aspen. The only benefit of riding that hillside came after about thirty minutes when the cowboy had ridden high enough to catch the warm rays of the rising sun.

Kevin's mare had humped up her back when he mounted, but he and Rodney reached the cattle without incident or conversation. Rodney had a very understated sense of humor, but rarely spoke. Suddenly, the brown mare dropped her head and all four feet came off the ground. She headed downhill fast and only slowed to give an extra buck.

Kevin first thought the worst—getting bucked off in dangerous terrain or the horse falling and pitching him over the top. Just as they neared the bottom of the hill along the creek, the horse crashed to the ground and off went Kevin. The mare opened a big gash on her head. Kevin, stunned, but relieved, picked himself up—no broken bones or blood. As Kevin got back on, Rodney rode up. Kevin asked, "Rod, did you see that?" Rodney replied, "No, Kevin. I had to ride back to get your hat."

Kevin's rodeo down the hill started the hillside cattle moving to the valley floor, and after gathering the other cattle from the willows, they more calmly drove them the next eight miles to Burnt Creek where they dropped them off.

Not long ago when he reflected on the brown mare—never known as anything other than "the brown mare"—Kevin said she had taught him more than any other horse he had trained. Not only had he learned to stay on a bucking horse, but as with all "cowboy" horses, the rider has to be constantly prepared for the unexpected. Most importantly, she taught him to be aware at all times of where the horse's attention is directed. When training or working a horse, the rider must know how to gain its attention so the horse will follow the rider's lead.

When Kevin started training horses, he says they were rougher than today. Over the past few decades, breeders have learned to take the buck out of most of them. His young age and tougher horses influenced his early training techniques. On a ranch the horse also has a job—often a demanding job—and getting a young horse ready sooner rather than later had certain logic. If a horse was unfinished, the cowboy and cow work completed its training. At that time, Kevin first halter broke the horse and then in preparation for the bit and bridle taught it to drop its head. After that and staying on the ground, he put the horse under saddle a few times. Then it was time to get aboard. He summed up his early philosophy when he said, "You can't break horses to ride, unless you ride them."

More than a hundred horses, a few horse wrecks, and thirty years later, Kevin has changed his techniques—maybe it was more age than philosophy. Yet now he acquires and trains only registered quarter horses. Many he buys from an Idaho breeder. Next, he spends more time on ground work including training with a rope and halter, using a rope to pick up the front and hind feet, working the horse under saddle, and teaching flexion and reining.

Even though Kevin's training techniques have evolved over the years, he cannot be considered a protégé of the unity, harmony or communication theories of horse training often called the school of "natural horsemanship." The most notable developers and practioners of it include Tom Dorrance, Ray Hunt, and Pat Parelli.

Kevin called those trainers the practioners of the "scientific method," in contrast to his more practical approach. However, Kevin has borrowed more from them than he might know or admit. For example, he said that if a horse has a kind disposition, he will draw on that kindness in his training. However, if the horse has a combative attitude, he will match his approach to that disposition.

Kevin has earned the reputation as one of the best horse

trainers and horseman in Sublette County and the surrounding region. Generally, he buys two-year-old colts that he will train, and when the horses turn four he will sell them. First, he demands good feet and legs. That is consistent with the old saying, "No feet, no horse."

Next, the withers must be shaped to hold the saddle on a working cow horse. In other words, they cannot be round. Third, the horse must have a good build or confirmation. Although Kevin does not look for big horses—sixteen hands or more—he does look for a good hip. Most of his horses have been fifteen hands or a little more. He likes his horses with a well-shaped head, good mind, and even disposition. Since they are trained as working cow horses, they possess a distinctive character. In addition, they seem to take on some of Kevin's own personality.

Aside from selling good horses, Kevin is honest and guarantees his horse sound and as advertised. He tells a potential buyer the strengths and weaknesses of the horse, and he lets the interested buyer take the horse and try it out for a week or two. If one of his horses comes up lame after a sale, he replaces it with a similar horse.

Today, Kevin owns and trains nearly thirty head of horses. Since many buyers prefer horses with color, that is, buckskins, red duns, grays, yellows and red or blue roans, he has all the colors of the horse rainbow. Yet, some of his best horses have been bays.

Long ago he got over any attachment to the horses he trains. Any or all of the thirty are for sale. However, four years ago he trained a buckskin that he planned to keep. But when moving cattle down the highway, a man from Utah drove by and later offered Kevin ten thousand dollars for the horse. Of course, he sold it, but within the year the buckskin, which had been badly managed by the new owner, came back. The man from Utah couldn't ride the horse, so in a fair trade Kevin gave him another horse. Kevin still owns and rides the buckskin.

From the age of five or six, when Kevin added his dreams to

his ambition, the sum always equaled cowboy. Since training horses was a natural part of cowboy life, as a teenager Kevin started riding other ranchers' problem horses and training colts. He loved horses, but at the beginning he did not expect that his horsemanship and later "Kevin Campbell" horses would lend so much to his identity. Kevin's horse brand, a flying U on top of an upside down U, is placed on the right shoulder and has become one of the county's more recognizable brands.

His heroes, those he admired the most, included his father, Walden, who helped him pick out his brand when Kevin was a teenager, and his father's best friend, Harve or "Slim" Stone. He said that his father was the toughest and hardest working man he knew, but he then went on to say, "My dad was my dad. Harve was my idol." It was no coincidence that Harve was a first class horseman and rode the roughest horses in the country. Harve's grandson, Boone Snidecor, is a friend of Kevin's and another respected horse trainer in Sublette County.

Kevin's hair is thinning, and he is more slight than sinewy, but befitting a Basin cowboy, he has a style and charm. He wears a weathered white cowboy hat, a red silk scarf neatly tied around his neck, a vest worn under a blue jean jacket, well worn blue jeans, chinks, and round toed boots and spurs. He goes out of his way to greet people and talk with them, particularly on horseback. He speaks slowly with frequent pauses. It is as if he has to formulate the sentence or two before he speaks. A friend jokes that he gets tired just waiting for Kevin to finish a thought. Like his better friends, who are all ranchers or cowboys, he has an engaging sense of humor. For example, until recently his telephone message recording said, "I am sorry, I can't take your call now, but leave a message if you want. And if you don't, I can't blame you."

Kevin deeply values his friendships, and those friends range from young men in their thirties to some well over sixty years old. With a little mist in his eyes, he says, "I damn sure haven't done everything right in my life. But I have done some things right. Otherwise I wouldn't have the host of good friends that I love and respect, and who feel the same way about me." He likes to say that his friends have made him part of what he is today. His friends all assume he means his better part.

He enjoys drinking with his friends. On more than one occasion he has truly exceeded his limit. Coors and Canadian Mist are his drinks of choice, and he has been a long-standing fixture at the Elkhorn Bar in Bondurant and the Green River Bar or the "GRB" in Daniel, Wyoming.

Originally in 1900, the GRB was built as a store and post office. In 1917, the building became a pool hall, and then in 1932, the building was moved to its present location and served as a bar and pool hall. Now it simply serves as a bar with a game room and paperback library in the back. Kevin prefers the GRB, and many think that he leases private pasture for his steers in that area just as an excuse to visit the GRB.

A Biographical Sketch

With no announcement on August 27, 1954, Kevin Walden Campbell made his first appearance at the hospital in Jackson, Wyoming. Surprisingly, a bottle of Canadian Mist was not at hand to celebrate the occasion. He was the first of four children born from the marriage of Walden Lorenzo Campbell and Patricia Joyce McGinnis Campbell. The three other children are: Katherine Ann born February 7, 1957; Colleen Patricia born December 8, 1961; and Lennie Joseph born January 14, 1968.

All the children attended elementary school in Bondurant and then middle school and high school in Pinedale. They all graduated from high school. They grew up as ranch children. They participated in 4H, and they helped calve, brand, hay, roundup, and winter feed cattle and horses. As Kevin likes to say, ranching was his and his siblings' college education.

Despite aunts and uncles living in the Basin, the immediate family shaped the children's lives and formed their memories of childhood.

Although all the children now live in Bondurant, Kevin and Lennie run the ranch. From 1976—1993, Katherine rode for the Jack Creek Association. She would give anything to relive those days. Katherine now lives in the original Campbell homestead and commutes to Jackson Hole. After a serious horse wreck and medical attention at St. John's Hospital in Jackson, she decided to trade riding the range for work as a medical doctor's assistant. However, she still rides roundup for the Campbell Ranch. Colleen lives in Bondurant with her husband, Bud Smith, and daughter, Jennie, who is four years old, and for years she has worked at The Bunnery, a very popular restaurant and bakery in Jackson.

Kevin has lived in an old "sheep camp" near the corrals at the original homestead. He pastures and works his younger horses there. More recently, he frequently stays with his girlfriend, Joy, in a "town house" just east of the highway near the Elkhorn Bar and restaurant. Joy and Kevin plan to build their own home on the Campbell homestead. Lennie and his mother, Pat, live on the Bill Bowlsby homestead that the Campbell family acquired in the early 1950s.

Reflecting a national trend where today fifty percent of marriages end in divorce, three of the Campbell family's third generation have been divorced. Colleen is the only sibling who remains married. Kevin and his former wife of nineteen years, Tammy, have one daughter, Heidi, who was born in 1977. As noted earlier, she rides for both the Jack Creek and Fisherman's Creek Associations. She also follows in her father's horse training footsteps. Her interest in horse training is a source of pride to Kevin.

Heidi looks very much like her mother, who is an

Walden and Pat Campbell, 1953.
Photo courtesy of Katherine Campbell Bond.

accomplished rider in her own right and works for Jackson saddlemaker and tack shop owner, Scott Carter. Years ago, Katherine married a well-regarded farrier and artisan, James Bond—no relationship to 007. The marriage did not last long. A few years ago, Lennie and his wife, Elizabeth, divorced. They have two young children: Walden, now ten, and Anna, who is six years old. Generally, they spend the week with their mother in Jackson and most weekends with Lennie at the ranch.

Walden and Pat

Walden Campbell had ridden bucking horses with Slim Stone. They chased and roped range calves, and figuratively did the same with the young girls of Bondurant and Jackson, Wyoming. They were young cowboys.

They enlisted in the Army and both served in the European theater. However, Walden was sent to Colorado Springs for basic training, and after signing up for paratroop training, he was sent to Fort Benning, Georgia, where his fear of heights prompted an immediate reassignment. Harve trained at Fort Hood, Texas, and although they were both shipped out to Europe, Walden and Slim Stone served in two different military campaigns. Since he witnessed many deaths among the soldiers in his Company, Walden thought that Slim might have been killed. At the end of the war, Walden was stationed in Switzerland, and one evening he walked into a bar patronized by many American soldiers. Through the darkness and smoky haze, he spotted Slim Stone, who sat drinking at the bar. It was a long night of celebration.

Soon they both returned home. Slim or Harve Stone returned to his wife, Lois. Walden returned to his family's ranch, but by 1949, Walden started looking for a true relationship, and he was captivated by Pat—beautiful and different than the local girls.

Walden's family was Scottish. Pat's family was Irish. He grew up on the family's homestead on Jack Creek. She grew up in Provo and Salt Lake City, Utah. He was rural. She was urban. His father was a farmer and then a rancher. Her father was a businessman. He was born in Idaho in 1921. She was born in Utah in 1929. He had an eighth grade education. She had been accepted at Radcliff College.

Seemingly opposites—yes, but did opposites attract? In this case the answer was *yes*.

In 1949, the twenty-year-old Pat McGinnis fulfilled a dream and landed a summer job at the V-V Guest Ranch in Wyoming's Hoback Basin. It sat right by the Hoback River and one step short of the Hoback Canyon. But it turns out that Pat wasn't looking for a Western adventure. She was looking for a Western way of life. When she met Walden Campbell that same year, she found it.

Pat and Walden were married on December 3, 1952. Earlier that year, building on his father's acquisition of the Bondurant homestead, Walden bought the Bill Bowlsby's place and that is where he and Pat lived until Walden's premature death.

Above all else, Walden was a rancher. He considered riding roundup his vacation. Yet despite a near tireless work ethic, he still enjoyed visitors, ski parties, cards, board games with his children, and the box of books his children read aloud during the winter. Their reading reminded him of the Zane Gray westerns he read aloud as an older child.

Although Walden had only reached the eighth grade, he enjoyed reading, valued education and had a natural talent for math. When Basin ranchers weighed and shipped their cattle, Walden's math skills were in great demand. He served first on the Bondurant School Board and then on the Board of the Consolidated Bondurant and Pinedale School District. His service spanned twenty years. He helped "put on" the annual Bondurant BBQ, and Walden and his children were active members of 4-H, a landmark institution in ranch and farm country.

Underneath his harder and more calloused exterior, Walden Campbell, like many ranchers, had a more thoughtful, civic minded and softer side. But no one underestimated Walden's toughness and resilience. Following a car accident, he lost the full use of his left hand, but he remained a very good roper. Anyone who has seen a rodeo or is even vaguely familiar with the roping of a calf or steer, can recognize the difficulty a roper faces when he throws the loop with his right hand and dallies with the same hand. However, in those early years a few Sublette County and Basin cowboys "tied hard and fast," including Walden.

Tying hard and fast means that the rope is "tied off "on the saddlehorn and once the roper's loop falls over the steer's head, the rope pulls taut, jerking the steer short and hard. If a cowboy's rope or cinch broke, he lost the steer or calf. Since it is dangerous, few cowboys tie hard and fast today.

After months of severe headaches that were misdiagnosed as migraines, in 1978, Walden was diagnosed with sinus cancer. As the disease rapidly progresses, the pain can destroy the equilibrium of the toughest man. Walden struggled to die with dignity. At age fifty-eight, on March 7, 1979, Walden Campbell died. His best friend, Harve "Slim" Stone, served as one of his pallbearers. He left a ranching legacy still honored today by his children.

Now, at seventy-six, Pat Campbell is the matriarch of the Campbell family and may have had that role for several decades. After Walden's death, it took hard work, frugality, and determination to keep the ranch afloat. She has earned the devotion of her children and the respect and affection of her community.

During certain seasons on the ranch like haying, everyone has a job in the hayfield, but a ranch wife still had the primary, if not nearly exclusive responsibility for raising the children and cooking for the family and crew. Except during winter, this division of labor resulted in somewhat separate and parallel lives. Even when they

Lennie Joe Campbell, 1995.
Photo by Katherine Campbell Bond.

helped during branding or roundup, as Pat did, women's memories were centered on the household and family. The men's memories focused on horses, cattle, and stories of ranch life.

Like some other ranch women, Pat is self-effacing. But her decision to settle in Wyoming's Hoback Basin and live a ranch life in an isolated community reveals a strong-willed woman. She has long managed the ranch's finances, and in a family where tradition still matters, she cooks and bakes on a beautiful and well-cared-for wood burning range.

She deeply admired her father. Her children, particularly Kevin, have a noticeable McGinnis look. Pat Campbell found the ranch life she was seeking and has no regrets. Few can say that.

Lennie Jo

That summer day in Evanston, Wyoming, Jack and Frosty entered the middle-weight division. They had traveled 160 miles from the Hoback Basin and faced tested competitors from Wyoming, Utah, Idaho and Montana. Spectators packed the arena.

If the two had weighed in like boxers and jockeys, they would have tipped the scales at over eighteen hundred pounds. Although the competition could have been intimidating, they felt confident and strong. When they pulled ninety-five hundred pounds, their confidence and power showed. They won a third place finish.

Jack and Frosty are two of Lennie Campbell's draft horses and his prized competitors in draft horse pulls—a competition for a team of horses hooked up to a sled that is given additional weight by fifty pound salt blocks or cement filled barrels. The teams and drivers begin by pulling a minimum weight, and throughout the competition more weight is added. Each pull must cover a certain distance, and the team that pulls the most weight over that distance wins.

Lorenzo Campbell, circa 1910-1914.
Photo courtesy of Katherine Campbell Bond.

The draft horses and driver, who usually owns the horses, are joined by two others known as "hookers." Not surprisingly, they hook the draft horses to the sled. They need to insure that the horses are calm, lined up evenly with the sled, and pulling in tandem. Also when they hook, there can only be about six inches of slack in the chain. Unless the horses are exceptional, without practiced and savvy hookers, a team has little chance of regular success.

That year was 2005, and it marked Lennie's third year of competition, but his knowledge, respect, and admiration for draft horses goes back years. Since his high school days, Lennie has used draft horses to hay and to feed cattle and horses during the winter, the third generation Campbell to do so. Lennie's grandfather and namesake, Lorenzo Edgar Campbell, who homesteaded in 1912, started the tradition almost a century ago when there was no alternative.

In the earlier days, the Campbell's horses mowed, raked, swept or piled the hay, and then pulled the fork or apron to the top of the beaver slide. Two men evenly stacked the hay. Each stack can contain one to four bents. Each bent holds about twelve tons of hay. Today, the Campbell's draft horses only mow.

However, in these days of ever rising fuel and equipment costs, the draft horses offer an appealing simplicity. The Campbells like to say, "Time on the Campbell Ranch is what we have the most of. That's why we still hay with horses." Yet when compared to the tractors pulling mowers or a swather, the horses are surprisingly efficient. When mowing, the Campbells use twelve horses or six teams. Among them are: Snip, Ed, Kate, Tonka, Ginger, Star, and Molly. Each year, the Campbells and their horses put up around seven hundred tons of hay. With two teams mowing, they can mow thirty tons a day, and with a full crew and decent weather, they can finish haying in thirty-five days.

Like his father, Lennie is a rancher and a skilled roper. He shares his father's work ethic and his ten year old son, Walden, bears

Lennie's father's name. Also, like his father, Lennie served on the Pinedale's District School Board. His father, Walden, is Lennie's hero.

At thirty-eight, Lennie is the youngest Campbell—fourteen years younger than his brother, Kevin. Therefore, the future of the Campbell Ranch rests in his hands. He can continue ranching for another twenty or twenty-five years, and it is possible that his son, Walden, could extend that tradition another fifty years.

Lennie also works well as a cowboy. He is well-built and well-spoken. He wears a light gray cowboy hat, silk scarf, a vest underneath a multi-colored plaid wool jacket, and batwing chaps. Unlike chinks that stop below the knees, these chaps extend to the ankle level of a cowboy boot and fan out like the wings of a bat, hence their name. Lennie has a preference for yellow horses, and in 2005 at the Sublette County gelding sale, he bought a three year old palomino gelding. Aside from branding, he rides with Kevin during turn out and roundup. Lennie shares Kevin's calm and almost rhythmic ability to cut cows out of a gathered herd.

Lennie has an engaging personality and shares the Campbell family's appreciation and respect for history and the preservation of the Basin's ranching and cowboy tradition. Lennie also has a sense of humor about his life as a rancher. For example, he told me that "when you work for someone else you can always quit, but when you work for yourself you can't."

Lorenzo Campbell

In late August, 1910, eager to reach the Fall River or Hoback Basin, Lorenzo "Lennie" Campbell saddled up his horse in Naf, Idaho, where his stepfather, John Naf, and mother, Lucinda, lived. Although he did not remember him well, his father, Levi Campbell, had a reputation as a gambler, woman chaser, and barfly. That explained his mother's decision to divorce and remarry. He and his ten brothers and sisters had a good life in Naf, but now it was Lennie's time to start a new one.

After a couple of days of riding, he finally reached the Fall River Basin—later known as the Hoback Basin. He had just turned twenty-one, and at that age he caught the eye of many a young woman. He was a handsome man, and fortunately his son and grandsons inherited those looks.

Lennie joined his brother-in-law, Shel Baker, and his slightly older brother, Arthur. In 1910, they all homesteaded on Jack Creek Flats, and they began building one or two-room log cabins. Within the year they all returned to their homes in Utah and Idaho. In 1911, Shel and his family moved to the Basin. Shel and Arthur formally filed their homestead claims in 1911. Lennie spent that same year working on his Basin cabin, but spent the winters in Idaho. He filed his claim in 1912. He built most of the cabin's furniture. As he had a penchant for hearts, the backs of the wooden chairs and the bed boards carried the heart design.

After a short courtship, on December 3, 1913, he married Luretta Lance, who was then only seventeen. Within the first year of their marriage, they had a daughter, Mildred. When they packed up the sheepwagon and began their trip to the Fall River Basin, she was only six weeks old. After ten days, they arrived in November, 1914. The first snow had already fallen, and initially they stayed with the Bakers.

Aside from the sheepwagon, their only possessions included a team of draft horses, a saddle horse, and the nonperishable food waiting in the log cabin. During the first years, survival depended upon working for other Daniel or Pinedale ranchers during haying season, carrying the mail from Daniel to Bondurant during the winter, and hunting deer and elk in the fall. Beyond that work for modest pay, they had to grub out sagebrush to make hay meadows and built fences and corrals. They proved up on their homestead claim in 1918.

During their second winter, Lennie and the family took a job feeding six hundred head of cattle and cleaning houses in Jackson Hole. Soon the ranch owner became impossible to deal with so they decided to return to the Basin. They put Mildred and their suitcases on a sled, and pulling her behind them, they skied from Jackson through the Hoback Canyon and up Jack Creek—a distance of at least forty-five miles. Luretta was the first and perhaps only woman to ski the entire Hoback Canyon.

Eventually, Lennie bought some milk cows, and the sale of milk and cream provided needed provisions and cash to start a small herd of Black Angus beef cattle. With the cattle he needed a brand. Out of devotion and respect for his stepfather, the Campbell's first Wyoming brand was JNF. His grandson and namesake now owns that brand.

But make no mistake, at first and for some years, Lennie was more homesteader and farmer than rancher and cowboy. He wore bib overalls, milked cows as would the next generation, and rode big muscular horses. His saddlehorses looked like a small version of today's draft horses. But his and Luretta's perseverance and hard work built the Campbell Ranch and allowed the next generation to develop their own identity and become Basin ranchers and horse trainers. Lennie Campbell perfectly fit Wallace Stegner's profile of the "sticker," who through determination, courage, and love of place beat the odds and settled some wild, but beautiful country. By most standards he was an ordinary man, who did extraordinary things. At the same time, he had a gentle hand with his children, and that gentleness extended to his livestock.

Aside from Mildred or "Molly," the oldest child, and Walden, the fourth child, Lennie and Luretta had five other daughters: Rhoda Ann born in 1918, Lillian Luretta born in 1919 who died of spinal meningitis in 1921, Lila born in 1928, and Mary Lucinda who was born in 1931 and died six days later.

Lennie's older brother and closest sibling, Arthur, sold his homestead to Shel Baker. After that sale, beyond returning to Idaho, little is known about Arthur's life. In 1931 at a youthful forty-four years old, Arthur died.

After fully living the life he chose, in 1958, Lennie died in the Jackson hospital. He was sixty-nine years old. He was eulogized by his best friend, Forest Walden, after whom he'd named his son. In 1976 at the age of eighty, Luretta died.

The Ranch

The Campbell ranch stands as one of only two ranches in the Hoback Basin still operated by the same family that homesteaded it. The other is the Pfisterer ranch. Further, the two ranches are the only family owned and operated ranches in the Basin. In the 1940s and early 1950s, the Campbells acquired the two other historically significant homesteads in the Basin—the Bondurant Lodge and the Bill Bowlsby homestead. After Bill Bowlsby's death, Marshall Purvis bought the homestead and ran it as a guest ranch—the C Heart C. Later it was owned by two men, Roy Fisk and Anson Hoyt, and then purchased by the Campbells.

Even though change in the Basin moves at a slower pace than other places, each generation of the Campbell family and each family member developed his or her own style and identity. Yet they are united by tradition, loyalty, the ranch itself, and a sense of history that supersedes that of other Basin residents. Although in the future that family tradition will take its own shape, with luck it will continue well into the 21st century.

Gerry Endecott mounting his horse, 1995.
Photo by Katherine Campbell Bond.

Gerry Endecott
and the Little Jennie

Like every other morning, Gerry awakened at 4:30 a.m.—too early to get out of bed or watch the Weather Channel—but he knew he could not fall asleep again. The rest of the roundup riders would not arrive until 8:00 a.m. Gerry had almost four hours to plan his day and the fall shipping schedule. Having gathered well over half of the Little Jennie's fourteen hundred Black Angus cattle, he pictured in his mind the cattle he would keep and those he would ship. Every day he rides, Gerry makes those mental notes and thinks about the ways to improve the herd and the ranch. Like other ranchers and cowboys, Gerry keeps a log of important dates and numbers in a pocket-sized daily minder or datebook. They are known as tally books. He keeps meticulous records, and in 2005, which marked his eleventh year as the Little Jennie Ranch manager, he had ten such books and a decade's worth of ranch and cattle records.

At about 5:30 a.m. and not wanting to wake up his wife, Rusty, Gerry quietly slipped out of bed. The stars still shone brightly in the Basin's early morning sky. The day was clear and later warm—at least for October. Gerry dressed and sat at the kitchen table. He poured his cup of coffee and ate breakfast. After glancing at the weather report, cable news, and the livestock report, Gerry pulled on his cowboy boots, put on his spurs, silk scarf, an extra warm shirt, a lined black jacket with blue trim, gloves, and his brown cowboy hat.

Although the first real morning light would not begin to brighten the day until 7:30 a.m., Gerry walked out his back door just after 7:00 a.m. His crew that day—Bruce, Rodney, and Greg—was just pulling up in their trucks. They talked about the day and the ranch chores. By the time Tom Filkins and I arrived at 7:50 a.m., they were already saddled. At 8:10 a.m., Kevin, his girlfriend, Joy, and brother, Lennie, pulled up. By then everyone else was mounted.

As the Campbells unloaded their horses, the plan for the day was discussed and a few jokes or stories were told. Sometimes these informal conferences can last ten minutes or longer. Today after about five minutes, we rode out. Tom, Joy, Kevin, and Lennie rode Parody Draw, and Gerry, his crew, and I rode Riling Draw, both above the Little Jennie and named for two Dell Creek homesteaders who settled near those two draws.

Joining our group that morning were Gerry's two dogs and constant companions, Katie and Gypsy. In Gerry's book, the two stand out as the best working dogs he has ever owned. Katie is a blue heeler cross and Gypsy a border collie. Even though they work cattle very well together, Katie is jealous of Gypsy, and she must always be ahead or first. Except vacations or trips to town, the dogs go everywhere with Gerry, including on the tractors, the four wheelers, and snow machines.

Once we dropped into a small basin, we fanned out in order to cover more country. The sun had melted the morning frost. When the sun hit the droplets on the taller grass, the water beads looked like a thousand sparkling crystals. The day warmed up.

A few hours later, each of us drove the few cattle we had found back to the small basin. Gerry, Katie, and Gypsy had found a few wild steers and a couple of big calves that were running as they came into the basin. Altogether we gathered fifteen head. Due to a late September snow in the high country, most of the cattle had already come down to the fields around the Little Jennie.

We started to push them up the jeep trail that crossed an open gate and then dropped off into the draw. After two miles, three steers and a calf looking for its mother ran back. Gerry galloped off, rode behind them, and drove them back to the waiting cattle. The four hundred pound calf refused to join the rest—a big mistake on his part, particularly since his mother was already at the Little Jennie. Gerry's loop, thrown at a gallop from at least fifteen yards away, landed perfectly around the calf's head. He dallied fast, and the calf dropped with an audible thud and loss of breath. Gerry dragged that calf through the gate and down the draw. After a few miles, he let the calf loose. At first, it didn't move, but slowly it found its legs and ever so slowly walked down the draw.

Gerry is a cowboy's cowboy or an all around cowboy. He raises, trains, and rides good horses. It seems like all of his horses want to work for him. Gerry explained, "I have had several very good horses and some good horses, but I liked to ride them all. An old cowboy told me that the horse is as good as its rider. I've never forgotten that, so every horse is good."

He is as comfortable with draft horses as he is with saddlehorses. He knows cattle, and the cattle know his dogs. He can ride in the steep high country as well as he can cut cattle from a gathered herd. He can rope with the best of them, and he is a good friend and good neighbor. When talking with his friends, particularly on horseback, he will express surprise by punctuating a friend's story with, "Oh hell."

Whether cutting cows, roping, range riding, or baling hay, like all professionals he is very competitive. But ironically, Gerry is relaxed around his livestock and friends—a relaxation bred by years of experience and self-confidence.

Gerry's first career was carpentry in his home state, Idaho. Unfortunately for Gerry, but fortunately for the Little Jennie and three other Sublette County ranches, an accident cut that career short. He lost two fingertips on his left hand. On March 15, 1968, at the age of twenty-five, Gerry arrived in Big Piney, Wyoming, and started his ranch life working for Bob O'Neil, whose father ran cattle on the Fisherman's Creek Allotment in the Hoback Basin. Eleven years later in 1979, O'Neil sold his ranch to a California family, and Gerry managed it for four more years until it was sold again.

Then Gerry moved to another well-known Big Piney ranch, the Miller Land and Livestock Company, where he worked for six years. In 1989, he managed the Antelope Run Ranch in Boulder, Wyoming, located south and east of Pinedale. Finally, on May 15, 1994, and twenty-five years after his first Wyoming ranch job, Gerry was hired as the Little Jennie's Ranch manager. The ranch was then owned by Bob Wagstaff, Sr., an attorney and a bottling company executive from Kansas City, Missouri. Gerry tells people, "I have lived in the three B's of Sublette County—Big Piney, Boulder, and Bondurant—and I was too poor to leave."

Recently speaking about his past decade at the Little Jennie, Gerry captured the essence of Basin ranch life: "Working in the Basin has been the job that I have been looking for all my life. I can't say which season is my favorite, because I like them all. Each season brings its own beauty to the mountains. I like the stillness of riding and watching a doe stand quietly when she doesn't think you can see her. In the winter you can snowmobile over the same places you rode a horse, and it looks like a new place. Everyday is a new look in any direction you turn."

The Little Jennie

After a casual acquaintance with ranching, most consider ranching a business—maybe not very profitable, but a business nevertheless. When a relationship with a ranch is longer and more intimate, that first impression gives way to the recognition that ranches are institutions embedded in the American West. Children who grew up on a ranch grew up differently than city kids. They were surrounded by horses, cattle, wildlife, and vast open spaces. Every year they saw birth, growth, and death. They had firsthand knowledge of the cycle of life and understood the fragility of life and the randomness of loss and death. They understood the seasons and the hardships of ranching in any weather. At a very early age, they acquired a strong work ethic, but they always took the time to look around them and appreciate the country.

If ranch life exhibits the features of a Western institution, then historic ranches emerge as distinctive institutions. Their distinction comes from longevity, history, and the memorable impact on those who owned or worked on them. If you were a real cowboy, you had to ride for one of these ranches. Their history and import even extended into the community where they were located. Famous Texas ranches like the 6666 (the Four Sixes), the Pitchfork, the Matador, and the King Ranch illustrate the institutional role of historic ranches. In Wyoming, the Pitchfork near Meeteetse and other historic ranches are now joined by the Little Jennie in the Hoback Basin.

The Little Jennie lies in a large rolling valley fed primarily by Dell Creek and Jack Creek. Its 3,011 deeded acres are surrounded mainly by the Gros Ventre and tangentially by the Hoback Mountains. The ranch is beautifully secluded, and the summer greens, blues, and purples in a changing light perfectly lend themselves to a scene that few artists or photographers could capture.

The ranch headquarters consist of a four thousand square foot owners' log home, a heated swimming pool, a ranch manager's log home, four guest cottages, a calving barn, machine sheds, a workshop, and a horse barn. The Upper ranch, which encompasses the original Shel Baker, Arthur Campbell, and the Fronks' homesteads, contains a log home, two guest cabins, and a variety of out buildings. The Upper ranch is like a walk back in time as is the deeply rutted dirt road that leads to it.

The real father of the Little Jennie Ranch was Thomas F. Kearns, Sr., of Park City and Salt Lake City, Utah. He named the ranch after his daughter, who was two years old when he bought the ranch. His daughter was named after Kearn's mother, Jennie Judge Kearns. Little Jennie's footprints are still visible near the hearth of the fire place. Jennie Kearns now lives in Wilson, Wyoming.

In 1952, Kearns had completed the acquisition of the original upper Dell Creek homesteads that included Andy Erickson's place. It appears that the original ranch also included George and Wilbert Parodys' homesteads, and David Riling's place. In 1958, Kearns acquired the Willie Jones place west of the ranch headquarters and then the Koontz place that sat northeast of the ranch headquarters. He built all of the current log homes, sheds and barns. He considered the Little Jennie his favorite "project." During Kearns' ownership, both Clure Smith and Billy Dockham, the Fronks' son-in-law, served as ranch foremen.

Thomas F. Kearns, Sr., was born November 27, 1899, the same year that Charlie Noble began summering his cattle in the Hoback Basin. He was born in Park City, Utah, to Thomas and Jennie Judge Kearns. He had a brother and a sister. It remains a mystery why the son of Thomas Kearns was named Thomas Kearns, Sr.

Thomas' father, born in Ontario, Canada, in 1862, was a successful self-made businessman, who first farmed with his family in Canada and Nebraska. Later, he worked as a freighter, driving a wagon full of supplies to the mining camps in the Dakota's Black Hills. He rode for the Black Hills Stock Association, and he worked in mines across Arizona and Utah. Eventually, he and a partner acquired and developed a Park City mining property, the Mayflower, which formed the basis for his and the family's financial wealth.

Kearns' father and his father's friend and partner, David Keith, bought and developed Utah's Silver King Mine and expanded that mine into a large property, the Silver King Coalition Mines. He was a politically active citizen, and in 1901, he was appointed as a Republican to the United States Senate. Later he was elected in his own right. In that same year he purchased the *Salt Lake City Tribune* and began a variety of real estate projects, including the Tribune Building and the Kearns Building. A little later Kearns' father formed the Kearns Corporation, a holding company for his other investments.

He was a devout Irish Catholic, yet worked and lived in Mormon country. He and his wife, Jennie, built and supported St. Ann's Orphanage in Salt Lake City. He died in 1918 and was a tough act for his two sons to follow. His oldest son, Edwin, and his wife, Margaret, ran the family's several thousand acre Nevada cattle ranch.

Thomas F. Kearns attended public schools in Salt Lake and, like his older brother, attended Santa Clara College in California. During World War I he served in Utah's 145th Artillery and then transferred to the U.S. Air Corps and became a pilot. After the war, in 1919, he married Kathryn Whiting, and in that same year assumed responsibility for the family's mining, newspaper, and real estate properties. He continued his father's financial support for the Salt Lake Catholic Church and St. Ann's Orphanage. At that stage of his life, it was not known whether he assumed the family businesses by default, business acumen, or some combination of both. Those who knew the family reported that near that time, Thomas was afflicted with the disease of alcoholism. Later in the 1940s, he spearheaded the creation of the State Board of Alcoholism and helped create local chapters of Alcoholics Anonymous.

In 1947, and after keeping his disease under control, Kearns with partner Paul Walton, bought and developed Clear Creek, then one of Utah's major gas producing fields. Revealing his skill as a businessman, in 1955 Kearns formed another partnership with Walton, and they began developing gas, oil, and mining properties throughout the Rocky Mountain West.

Despite his affection for the Little Jennie and for no known reason, between 1959 and 1960 he sold it to Cliff Pearce, who turned around and sold it to a doctor, who within weeks defaulted on his loan. After much legal wrangling, the ranch reverted to Cliff Pearce, who in October, 1961, sold it to Bob Wagstaff of Kansas City, Missouri. At the age of sixty-nine in January 1967, Thomas Kearns died.

When historic ranches change ownership, often in the minds and memories of the surrounding community, one family becomes identified with the ranch. This was the case with the Wagstaff family and the Little Jennie. The Wagstaff family and later the Wagstaff Land and Cattle Company owned the Little Jennie for nearly forty-five years. During those years they greatly expanded the ranch. They purchased the Upper Ranch and then the Bosone place where Walden Campbell's sister, Mildred or "Aunt Molly" lived with her husband, Jim Bosone. In September, 2005, they sold the Little Jennie to Stan and Carol Thomas of Atlanta, Georgia. Although the original asking price was seventy-five million, the ranch reportedly sold for between fifty and fifty-five million.

Ever since he was seventeen and worked as a Park Ranger in Yellowstone National Park, Robert Wilson Wagstaff dreamed about owning a ranch in the pristine country of northwestern Wyoming. Thirty-five years later the Little Jennie fulfilled his dream.

Born 1909 in Independence, Kansas, Bob Wagstaff graduated from the University of Kansas, and in 1933, he graduated from Harvard Law School. From 1933 to 1934 he practiced law in

Independence, and then from 1935 until 1945, he worked in the legal department of Kansas City's Sinclair Refining Company.

In 1936, he married Katherine "Kitty" Hall. She became his lifelong partner, and that partnership rekindled his ardor for a Wyoming ranch. In 1937, on a belated Western honeymoon, the two traveled to Wyoming's Hoback Basin and stayed at the Triangle F guest ranch. As he looked out one of the large windows in the lodge that faced southeast, Bob saw the Gros Ventre Mountains and below them the future site of the Little Jennie. He said to Kitty, "Someday we are going to own a ranch in that valley."

In 1945, Bob started as a lawyer for the Vendo Company, a company that made the small upright self-serve soda machines for Coca-Cola. In 1961, when he left and started a new career, Bob was chief operating officer and vice chair of the Vendo Board. In 1961, he bought the Kansas City Coca Cola Bottling Company. That same year, Bob and Kitty bought the Little Jennie—twenty-five years after he stared out that window at the Triangle F and made his pledge to Kitty.

Although they first directed their Denver real estate agent to find a ranch in Jackson Hole, the Little Jennie was the best and most beautiful property to hit the market. After the purchase, every year in mid-June Bob and Kitty left Kansas City and until Labor Day stayed at the Little Jennie. They were devoted to the ranch and ranch life.

During their active ownership Bob and Kitty temporarily leased parts of the ranch to Northwest Exploration—presumably to determine if any commercially viable oil or natural gas deposits lay beneath the ranch's surface. Similar exploration on other Basin ranches began as early as 1934 with a Gulf Oil lease, and exploration expanded during the late 1970s and early 1980s. While nothing was developed during these years, in 2004, the Bridger-Teton National Forest planned to lease another 175,000 acres in the Wyoming Range, and 130,000 of those acres were located mainly within the Hoback Cattle and Horse Allotment. The acreage contains some of the area's most scenic hiking and horseback riding trails as well as prime camping and hunting areas. The rest of this story will unfold in *Part Six: A Glance Into the Future.*

Back in Kansas City, in 1962 Bob co-founded the Kansas National Bank and Trust Company, and in 1969, he was appointed to the Board of the Kansas City Federal Reserve Bank. Finally in 1972, he took over the Coca-Cola Bottling Company of Mid-America. Aside from the Little Jennie and his Kansas cattle ranch, Bob was an active member and lay leader of St. Paul's Episcopal Church, Kansas City, and for fifteen years he served as a board member of St. Luke's Hospital. After a long illness, he died at age eighty-two on November 29, 1991—thirty years after he'd bought the Little Jennie. His wife, Kitty, died on October 21, 2003.

During the Wagstaff family's forty-five year tenure, they retained only four ranch managers or foremen. The first foreman, Bill Allen, spent seventeen years on the Little Jennie. When Bill worked and lived on the ranch, during the summers the Wagstaff children— Bob, Tom and Katherine—spent many of their high school and college years on the ranch.

Tom spent most of his summers working for Bill. In 1978, Bill Allen retired, and after him came Mike McGinnis, who had a relatively brief two year stay. In 1980, Mike was succeeded by Bill's nephew, Dennis Allen. Dennis did not enjoy the same reputation as his uncle, but managed to stay nearly fifteen years. In 1985, as his father aged, Tom Wagstaff assumed the responsibility for the ranch's financial management and the hiring decisions. His older brother, Bob, lived and still lives in Anchorage, Alaska. He and his family were too far away to help manage the ranch. In May, 1994, Tom interviewed and hired Gerry and Rusty Endecott.

For fifteen years, Tom Wagstaff continued his father's legacy at the Little Jennie. However, the demands of his legal career, his family, the launch of his own law firm, and the management of two ranches left less family time and resources for the Little Jennie. Any capital improvements had to come out of the ranch budget.

Reassured that it would continue as a working cattle ranch, the Wagstaffs turned over the keys to Stan and Carol Thomas. Stan's commitment to the Little Jennie emerged quickly when he immediately purchased two new tractors, a round baler, and ten new saddles and tack. Although his financial wherewithal came from the development, leasing, and management of open air malls in the southeastern United States, he had a background and passion for cattle ranching, particularly Black Angus genetics and cattle breeding. For example, he plans to select and buy all of the Little Jennie's bulls. While Stan and his family have owned the Little Jennie for only a short time, his passion, early investment, and commitment suggest that he too may begin a new legacy—something the Little Jennie richly deserves.

Gerry and Rusty

On August 13, 1943, Gerry arrived on the scene in Squirrel, Idaho. In jest, some like to say that it sits next to Chipmunk, Idaho, but it was a small Idaho town built around agriculture. It has become even smaller today.

Gerry entered the world as the fourth child of Hilda and Richard Endecott. He had an older brother, two older sisters, and two younger brothers. Born in 1946, only his youngest brother, Jack, had the luxury of a hospital delivery.

His mother was born in Ely, Nevada, but her mother was German and her father Polish. Gerry's father was born in Und, Nebraska. While his grandparents both claimed Iowa as their birthplace, Gerry's father was a rancher and farmer.

Gerry and his siblings first attended a nearby country school. When the school closed, the family moved to Ashton during the school year. Ashton lies fifteen miles from Squirrel, and bus service did not begin until Gerry was a high school freshman. Gerry has four grown children—two live in Wyoming, one in Nebraska, and the last in Montana. All three of his daughters work on ranches.

They were in their signature cowboy boots, red rodeo jackets with their logo on the back, and cowboy hats sat atop their red hair. With acoustic guitars hung around their necks, the two sisters, Rusty Endecott and Susan Peak, known as Wyoming Red, took the stage of the Roxy Theater. It was Friday afternoon during the third weekend in May. Since a milk cow owned by one of that evening's star performers had died, he canceled. Wyoming Red and other musicians were asked to audition for the evening show. Much to their surprise and delight, Rusty and Susan were selected to kick off the evening. It marked their first appearance at the annual St. Anthony, Idaho Cowboy Poetry Gathering.

When they took the stage that night, a large crowd of over five hundred reflected the excitement of the first day of the Cowboy Poetry Gathering. A little nervous, Rusty and Susan opened with a fast moving tune, *Sarah Hogan*. When they sang *Back Home on the Range*, Wyoming Red began to feel the historic 1930s movie theater and opera house sway to the rhythms of their music. They could have played all night, but Rusty and Susan had only one more song. They closed with *Cool Water*. They received a standing ovation. They were followed by cowboy poets and humorists, Phil and Don Kenington. Closing the set the first night was solo musician, Rand Hillman, who later formed the Fall River Boys. As the audience filed out, some stayed in the theater lobby looking at the musician and poets' tapes and CDs, others went to the Star Bar and the Trail's Inn and awaited the jam sessions featuring the Gathering's musicians.

On Saturday, in recognition of their stage presence and performance, Wyoming Red received St. Anthony's Cowboy Poetry

Gathering's third annual Golden Note Award. Not surprisingly, over the next decade this friendly event became Rusty and Susan's favorite place to play.

Not quite thirty years before Wyoming Red's first performance at the Gathering, Rusty and Gerry met on a blind date in Idaho. Two friends arranged it. After a dinner of steak and fried potatoes—Gerry's favorite dinner—Gerry, Rusty, and the two friends drove to the local bar that had a live band and dance floor. When Gerry asked Rusty for a dance, she knew immediately that he should be in her future. And he was. They were married on January 26, 1968.

A year later, they traveled to Bob O'Neil's ranch in Big Piney. Over twenty-five years after that, they arrived at the Little Jennie, where Rusty has lent as much of her character and style to the ranch as Gerry has. Aside from singing, playing the guitar, and reading a good book, Rusty helps calve and hay, and in the fall she rides roundup. The most memorable event for their friends is the occasional Christmas party they host. In the late afternoon, it begins with a horse drawn hay wagon loaded with guests singing Christmas carols. After the hay ride, the guests find refuge from the frigid air in the warmth of Rusty and Gerry's log home on the Little Jennie. The smells of oyster stew, chili, and corn bread fill the house. Good conversation, Rusty's guitar, cakes, cookies, and pies top off the evening.

Although born in Afton, Wyoming, Rusty grew up in a musical household in Palisades, Idaho. Her father played the piano and her mother sang. Rusty was "born to sing" on September 13, 1944. With a brother, Daniel, five years older, and her sister Susan, five years younger, Rusty landed exactly in the middle. Her father helped build the Palisades Dam and Reservoir that holds and transfers Snake River water into irrigation water for Idaho ranchers and farmers. The children of those workers still hold reunions, and they are known as "the dam kids' reunion."

At age thirteen, Rusty started playing the guitar. Since her sister shared that talent, they played and sang together. However, it was just fifteen years ago that they formed Wyoming Red. They have built a wide and loyal following. Although they have played in a few Wyoming towns like Riverton, Lander, and Cody, they have had more bookings in California, Montana, Idaho, Utah, and Canada. When possible, Wyoming Red plays for the annual Bondurant BBQ. Often the Little Jennie donates a steer, and Gerry helps cook and carve the beef. On occasion, some have witnessed Gerry keeping time to the music with his carving knife and fork.

Every year on one Sunday, Rusty and Gerry are joined by Tom Filkins, his wife, Marilyn, Kevin, and now his girlfriend, Joy, and they take a day ride to someplace they have never been. It usually takes place during late summer or early fall and covers high country and sometimes very high country. It is a tradition that they all share, and later, whenever they ride near one of those Sunday destinations, they exchange memories.

Soon Gerry and Rusty will have nearly forty years of their own memories to share with each other, their family, and friends—memories of ranching, riding, haying, making music, winter feeding, snowmobiling, and enjoying good company. Neither is built for retirement, and today Gerry is still the cowboy he was ten years ago or more. Like all couples married that long, they know the other's good and bad habits. Their relationship's goodness flows like an undercurrent of a river, but the bad or irritating part bubbles up to the surface. For some those bubbles bring bitterness, but in Rusty and Gerry's case the bubbles pop with humor. That speaks to their integrity, and how they value their life together. They have a long life ahead, and if not for them, many others may have missed the view of higher ground.

Tom Filkins
Association Rider

The Horse Wreck

Just before 7:00 a.m. on June 22, 2004, Tom turned his blue and white pickup truck into the cow camp. He drove down the steep short hill and pulled up to his "parking space" just short of the front porch. He took the last swallow of his coffee and screwed the cup back on the thermos. He opened the truck door and stepped out. His dogs, Doc and Skeeter, jumped out the back of the pickup and followed him to the cow camp's front door. Tom opened the door and saw the mice scurry away. He set the thermos on the kitchen table. The sun peeked above the mountains in the east, and Tom thought to himself, a good day for fencing. Then it dawned on him that this year marked his tenth consecutive year as the cow boss for the Hoback Stock Association. That morning it had not seemed that long.

After picking up his blue rope halter at the tack shed, Tom

Tom Filkins at the Hoback Cow Camp, 1995.
Photo by Katherine Campbell Bond.

walked a few more steps to the wrangle horse pasture. He opened the gate and slipped the halter on the sorrel wrangle horse. He saddled up by the tack shed, picked up his bullwhip that was hanging on the hitching rail, and stepped into his stirrup. As he rode out, he saw the saddlehorses above the aspen grove that stood high on the pasture's north end.

Shortly, the bullwhip cracked, and the horses started running down the hill toward the corral. Tom kept cracking the whip behind them, and finally the last two most reluctant horses walked into the corral. Tom got off the wrangle horse and closed the corral gate. He unsaddled and put his horse back in his pasture.

Keeping the halter cradled in the crook of his arm, Tom opened the corral gate, shut it, and walked toward his big bay horse, Jug Head. The herd leaders, including Jug Head, ran and snorted around the corral. After they settled down, Tom put the halter on Jug Head and walked him over to the tack shed. At any time of year Jug Head was tough to handle and more so in early summer. Some called him mean. Others said he was "a buzzy" or "squirrelly" horse. While talking to him to quiet him, Tom saddled the horse and tied him to the rail. Jug Head tried pulling off the hitching rail, but he failed to get free and momentarily settled down.

Hans Graf, a Swiss shipping company executive and long time Basin seasonal resident, had given Jug Head to Tom. The horse had proven too much for Hans, and Tom was looking for a big powerful horse that could manage the steep and hilly Basin terrain—ostensibly it was a good match. Either the horse was named for the slow-witted character in the 1950s *Archie* comic book series or was given the name because he had a head as thick as a jug. Whatever the origin, it did not bode well for the horse's disposition.

At 7:45 a.m., as Tom grabbed the bullwhip and started walking towards the cow camp cabin, Scott Jackson, that year's second rider, drove up. His family lived just a few miles away. Scott was hired to ride through July, and then he helped the Campbells hay.

He was fourteen that summer and was headed for ninth grade.

First, Tom offered his traditional top of the day greeting, "How's Scott this morning?" He then told Scott that they would fix fence that day and start with the Pape pasture a few miles down the Upper Hoback Road. The pasture was and still is used as the place where, during roundup, the Pape Ranch's heifers and bulls are held until they are pushed up the highway and over the Rim. The pasture is located on the very south side of the Reseed Pasture and not far from the highway.

Scott caught his horse and saddled him. Tom and Scott rode south up the cow camp road and stopped just across the Upper Hoback Road and beyond the road's cattleguard. After opening and closing the wire gate, they rode east and after a few minutes, they rode near some culverts that ran underneath the road. Jug Head threw his head and pranced. Tom pulled him up and said, "You damn goofball." Taking the edge off the horse, Tom backed him up and then saw his headstall break. It fell off Jug Head and hit him on the chest. At full speed the horse dove down a sharply falling embankment on the right side of the road. Big boulders were strewn near the bottom of that bank, which was close to Bill Stong's old homestead.

Scott saw Tom drop down the bank and knew he was off balance. Jug Head made a quick move to the left, and Tom flew off the horse, hitting the ground hard. Scott jumped off his horse and ran towards Tom. Tom could barely speak. Not only had the wind been knocked out of him, but he was badly injured. Scott knew it was serious, too. Due to his sharp breath-taking pangs of pain, Tom was deeply flushed.

The only good news arrived when Scott noticed that Tom's head had missed a boulder by a mere four inches. It was also fortunate that they were just minutes from the cow camp.

Showing an uncommon presence for a fourteen year old, Scott suggested that he would ride to the cow camp and drive Tom's truck back to the accident site. Scott rode back and near the gate at the cattleguard, he found Jug Head. He brought both horses through the gate and after getting two halters from the tack shed pegs, he tied both up to the hitching post.

Scott drove back to Tom, whose pain was getting more intense. Scott helped him into and then out of the truck. Again, leaning on Scott, Tom made it into a chair at the kitchen table. Scott thought that Tom had passed out, but he had just closed his eyes in pain. Scott called Tom's wife, Marilyn, who worked as Deputy County Attorney in Pinedale about an hour away. Finally Marilyn arrived, and they drove immediately to the St. Johns Hospital in Jackson.

After Tom received emergency medical attention, the attending physicians and nurses discovered that he had broken eight of twelve ribs. Fortunately, none had punctured his lungs nor had he ruptured his spleen. Since ribs can only heal naturally, his salvation came from painkillers. After five days in intensive care, Tom was moved to the regular wing of the hospital. However, he thought that his recovery was too slow, and he complained of nagging discomfort. Shortly, the doctors discovered that he had lacerated his diaphragm. When they operated, the surgeon sewed it up with Gore-Tex sutures—the same sturdy material used for some outdoor clothing.

Just before Tom's scheduled surgery, Kevin Campbell arrived at the emergency room with a concussion and broken wrist. Kevin's surgery slightly delayed the repair of Tom's diaphragm. Ironically, Kevin sustained those injuries in another horse wreck. He had been working his steers on Cottonwood Creek when his horse stepped in a badger hole and tossed Kevin over his head. Kevin's horse had a broken shoulder, and briefly unconscious, Kevin was later found disoriented and walking along the highway.

Tom's recovery took over three months. During the first month he sat and slept in a recliner. If he lay prone, the pain kept him from sitting up or even getting out of bed. Later when he lay in bed, Tom tied a rope to the bottom end of the bed frame, and used it to pull himself into a sitting position. In spite of his injuries, Tom rode roundup that year. Of course, Kevin's recovery was faster, but that fall he still wore his wrist cast.

Tom and Kevin's horse wrecks reminded everyone that a cowboy's life can pose more danger than romance. They often ride alone miles from cow camp or a ranch. Cell phones and GPS are not standard equipment, and since the rugged country interferes with their reception, they probably never will be commonplace. No cowboy dwells on it, but riding a twelve hundred pound animal at high speed in tricky terrain is simply risky business.

Tom

He stands well over six feet and tips the scales at a good bit over two hundred pounds. He isn't musclebound, but he's strong. Even at fifty-two, he can toss fifty pound salt blocks like they were half that weight. But his back has paid the price of years of horseshoeing and truck driving. He has close cropped sandy hair and blue eyes. Years ago a small piece of metal shrapnel pierced one of his eyes and somewhat impaired his vision. In sunny or snowy weather, sunglasses are a given feature on his face.

Above all Tom is a cowboy and even a cowboy humorist. He wears a white short brimmed cowboy hat with a narrow buckled black leather hatband. After only a year, the hat is already sweat stained around the band. His old hat was so worn that the brim had waves and drooped down on his forehead. Long ago the white of that old hat had turned brown. A few cowboys had threatened to take up a collection so Tom could buy a new hat.

He wears the trademark silk scarf—usually black—a tan vest, blue jeans, and chinks. Buckaroo-style, he tucks his jeans into his tall black Olathe cowboy boots. Today, he is the only Basin cowboy to dress buckaroo-style—a style that particularly typifies cowboys who ride in the Sierra Nevada Mountains.

For convenience, when he pulls off his boots, he leaves his spurs on the boots. Together, they are placed on his boot dryer.

Similar to Kevin and Gerry, Tom seems almost fearless on horseback. A few years ago he rode off the heavily timbered and precipice-like side of nine thousand foot Crazy Mountain. The several hour ride up the mountain trail on the west is steep enough. When on the top and even the with no fear of heights, the average cowboy keeps his horse several paces back from the edge that Tom rode down.

When they were still young men, after a healthy afternoon of drinking at the Elkhorn Bar, Tom, Kevin Campbell, Kent Snidecor, and Steve James trailered over to Cliff Creek. After several miles, they unloaded their horses, mounted up, and rode up a wall-like red rock cliff. Earlier, a private plane hired by the Stock Association had spotted a few steers on the top of that cliff. Hours later they came down with the steers, which were initially unwilling to start down the steep mountainside. No sober cowboy ever tried that ride.

When they gathered those steers in the early 1980s, Tom was riding for Kent Snidecor, who was then the Stock Association's cow boss. Not only did they ride together, but their families shared the cow camp and called it home.

Tom had married his wife, Marilyn, in 1979, and Kent was then married to Cheryl Stone, Harve Stone's daughter. Kent and Cheryl's only son, Boone, was born at the cow camp, and a little later Jake, Tom and Marilyn's oldest son, arrived. Since the cow camp had only three rooms—a small kitchen and living room combination, a bedroom adjacent to the kitchen, and a separate bedroom on the other side of the kitchen—for those two years it was a very cozy place indeed. In those early years, an outside pump was the only source of water—no running or hot water indoors.

During this same time, Tom, Kent and Kevin Campbell found themselves photographed by Jay Dusard and later featured in his *North American Cowboys: A Portrait*. That collection is now a limited edition publication costing over a thousand dollars a copy. Dusard's *Portrait* also featured another Basin resident, Julie Hagen, who then worked at the Little Jennie. Her photo is often known as the Mona Lisa of the West. Later both Kent and Tom rode for the Little Jennie.

Tom's cowboy sense of humor began in the 1980s, but hit full stride in the 1990s and beyond. Perhaps that sense of humor had its origins in his relaxed attitude towards life. He works hard, but Tom is not a worrier. He refers to gloves as "hand shoes." He calls Pinedale –"Pine Nut" and the weekly newspaper, the *Roundup*—"the Round Down." When driving his truck, Tom can pour coffee into his cup without taking his eyes off the road. He said he learned that basic skill in "Truck Driving 101."

Although Kevin, Gerry, and Tom enjoy joking and laughing, often Tom is the one who gets the humor ball rolling. For example, very early on a beautiful fall morning when the aspens had just started to turn, Tom, Kevin, and I were pulling our horses up the Cliff Creek Road. After a cup of Tom's coffee, Kevin was just starting to wake up. As we passed a ravine stunningly dotted with yellow aspens, Tom asked Kevin if he brought his camera—since Kevin's sister, Katherine, is the photographer in the family, that is something that Kevin never did—but not missing a beat, Tom suggested that better yet, Kevin should take out his paints and easel. Similarly, Tom and Marilyn bought a German chocolate cake at a church bake sale, but wanting to lose weight, they gave it to me. When Tom brought the cake to cow camp, he said that I should take the cake home, put it in the oven with no heat, and after Sherrill and Lily get home, take it out of the oven, and show them the cake that I had baked.

Aside from his sense of humor, Tom possesses many talents. In another time he might be called a renaissance man. In this one, he would be known as a "jack of all trades." Not only can he do everything with horses and horse gear, but he is an exceptional mechanic. In the Basin when he might work on his or someone else's truck, he refers to his work as "mechanic-ing." Accordingly, Tom is a loyal listener to National Public Radio's *Car Talk*.

Although Tom holds just a high school diploma, he is noticeably more talented than his education might suggest. Now, during the winter Tom plows roads for the Wyoming Department of Transportation, and he leads commercial snowmobile tours. He has worked in the oil fields and driven semi-trailer trucks all across the West. He is the quintessential self-sufficient man.

His Background and Family

Tom was born and raised in upstate New York and his love of hockey also had its origins there. His wife, Marilyn, was born and raised in Bethesda, Maryland. Like other Easterners during the 1970s, Tom and Marilyn felt the magnetic pull of life in the West, and separately they made the transition to life in Wyoming. With ease, Tom took up life as a cowboy. Their romance with the West turned into a romance with each other, and they were married in 1979. That began their life in the Hoback Basin and their attachment to the Hoback Stock Association.

Although the Filkins had spent a decade in Cody, Wyoming, they returned to the Hoback Basin in 1994, and the lives of their two sons, Jake and Wade, have been defined by the Hoback Basin, its ranchers and cowboys. Both boys have helped Tom and the Stock Association during turnout and roundup, and they have done that riding for both pleasure and pay. During the Sublette County horse pulls, Jake and Wade have also worked as hookers for Lennie Campbell's team of draft horses, and using those same horses, Wade has helped the Campbell family mow hay.

In his mid-twenties, Jake, the oldest, is a skilled carpenter. He and his wife, Angel, now live in Fairbanks, Alaska, but they are looking forward to their return to Wyoming. Wade, who is a gifted horseman, finished his engineering degree at the University of Wyoming in 2005, and in late 2005 accepted a job as a water engineer in Sheridan, Wyoming. He also would like to return to the Hoback Basin.

After riding for pay, working the oil fields, raising their sons, and taking a variety of odd jobs, Marilyn finished a bachelor's degree and completed her law degree at the University of Wyoming. She briefly entered private practice in Pinedale and then served as a law clerk in Green River, Wyoming. For the past several years she has served as Deputy County Attorney in Sublette County. She is also recognized as an accomplished fiddle player.

Tom and Marilyn made a conscious decision to live and cowboy in Wyoming's Hoback Basin, but that decision entailed sacrifices like fewer professional opportunities, less income, more hardship, greater isolation, longer winters and fewer amenities. Yet that is the life they chose. However, despite Jake and Wade's affection for the Hoback Basin, they have made their own way, and even if they return, they will likely supersede the earlier hardships of life in the Hoback Basin.

Victor Mack, Jr.
and the Mack Family

Nationally, 1953 was a swing year. It swung between the immediate post-war America and the changes that would follow in the late 1950s. Selling nearly four million sets, television made its first meaningful debut in 1950. Dwight Eisenhower had been elected to his first term in 1952, the year Kellogg introduced Frosted Flakes. Joe McCarthy briefly raged across the national stage. The Korean War ended in 1953, and the Cold War began. A housing boom exploded in the suburbs, and unless a minority or poor, life was generally prosperous and comfortable.

A little later the TV shows, *Father Knows Best, The Life of Riley,* and *Leave It to Beaver* became the metaphors for the time. But foretelling change, J.D. Salinger's *Catcher In the Rye* was published in 1951. *On the Road* by Jack Kerouac came out in 1955, and in 1964 the U.S. Supreme Court ruled in Brown vs. Board of Education that separate but equal schools were unconstitutional. What demographically united everybody born between 1946 and 1964

Jo and Mack, Sr., 1996.
Photo courtesy of Jo Mack.

was their status as baby boomers and their later reputation for independence.

Some of these economic and cultural trends reached Wyoming. Others came later, and some never arrived at all.

Born in that swing year, 1953, Victor Mack, Jr., reflected a generation's energy and curiosity. Like all of us, Vic would evolve into his own person. Everybody is more than just the sum their parts. But Vic Jr. gained his ranching pedigree from his father, his grandfather, and even great grandfather. His artistic predisposition came from his mother. His appreciation of history and love of a good story came from both.

Above all, three generations of the Mack family have felt the pull and attraction of the Hoback Basin. Wherever they have lived and ranched, the magic of the Basin drew them back. Vic's mother, Jo, stated it best when she said, "God lives there." But she could have added that hardship is the expected price of admission to see and enjoy His handiwork.

Vic Sr. and Jo

Josephine, "Jo," Fisk was born in Hollywood, California, in 1933. Even during the 1920s, California and southern California had witnessed extremely rapid growth in population and wealth, which included agriculture, oil and retiree savings. By 1933 the Great Depression rocked California, and by 1934, twenty percent of its population was dependent on public relief.

Fortunately for the Fisk family, Jo's father, Roy, had received his PhD from the University of Southern California and then became an assistant professor of microbiology at USC. As a sign of the times, Jo's mother, Marcella, was a stay-at-home mom. Originally Jo's parents had come to California from Washington State, and she has one brother, Roy Jr., who still lives in the Hoback Basin.

The roller coaster economy of California and low cost investment options in other western states prompted many residents to pause and think about a more rural and real western life. Who knows how many of them were influenced by the "Old West" gunfights staged by the motion picture industry in the hills of the southern San Fernando Valley, now known as North Hollywood?

In 1948, when Jo was fifteen, the Fisks entered into a financial partnership with friend and surgeon, Anson Hoyt, and purchased Bill Bowlsby's old homestead on Jack Creek Flats. By then the original Bowlsby homestead included another 160 acres that had been owned by Bill's son, Banty. This made a solid 320 acres that Marshall Purvis ran as the C Heart C Dude Ranch, which the Fisk and Hoyt partnership bought and divided between them.

Although Roy Fisk was careful not to forsake his research commitments for this new undertaking, the move marked a risky and dramatic change. Jo felt that change like freedom—a break from the confines and conventions of southern California. It didn't matter that their electricity came from a fractious light plant or that during the winters their water was sometimes melted snow.

About one hundred and eighty lifestyle degrees from southern California, Victor Mack, Sr., was born in July, 1926, joining his sister, Winnie, on a horse ranch in Big Sandy, Wyoming. His grandfather, Byron Leroy Mack, homesteaded it in 1904-1905 and eventually expanded the ranch to one square mile. Later Vic's father and grandfather worked together and raised remount horses for the U.S. Army.

A remount is a horse raised to replace another, and before the mechanization of the U.S. military, it was a big business in the West. During this period, wolves posed a constant threat to the colts, and the Mack family often found colts killed and eaten by them until the family and other area ranchers took steps to control their numbers.

After his grandfather's death in the early 1930s, Vic's father, Elwin, always called "Babe," moved the family near the New Fork

River and purchased a privately owned "horse camp." The Macks then bought a band of twelve hundred sheep, and they supplemented their income by managing the desert horses, as did their neighbors. Every year, they ran the mares and yearlings, often known as "broomtails," off the desert.

They castrated the colts, kept the best horses, and broke them to ride. The horses were branded and later sold. After culling the colts, the Macks put a domesticated stallion with the mares and turned them back out on the desert. That stallion helped leaven the wildness of the colts and made them more reliable riding horses. As Vic grew older, he joined his father in this venture and was breaking horses to sell. That required real horsemanship and a good dose of courage, if not a touch of craziness.

Like so many small western ranch communities and camps, the weather and wind have removed all remnants of the original horse ranch, save for an occasional unintended monument of rocks.

In the late 1930s, Babe and his family moved to the Hoback Basin, where they leased land off of Dell Creek and raised sheep. In the early 1940s, Babe purchased the original homestead cabin and forty acres from Green Beeman. He paid four hundred dollars for it, and that property was just off the Dell Creek Road, too. This modest beginning created the Mack family's first foothold in the Hoback Basin, which later became the defining element of all their lives. In 1945, Babe sold the horse ranch and shifted from the sheep business into the cattle business.

After a World War II stint in the Navy, Vic Sr. returned to the Basin and worked with his father raising cattle. But even in the Basin, the U.S. government offered its Bondurant version of the G.I. Bill. It was called the G.I. School and provided a monthly educational program on agriculture and ranch management. Each veteran who attended received a modest stipend, and the school was taught by Jim Boscone, Walden Campbell's brother-in-law.

After each session and armed with their stipend, many went

to Floerke's bar and waged war with the bartender. For those who, after a few drinks, wanted to wage war with each other, the rest of the bar laughed and chimed, "Hit'em hard with those whiskey gloves."

In 1951 after a G.I. School session, Vic joined his friends at Floerke's and much to his surprise and delight met Jo Fisk and her parents. It was fall and the Fisks were getting ready to return to California for the winter. Suddenly, the pace of their lives accelerated. Tiring of the ranching business that he never understood, the Fisk family partner, Anson Hoyt, decided to sell his upper half of the ranch, the old Bill Bowlsby's place, to recently married Walden and Pat Campbell. Keeping their part of the ranch, Jo's family also decided to return to California, where later her father became medical director of Hyland Laboratories.

Attuned to these changes, Vic, Sr., hoping to keep the coals of their new relationship warm, acquired her California address, wrote letters, and visited her that same year in Los Angeles. Her passion for him and the Basin brought her back, and in 1952, they were married. Fearing that a secretly planned shivaree in the Basin might get out of control, they drove to Idaho Falls and said their vows there.

By then Vic, Sr., had become a practiced stockman and an exceptional horseman. For the next four years they worked on a few Basin ranches and began building a cattle herd and saving some money. In 1956, they settled on the Banty' Bowlsby homestead that Jo's parents owned. They built the first part of their log home in 1957 and added more rooms later. In 1971 Jo and Vic, Sr. added another 120 adjoining acres then owned by Banty Bowlsby and his wife, Virginia, who continued to live in their home on the property until their respective deaths.

By 1957, Vic, Jr. was four, and his sister, Joni, was a year old. That log house was their first and most memorable home. During the next seven years they grew up in the openness and freedom of the Basin. It left an indelible mark on both children.

During this time, Jo began to paint again. She had first drawn and painted during her high school years. In order to find the time to paint, she told the two children that if they could play by themselves without disturbing her, she would give them half of the sale price of each painting. It worked.

Although they kept their Basin property as their "home" ranch, in 1964, the Mack family relocated their ranch operations to Riverton, Wyoming. By then they were running two hundred cow-calf pairs. Each spring, they trucked their cattle to the Hoback Basin where the cattle's weight gains exceeded the gain of those pastured on other allotments. Managing those cattle and all of the other ranch chores, including haying and calving, kept each family member in more than full time jobs. Growing up this way, Vic, Jr. and Joni learned hands-on ranching. While living in Riverton, they also completed public school. Later Vic, Jr. attended Central Wyoming College in Riverton and then graduated from the University of Wyoming.

In 1978, the cost of irrigation water from the Riverton reclamation project rose, and that price increase and a desire to be closer to the Hoback Basin prompted the Mack family to sell the Riverton ranch. With the proceeds they bought a ranch on Cottonwood Creek south of Daniel. The ranch had been homesteaded by Frank and Effie Ball. During those years, the restoration of the house was Jo's art project and, of course, she still helped with all of the ranch work.

The ranch covered a lot of territory. Beyond its twenty-seven hundred deeded acres, they had an allotment of three thousand adjacent acres of BLM land. They also retained their permits and private pasture in the Basin and now had permits on the Upper Green and the Little Colorado Desert. Aside from using all permits and riding for two stock associations, the other ranch work—fixing fence, irrigating, and haying—took all the time they had. During those first years on the Cottonwood Creek ranch, between riding the Drift, the Upper Green and the Hoback Basin, Vic, Jr. rode over thirty

Vic Mack, Jr.
Photo courtesy of Jo Mack.

days straight.

By the late 1980s ,Vic, Jr. and his new wife, Lucy, were taking more responsibility for the ranch work. In 1992, Vic, Sr. and Jo sold the ranch to Leon Hirsch, the founder of U.S. Surgical which commercialized the surgical staple. Although a very wealthy out of state resident and gentleman rancher in Montana, Hirsch went on a Sublette County ranch buying spree in the late 1980s and early 1990s. When he bought the Mack place he already owned thirty-five thousand head of cattle in the county. Since then Hirsch has sold all of his ranches except the home ranch near Merna, the old Harrison place. He and his wife were divorced, and she now owns the home ranch that had been owned by Gordon Jewett after the Harrisons.

Later in 1992, Vic, Sr. and Jo bought a home on Tyler Avenue in Pinedale where they spend the winters and return to the Basin during the summer. They enjoy their life, and Jo now has enough time to paint. But the cowboy images of the Basin and its wildlife cannot be erased from her memory or palette, and Vic, Sr., who knows he has been fortunate, is simply a delight.

Vic, Jr., and Lucy

When Vic, Jr. turned fifty-three in 2006, he marked thirty years as a member of the Hoback Stock Association. In 1976, the Macks purchased their first permit on the Bridger-Teton National Forest in the Hoback Basin. That purchase stamped an indelible impressions on Vic, Jr.'s memory. First, the sight of cattle on the wide open range was a new experience. Second, Walden Campbell riding with his son, Kevin, introduced young Vic to the Basin and a new way of working cattle.

Walden became a mentor to Vic, and that teacher-student relationship revealed some of Vic's life long traits. Vic doesn't just hear, he listens. That will not surprise anyone who knows him. He has been and is eager to learn, and a person cannot learn if he or she can't listen. Whether it was Walden Campbell or Jackson saddlemaker Doug Scott who were the teachers, Vic absorbed the lessons—but maybe not at first.

He even showed that sponge-like quality when listening to oldtimers' stories, and he retained vivid childhood memories of places, smells, and tastes like ice cream at Floerke's store or the fishing pond stocked with big trout visible from Floerke's second floor fishing shop. That trait turned him into a good storyteller and entertaining historian. That talent brings up another quality: talking. Vic can talk, but he can still listen.

Unquestionably bright and brightly funny, Vic's mind works so fast that his mouth often cannot catch up. Yet, with the contradictions embedded in complex men, Vic can enjoy quiet, too.

Vic stands at medium height—maybe a little less. He is thin, but solid. He has noticeably sharp facial features, sometimes outlined by a well trimmed beard. Although he puts more of a roll on his hat brim than most Basin cowboys, he wears silk scarves, cowboy shirts, a Carhartt jacket, and chinks with his brand, the Three Quarter Circle, just above the knee. The brand had been his grandfather's brand.

In 1970s Wyoming, a good cowboy with a college education and sense of humor should have been irresistible bait for many women, but Vic just couldn't seem to catch one. That is until he needed a new Ford pickup truck. He had heard from friends that the best price in the region could be found at a well regarded Ford dealer in Lyman, Colorado. He made an offer, and the dealership delivered the truck to the Cottonwood Creek ranch. Vic asked if any available women lived in Lyman, and the dealer said yes—a schoolteacher.

Before long Vic received a letter from Lucy, the schoolteacher. After a few letters between them, Lucy decided to visit Vic in Wyoming. Even knowing her arrival date, Vic was riding the Upper

Green the day she arrived. Fortunately, she was patient, and Vic's father and mother took up the social slack.

Finally, Vic arrived and what an arrival it must have been. They were married on July 3, 1982. Thereafter, Vic likes to say that in a reversal of western history, he was a mail order groom. Lucy and Vic have one daughter, Megan, who was born in 1984. For two summers Megan also rode for the Hoback Stock Association and now is a range management major at the University of Wyoming.

As the reader might now suspect, like some of his predecessors in the Basin, Vic, Jr. is distinctive and even today he stands out in comparison to other Basin cowboys. Perhaps his most distinctive talent is his art. Vic is not only a skilled saddlemaker, but makes bits, headstalls, spurs, and chinks.

When asked how and why he started his art and craft, Vic said, "poverty was the driving force. In saddle shops I saw all of the well crafted items I wanted, but couldn't afford. If I wanted to have that cowboy gear, I knew I would have to make it."

Armed with books and his own experience on horseback, Vic started to teach himself saddle making. He quickly learned that "experience is a cruel and expensive teacher." He then met Doug Scott, a Jackson saddlemaker, who taught him the basic elements of the art. Despite those lessons, his first saddle was, as Vic described it, "a botched job." But he has kept that saddle as a reminder that a novice in any endeavor needs a teacher.

Fortunately, after that first saddle, he met Ralph Foster, a Riverton saddlemaker, who encouraged him and reinforced his desire. Vic has continued his saddle making and other leather work, and he now makes saddles for others. He could well build a successful business out of something he truly enjoys.

After the sale of the Cottonwood Creek ranch, Vic and Lucy picked up where his parents had left off. However, with little ranch land available in the Basin, Vic and Lucy bought a ranch near Farson, Wyoming, a small town about fifty minutes south of Pinedale. They continued to summer their cattle in the Basin and cherish its history.

Although the Mack family has kept a focus on the business of ranching, their home has always been the Basin. It has nurtured them, and they have returned the favor. They have hung their souls on the Hoback Basin's sagebrush flats, ridges and mountain tops. Wherever life or death may take them, their spirits have already found home.

My history of the Hoback Basin has now just about come full circle. This chronicle began over a century ago, and has worked its way through the intervening decades. It has introduced and given life to the Basin's pioneering cowboys and ranchers. Part Five has now bridged that past to the present and today's cowboys. Completing the circle, Part Six, the conclusion, will peek into the Basin's future and see what element of its history and tradition, if any, will remain.

Cliff Creek
Photo by Sherrill Hudson.

Part Six

A Glance into the Future

PAUL JENSEN

This book's previous pages have told the story of the Hoback Basin's history, the characters that animated it, and those who keep the cowboy and ranching tradition alive. The portraits of those individuals have made them come to life for the reader and revealed their grit, skill, and humor.

The Hoback Basin pioneers and early cowboys captured the essence of those who first settled the Western frontier. We have learned that most were "stickers," those, who beat the hardship, weather, and isolation, and survived. Over the years, popular culture has romanticized their lives, and yet their lives were so contrary to that romantic vision. My goal has been to create a balance between their harsh realities and the more heroic and touching moments.

Over the past century, much has changed in the Hoback Basin, but change there moves at a very slow pace. While the cowboy tradition remains intact, the Basin seems to have no need for the near ubiquitous technologies found in other places like Blackberries, MP3s, iPods, and high speed Internet connections.

At the same time, some forces that are still at play in surrounding communities may eventually impinge on the Hoback Basin. Those forces include the ever escalating real estate prices of Jackson Hole, Wyoming, driven by phenomenal out-of-state wealth, and the large scale natural gas development near Pinedale and Big Piney, Wyoming, that is soon to come on line.

The purpose of this concluding Part is to assess these forces and the likelihood that they will bring about a change big enough to threaten, if not extinguish, a century old tradition and way of life. We will look out about twenty years to 2025. Certainly forecasting the future is a tricky business, but we are only looking for the major contour lines of change and those that can easily be seen on the horizon.

The Future of the Cowboy
and Ranching Heritage

In 2002, nearly ninety-nine percent of Sublette County's private lands were ranched. Much of the public land has also been available for grazing. Additionally, Sublette County with 1.2 persons per square mile remains a rural county where ranches still dominate most of the landscape. They stretch from the foothills of the mountains to the shores of the rivers and creeks. Visually and culturally, the county has stayed consistent with its image as the "last frontier" of Wyoming. Soon that may change.

Not surprisingly what rings true for the county as a whole rings even truer of the Hoback Basin, the north end of the county. The future of the Hoback Allotment and the few larger Basin ranches are closely tied together. The more than a hundred thousand acre Allotment overwhelms the rest of the Basin's natural features and architecture. It gives the impression of almost unlimited open space, but without the larger ranches, which mainly compose the Hoback Stock Association, the Allotment would shift more and more into other uses, whether recreation or natural gas development.

Beyond the checkerboard pattern of modest homes along Highway 191, today four ranches sustain the Basin's heritage and the Stock Association. From the south end of the Basin towards the north, those ranches are the Pfisterer ranch, the River Bend Ranch, the Campbell Ranch off the Jack Creek Road, and the Little Jennie Ranch further north and off the Dell Creek Road. A reader of Part Five has become very familiar with the Campbell and Little Jennie Ranches. Those two also run nearly half of the cattle placed on the Hoback Allotment.

The third generation of the Campbell family intends to operate their ranch for at least the next twenty years. During the next decade Rusty and Gerry Endecott may step aside as the Little Jennie's ranch managers. However, it appears that the new owners, the Thomas family from Atlanta, Georgia, will continue the Little Jennie as a working ranch. Since both ranches are "off the beaten path" and confront severe winters, they are less amenable to subdivision than areas closer to the highway.

The Pfisterer family was introduced and briefly described in Part Three. Since the family keeps its business very private, I cannot pretend to know their plans, but the sale of their ranch by the third or fourth generation would constitute a dramatic break from the family's history and tradition.

The River Bend Ranch, owned by Gil Ordway, a successful midwestern businessman and entrepreneur, located its headquarters just off of the highway. It is the most accessible of the four ranches. It has been well managed by Bill Saunders, his wife, Martha, and their son, Tony, and his wife, Stacy, who works in Jackson, Wyoming. Tony is a very accomplished roper, enjoys the respect of other Basin cowboys, and runs a successful fall hunting camp in the Gros Ventre. In 2006, Bill celebrated his eighty-first birthday, and in his day he gained a well deserved reputation as a good cowboy. He still cuts out his cows during roundup, and Martha helps brand, hay and ship cattle. They enjoy their life.

Most of the River Bend ranch property is located across the highway and encompasses some of the Basin's historic homestead sites, including the Shideler place and the Mont Johnson homestead. Both are now hayfields. For a number of years, Gil Ordway has owned an old guest ranch in Wilson, Wyoming, named Fish Creek. Wilson is located about twenty minutes west of Jackson on Highway 22. He has placed a conservation easement on Fish Creek, ensuring that it will remain open space in perpetuity. In 2004, he placed a similar easement on the River Bend Ranch. The easement will protect most of the privately deeded land south of the Hoback River and guarantee that the entire ranch remains in productive open space. The easement will also preserve some of the Basin's most historic property.

Beyond the four Basin ranches, the Pape Ranch in Bronx, Wyoming, near Daniel, has served as a linchpin of the Hoback Stock Association. Norm's two sons, Fred and Dave, will operate their ranch beyond 2025. If they continue the family tradition and run some of their cattle on the Hoback Allotment, they will help further ensure the longer term future of the Hoback Stock Association.

Of course, premature death or illness among these ranchers or other unexpected contingencies could alter this most likely scenario. However, even then the Basin's ranching and cowboy heritage will endure through the next fifteen years and most likely beyond.

Real Estate
and Development Prospects

Beginning in 1972, the Hoback Ranches, a six thousand acre low density and rustic residential property, started the idea that a real estate boom in the Hoback Basin was "just around the bend of the river." For over thirty-five years, the hope that Jackson Hole's popularity and real estate prices would float up the Hoback Canyon has remained just that—a hope.

Today, the Hoback Ranches hosts twenty year-around residents and 140 seasonal homes. Beyond the Hoback Ranches, a few other beautiful homes are sprinkled along the Upper Hoback Road and well off Highway 191, but the Basin's residential development promise has never materialized. Whether it is the harsh winters, the lack of amenities, the minimum ten acre zoning, the rough lifestyle or just the "atmospherics" of the place, the Basin has yet to attract investors and developers or really test its growth potential. It has been a developers' "no man's land." Most Basin residents consider that a good thing.

In contrast, real estate prices and profits in and around Jackson Hole have reached stratospheric levels. Since the inventory is declining and only two percent of all land is left for development, those prices are likely to persist. For example, in 2005, just over eleven hundred real estate transactions produced $1.3 billion in sales or an average sale of $1.2 million. Seventy-three of those transactions sold for over three million, and thirty-four sold for over five million.

By comparison, the real estate market of Sublette County in 2005 produced 154 transactions with an average sale price of $262,944

Rather than reaching up the Hoback Canyon, the tentacles of Jackson development spread over Teton Pass and west into Victor and Driggs, Idaho. This growth in Teton Valley, Idaho, extended into the hills surrounding the two towns and the areas near the Grand Targhee Ski Resort. In 2005, 889 homes sold for an average price of $242,407. Total sales volume grew 216% from 2003 to 2005. The growth in Victor and Driggs started when they became the bedroom communities for those who worked in Jackson, but could not afford to live there. They were commuter communities Rocky Mountain style, but between 1990 and 2000 the population of that county grew 74.4 percent. Between 2000 and 2004, it grew another twenty-one percent. The 2004 population was 7,253.

Adding to Teton Valley's growth prospects is the new development proposed by Jon Huntsman, whose family built Huntsman Chemical. He holds the number 198 position on the *Forbes 2005 Richest Americans List*. He has acquired 1,341 acres between Victor and Driggs, and although the plans for his development are still evolving, it envisions a golf course, a hotel, custom built homes, townhouses, ponds and streams stocked with cutthroat trout, and hunting fields stocked with pheasants.

The region's other development tentacle stretched south down the Snake River Canyon and into Alpine and the northern end of Star Valley. Sales volume in the Star Valley rose fifty-five percent from 2004 to 2005. In 2005, the Valley's average home sale price was $175,182. Its growth began as a commuter town for Jackson workers, too.

Due to the growing amenities, beauty, available land, and proximity to Jackson Hole, Teton Valley, Idaho, looks to emerge as the next major development corridor. At a minimum, the Star Valley will continue its growth as a commuter community. In all likelihood, the Hoback Basin will remain outside of the growth zone, but become an increasingly attractive recreation area for Jackson residents and visitors who are seeking fewer people, less congestion, and more unspoiled or untouched country. They can also find cowboy life as they imagined it.

For Basin residents and the preservation of a distinctive history and life, this growth in recreation, in contrast to Jackson style residential development, should appeal. It would bring more economic opportunity and amenities, but not the suffocating kind that has afflicted Jackson and other similar resort towns. For example, it is impossible to imagine a PGA Tour or Arnold Palmer designed golf course in Bondurant, Wyoming. But at some stage when Jackson Hole and Teton Valley, Idaho, have exhausted all of their potential, the Hoback Basin may finally find its glory days as a destination resort and all that it means. Those days are far, far in the future. If the development is well planned, it is unlikely to injure the Basin's beauty or ranching heritage.

However, one exceptional real estate transaction stands in stark contrast to the generally limited nature of the Basin's current real estate market and growth prospects. It has the drama of a TV miniseries set in the West. After four decades of hard work, one Hoback Basin rancher finally cashed in. A local real estate agent and his Midwestern partners, who bought the ranch, began to subdivide the property.

Before the partners actually developed the property, the

self-made founder of a Nebraska tech company bought out the real estate partnership but had little appreciation for his property's historic value, its most productive use, or the community in which it was located. He decided to raise buffalo, but not for profit.

The hardworking rancher who cashed in is Bob McNeel, who in the mid-1950s bought the Charlie Noble ranch from Charlie's grandchildren. Bob was born in 1926 in Etna, Wyoming, located in the Star Valley. At thirteen, he came into the Basin to hay for Albert Miller and continued that summer work until he started working for Charlie Noble. Bob ranched in the Basin for forty years and had a very close relationship with the Hoback Stock Association. He served as range boss and the area's brand inspector. He was a fixture in the Basin yet a transitional figure between the originals like Charlie Noble and today's cowboys. His first wife, Lois Hicks, died, and he later remarried.

By the time Bob sold his ranch, he had added the Elmer Nutting and Bill Stong homesteads. Earlier he had sold one of his hayfields, the "Shideler field" to Gil Ordway and the River Bend Ranch. In the late 1990s, he sold the rest of his ranch to a real estate partnership called Firebrand that was spearheaded by Steve Robertson, a Basin resident, outfitter, cowboy, Jackson real estate agent, and a member of the Hoback Stock Association. His partners were successful businessmen from the Midwest. Their mission was to preserve as much of the Basin's historic ranch landscape as possible.

Firebrand paid $ 3.2 million for the close to eight hundred acre McNeel ranch. Firebrand intended to subdivide the property into large residential tracts and thereby recoup their initial investment and earn a healthy return. The company had begun building access roads when Joe Ricketts, the founder of the first online brokerage, Ameritrade, decided to buy that acreage for substantially more than Firebrand paid for the ranch. He bought 520 more acres from Hans Graf, a wealthy seasonal resident, which included a large home, two guest homes, and an indoor arena with horse stalls. That acreage included the old Jesse Budd homestead.

Bob McNeel, his second wife, Paula and their son, Robbie, used his proceeds to buy another ranch, the Mack place, on Cottonwood Creek south of Daniel. In 2005, Bob and Paula were finally divorced. Robbie attended the University of Wyoming and due to a woodstove fire, the beautiful two-story Victorian home on the Mack place burned down.

Steve Robertson and his partners bought another ranch, the Pete Olsen place, on the New Fork River near Big Piney, Wyoming. In keeping with their mission, they have kept it as a working ranch, but their plans to sell land for prospective home sites has yet to bear financial fruit. Their New Fork cattle now summer on the Hoback Allotment. As a rancher and cowboy, Steve stands out as a well informed and vocal opponent of the misuse and abuse of the county's National Forests, particularly the Wyoming Range. He believes that the U.S Forest Service's failure to anticipate the impact of technological change has led to an escalating footprint of snow machines, ATVs, RVs, and energy development.

Aside from raising one hundred forty buffalo and enhancing the homes on his property, Joe Ricketts is still struggling with the best use of his land. At various times, he has proposed starting a dude ranch. With no concrete plans in hand, in 2004, Joe proposed to the Hoback Stock Association and the U.S.Forest Service that he be allowed to "fence off" the river so his prospective dudes would not be frightened away by the cattle drinking at the river. Numerous practical problems plagued the idea of substituting water tanks for the river. For instance, cattle will denude whole areas around the tanks, and calves will be too small to drink from the tanks. Also Mr. Ricketts gave no thought to the precedent that his proposal would set for other landowners who had rivers or streams running through their property. The proposal was rejected.

Due to this confluence of events, the prospective success of an expensive large tract subdivision in the Hoback Basin has never been tested. However, since Joe Ricketts has periodically threatened to subdivide his property, the test may come sooner than later.

Natural Gas:
A Boom or a Ka-boom?

The story that will soon unfold about energy development in Sublette County is similar to the ones that can be told in many communities throughout the Rocky Mountain West, particularly in Wyoming, Montana, and Colorado. No national, state, or local imperative dictates the plot and pace of these stories. They are a matter of federal government policy and not choice. Many scenarios can promote energy development, energy company profits; create jobs and tax revenue; enhance community values; sustain multiple use of public land; and protect the environment. Unfortunately, the current policy's rush to drill does not encompass any of those scenarios nor respect century old traditions and values.

The Gas Play in Sublette County

During the past few years and for at least the next twenty years, natural gas and oil development has been and will continue as the main driver of change in Sublette County. That change could easily and totally transform the Hoback Basin. Now we are just in the first act of a three act drama. During the first act, the county's traditional industries and economic life barely began sharing the spotlight with energy. In 2002, agriculture and ranching had a market value of just over twenty-seven million. In 2003, county tourism and travel accounted for almost thirty-one million in spending. Under any circumstances, those two elements of the county's "domestic product" should have provided a stable economic foundation for a 2004 county population of 6,654 that includes all age groups. Each of those traditional industries depends on a healthy environment and wildlife population. Further, during the first act, energy's dual role as a source of benefits and problems was just beginning to emerge.

The curtain has just risen on the second act of the drama, and in comparison to the first, it offers the prospect of explosive growth and change in the county's community life, economy, and environment. That growth also could jeopardize the more traditional elements of the county's economy such as, tourism and recreation.

This growth will initially be fueled by thirty-one hundred new wells in the Jonah Field located in southeastern Sublette County and thirty-two miles from Pinedale. The Jonah Field sits on land owned and managed by the Department of Interior's Bureau of Land Management (BLM). The architect and operator of theses new wells is Encana Oil and Gas USA which is based in Denver, but whose parent company, the Encana Corporation is Canadian and based in Calgary.

The Jonah Field's sixty-six thousand acres is dominated by sagebrush flats and rolling hills, and historically it has been home to pronghorn, sage grouse and grazing cattle. The Field currently supports 554 wells and contains hundreds of miles of roads and pipelines. The new wells represent a 560% increase over the current base.

The new project area encompasses 30,500 acres. The new wells' rate of development would be 250 per year and the total surface disturbance between fourteen thousand and twenty-thousand acres. In return, Encana will accelerate on site mitigation including measures to reduce emissions, minimize and reclaim surface disturbances, and over time contribute about twenty-four million dollars to an offsite mitigation fund held by the state of Wyoming's new Wildlife and Natural Resources Trust Account.

BLM has also created a state and federal interagency group that will recommend what projects the Trust account should fund with the Encana money. The Jonah Field reserves are estimated at eight trillion cubic feet. It has been projected that well drilling and production will continue around fifteen years or many more, and the value of the produced gas will approach twenty billion.

The other staging area for the drama's second act is what is known as the Mesa or the Pinedale Anticline. It is also owned by BLM. Although south of Pinedale, it is closer than the Jonah Field. Over its history, it has sustained rich and varied multiple uses including sage grouse habitat, mule deer, pronghorn, and cattle. The Mesa also offers a breathtaking view of the surrounding mountains and valleys.

In spring, 2006, four companies—Anshutz, Questar, Shell, and Ultra—operated 293 wells. Due to the Mesa's value as winter habitat for mule deer, until recently, BLM has not permitted winter drilling. In 2004 and on a pilot basis, BLM gave Questar permission to drill during the winter. In 2005, all four companies have proposed that the winter "stipulations" or restrictions be lifted. They cite more and better year-around jobs, a produced water pipeline transportation system in contrast to trucks, and an overall footprint of shorter duration.

Although the numbers fluctuate and if allowed by BLM, the companies could drill nine thousand or more new wells. The Pinedale Anticline is estimated to hold twenty-five trillion cubic feet of natural gas reserves. Together with the 3,100 Jonah Field wells, during the next fifteen or more years the county could expect to see the benefits and costs of an additional twelve to fifteen thousand new wells, an increase of 1,329 %.

Neither of these developments has had nor will have any direct impact on the Hoback Basin. However, recently the plot encompassed the Basin, and the drama became more controversial. In late 2004, the Basin faced the first real and immediate prospect of energy development. The U.S. Forest Service officials of the Bridger-Teton National Forest in Jackson, Wyoming, proposed a lease auction of 175,000 acres of the Wyoming Range stretching from beyond Merna and over the Rim into the Hoback Basin. BLM would conduct the auction, and the Hoback Basin parcels included some of its most pristine, prominent, and historically valuable acreage like the South Rim, Noble Basin, and Cliff Creek In fact, the proposed lease ripped right through the Hoback Allotment. That 175,000 acres of proposed leases came on top the 150,000 acres of the Wyoming Range that had already been leased.

The most recent Environmental Impact Statement (EIS) that covered the new 175,000 acres had been conducted in 1993. Further, the new Resource Management Plan for the Bridger-Teton intended to guide the future uses of the Forest was, and in 2006, is still a work-in-progress. Next, the U.S. Forest Service refused to conduct public hearings on the proposed lease. Last, the office often contended that leasing a parcel was not the equivalent of developing or drilling on the parcel, particularly since a permit to drill application would trigger an Environmental Impact Statement. Since once a lease is awarded, the Forest Service cannot suspend the lease nor deny the company the right to drill, that contention was a bureaucratic sleight of hand.

Not surprisingly, a bipartisan storm of protest thundered

through the U.S. Forest Service. Opposition from Wyoming's U.S. Senator, Craig Thomas, Wyoming's Governor, Dave Freudenthal, state legislators, and many mainstream citizen, recreation, and environmental groups prompted the Forest Service to withdraw the plan.

In 2005, the Forest Service came back with a proposed 44,600 acre offering in the Wyoming Range. This time the lease started beyond Merna and extended north just to the Rim. The 31,000 acres temporarily withdrawn were all the proposed parcels in the Hoback Basin. With thousands of new wells already approved by BLM, few could see the logic of opening up an undisturbed part of the National Forest which had other higher values and uses. That is why Governor Dave Freudenthal and the National Outdoor Leadership School (NOLS) based in Lander, Wyoming, remained steadfastly opposed to the new plan.

Then in November, 2005, the Forest Service announced its plan to auction two parcels in the Wyoming Range by December, 2005. The two parcels totaling 1,280 acres were part of the 44,600 acres that the Forest Service planned to lease. That drew immediate public and legal protests from NOLS, Trout Unlimited, the Hoback Service and Improvement District, the Wilderness Society, the National Wildlife Association, the Wyoming Outdoor Council, the Jackson Hole Conservation Alliance, and others. In early July, 2006, those protests to the Interior Board of Land Appeals prompted the Board to temporarily "stay" the development on that acreage until BLM addressed the merits of the appeal, including air quality, the future of the Canadian lynx, and the cumulative impact of energy development in the Upper Green River Valley.

Beyond that controversy, a current National Forest leaseholder, Plains Exploration and Production Company, plans to conduct exploratory drilling near the Hoback Ranches in the Basin. In late January, Big Piney Ranger District sponsored two public hearings— one in Bondurant and the other in Pinedale—and the district is conducting an Environmental Impact Statement.

Of course, at first glance, these two small development initiatives may seem innocent enough. However, if exploratory drilling discovers economically viable reserves, then pressure to auction wall to wall leases will ensue, and a beautiful rural and ranching community will become another energy thoroughfare.

Not even waiting for the results from these two small developments, early in the week of March 21, 2006, the U.S. Forest Service announced its plans to conduct a lease sale of twenty thousand acres of the Wyoming Range, and thereby accelerated the construction of a new energy thoroughfare. That twenty thousand acres lying west of Merna and stretching north represents about one half of the just over forty-four thousand acres the U.S Forest Service proposed to lease in late 2005. The auction scheduled for April 4, 2006, has been protested by the same groups that protested the recent leasing of the 1,280 acres. None of this proposed acreage reaches into the Hoback Basin. However, the USFS conducted another Wyoming Range lease sale in early June 6, 2006 that leased twelve thousand more acres. Most of the balance, 11,263 was leased in August 1, 2006 and that was protested, too.

None of the protests deterred BLM or the Forest Service, and the auctions were conducted as scheduled. With respect to the April 4, 2006 auction, three companies paid a total of $2.246 million for eleven parcels, only $112 per acre. The three companies are Kirkwood Oil and Gas, LLC; Stanley Energy; and Hanson & Strahn, Inc.—all small companies.

The June 6, 2006, lease sale sold its thirteen parcels covering twelve thousand acres. The sale of those parcels earned $1.34 million, and Van Bullock of Colorado's Bullock Oil Properties bought five of the thirteen parcels. The August 1, 2006 lease sale of 11,263 acres in ten parcels netted $905,852.

One bright spot emerged on the Wyoming Range's horizon in late March, 2006. Wyoming's governor, Dave Freudenthal, negotiated an agreement with the U.S. Forest Service that protected the 131,000 of the Range's roadless acres from drilling leases until 2008. That is the year the Bridger-Teton National Forest's Resource Management Plan is scheduled for completion. The 131,000 roadless acres represent nineteen percent of the seven hundred thousand acres of the Bridger-Teton encompassed by the Wyoming Range.

Again on June 1, 2006, Governor Freudenthal shone more light on the Wyoming Range when he sent a letter to the Wyoming Director of the Bureau of Land Management, Bob Bennett, opposing the June 6 lease sale and any future sales.

When in mid-June, 2006, Wyoming Senator, Craig Thomas, R-Wy, declared his opposition to energy leases in national forests and specifically the Wyoming Range, he added more power to those fighting any further energy development in the Wyoming Range. Senator Thomas now needs to translate that commitment into national legislation.

As the helter-skelter nature of energy development continues, it is essential to schedule an intermission in this three act play before it becomes a tragedy. The Sublette County citizens, the state, region and nation need to see what common sense, early evidence, and history can teach us about how to take control of our own lives and future.

Natural Gas: How Much is Enough?

In 2004, Americans consumed 22.430 trillion cubic feet (TCF) of natural gas. The U.S. produced 18.758 TCF or just over eighty percent of total consumption. It imported 4.259 TCF or just short of twenty percent. The overwhelming majority of imports came by pipeline from Mexico and Canada. Over the next twenty years the Energy Information Administration estimates that U.S. production will grow by a half a percent annually, and by 2025, U.S. production will represent seventy-eight percent of total U.S. consumption and imports will rise to twenty-three percent of consumption. Throughout those twenty years the wellhead price has been forecast to remain high by historical standards, but fairly stable. For example, in 1990, the average well head price was $1.70 per thousand cubic feet. In 2000, it had risen to $3.69 per thousand cubic feet. It stood at $7.50 in 2005, and that represents a 320 percent increase from 1990 and a thirty-seven percent increase from 2004. The wellhead price is forecast to average $8.87 in 2006 and $8.70 in 2007.

As of 2004, the nation's current dry gas proven reserves stood at 192.513 trillion cubic feet. When the oil and condensates have been removed from natural gas, it is known as dry gas. At current rates of consumption those reserves would last just six years. However, in the past, the nation has been able to find new gas reserves greater than annual production. Since 1997, the discovery of new reserves has averaged 13.4 billion cubic feet per year. Only a few states replace or find reserves greater than their annual production. They include Texas, Oklahoma, Wyoming, and Colorado.

In the past and the foreseeable future, the U.S. will produce nearly eighty percent of its consumption and its pipeline imports will be relatively secure. Canada and Mexico are not Iran and Iraq. Of course, the natural gas picture is the near mirror image of that for oil. In short, neither national security nor short term benefits versus longer term value offer a credible case for drilling every extra trillion cubic feet of gas that can be found, and as we will learn shortly that proposition holds for Wyoming, too.

In 2005, Wyoming ranked third among thirty-two states that produced natural gas. Producing just over a trillion cubic feet, Wyoming accounted for eight and a half percent of the nation's natural gas production. Texas produced thirty-five percent of total U.S. production and ranked number one. It should have come as no surprise to Wyoming and Sublette County residents, when Texas based companies like Halliburton, became the major contractors and beneficiaries of the state and county's energy boom. Oklahoma ranked second. New Mexico took fourth place. Louisiana dropped to fifth and Colorado finished sixth.

Each of the five states that ranked below Texas produced two trillion cubic feet per year or less, but the top six states marketed seventy-seven percent of the nation's natural gas. The Jonah Field and the Pinedale Anticline can produce more than forty percent or more of Wyoming's marketable production. The rest of Wyoming's gas comes or will come from the ten thousand to fifty thousand coal bed methane wells in the Powder River Basin, and nearly eight thousand coal bed methane or natural gas wells planned by BLM in other parts of Wyoming, including the Atlantic Rim, South Piney, Seminoe Road, Continental Divide-Creston, and of course, the Wyoming Range.

Based on earlier projections, over the next twenty to thirty years, the two current Sublette County gas fields could produce a total of thirty-three trillion cubic feet. As we have learned, that's a lot of wells and a lot of gas. But remember, if it were possible for the two fields to supply the nation's total natural gas needs, both the Jonah Field and the Pinedale Anticline would be exhausted in about a year. That underscores the need for energy development that enhances the long term value of the gas reserves and the continuity of supply. Like the Strategic Petroleum Reserve, gas reserves guard against the country falling off a supply cliff when domestic production drops off as it inevitably will.

No doubt, the two Sublette County fields have and will continue to produce a significant quantity of gas. If the pace of development were slower, the gas would remain just as valuable and the impact on the national energy picture would be negligible. However, reflecting President Bush's version of national energy policy, BLM and the U.S. Forest Service are accelerating development, particularly in Sublette County. For example, when BLM issued its final Jonah Field Environmental Impact Statement in January, 2006, it declared that the 3,100 new wells would ensure that thousands of acres could not support any alternative use. If winter restrictions are lifted on the Mesa in 2006, a similar outcome is possible. Setting aside an accurate assessment of community benefits and costs, a twenty year moratorium on any use or value beyond energy is a very high price to pay, particularly when neither national security nor realistic energy policy really require it.

The Impacts

If Sublette County energy development will produce large scale land use changes and related effects on wildlife habitat and wildlife, its impact on the socio-economic profile of the county and the fabric of its life could be just as great. Unfortunately and despite many studies, today no person or institution can offer a clear, valid and reliable assessment of the industry's community impact.

The first shortcoming of past socio-economic and environmental studies is that none have assessed the combined impacts of the Jonah Field, the Pinedale Anticline, and any other prospective development. More importantly, none have even mentioned, much less analyzed, the cumulative impacts of all developments over their lifetime. As a result, no one will know when a small incremental change in the demographic profile of the county, its air quality, or its wildlife habitat might lead to sudden and very big change. This phenomenon is known as the "tipping point," and an idea recently made popular by author, Malcolm Gladwell, in his book, *The Tipping Point, How Little Things Can Make a Big Difference.*

Between 2000 and 2004, the county's population grew by 734 people or 12.4 percent and totaled 6,654. The 2000 population was 5,920. That compares to a 1990 population of 4,843, and a projected 2014 population of 8,500. The components of that population growth between 2000 and 2004 included ninety eight more births than deaths and the 643 people who moved to the county from someplace else in the United States.

Who made up those 643 arrivals? First, many appear to be children arriving with their parents. Next, according to a 2004 Sublette County District One Middle School mobility study, forty percent of those who started fourth grade had left by the eighth grade. Clearly, a significant percentage of those who moved to the county, were transient workers with their families. In keeping with that lifestyle, they had not planned on staying long. Third, in 2000, the twenty-six percent of the county's 3,552 homes that were devoted to seasonal or recreational use suggested that another portion of those 643 new "immigrants" were people who had started new careers or were retired or semi-retired families. They tended to be professionals and were attracted to the area by its outdoor amenities, recreation, and natural beauty—values prospectively threatened by the energy industry. Many located in the "rural" north of Pinedale where in 2005 the average home price was the highest in the county: $317,394. Last, energy development also accounted for some of the "newcomers," but the energy companies' executives and managers were the ones who relocated and have become longer term residents.

The recent population increase can be attributed to many sources and the energy industry has been just one. However, the future fast pace of development may prompt more permanent newcomers from the industry, and growth in the other categories of energy company employees. Although a subject for further study, the energy industry's economic and compensation structure in the county looks more and more like a pyramid with the companies' executives and managers sitting on the top. Just below them are the mainly Texas contractors like Halliburton and Schlumberger who run the rigs and other more technical elements of gas production.

One more step down the pyramid are, the skilled and semi-skilled workers who routinely work for the contractors or who go where the better paying jobs in the industry can be found. Either they are single or their families live in their "home" states. They tend to cluster in the "man camps," trailer parks or the year around residential hotels. In 2006, they likely numbered just over four hundred residents with at least another man camp planned in 2007 that could accommodate two hundred residents.

Next to the bottom of the economic pyramid are the skilled and semi-skilled Sublette and Sweetwater County workers. They work as roustabouts, construction laborers, welders, truck drivers, heavy equipment operators, and vehicle repairmen and in a wide variety of other assignments. For most, their income is more, if not much more, than they had earned earlier. At the pyramid's base are the more transient workers. They often are those who hear about the county's growth and energy industry, and move their families to Pinedale without a guaranteed job. They find a job, but for whatever reason, it doesn't work out as expected and within a year or two they depart for wherever they hear the next best opportunity can be found.

This pyramid concept indicates that more of the energy industry's employment growth and benefits in Sublette County will flow to the employees other than Sublette County's gas field workers, who have been long time residents. In 2000, of county workers twenty-five years old and over, fifty-six percent had less than one year of college and most of those had only a high school diploma or less. That educational level and the absence of a quality skills training center will limit the upward mobility of its residents and do little to stem the migration tide of its more talented young people. Already the county's energy companies are recruiting laid off auto workers in Michigan, and eventually the newer immigrants will come from other states that have unemployed skilled workers.

The Tipping Point

The likely influx of many more newcomers suggests that the county may reach a socio-economic tipping point where the change is sudden and dramatic, and alters the whole character of the community. To better understand this phenomenon, let's look at another Wyoming community.

Sublette County citizens need not look further than their northern neighbor, Jackson Hole. Until the early 1990s, Jackson was a local community with a shared history and local characters who enlivened it. They included Paul Petzoldt, an extraordinary mountaineer, who in 1924 at age sixteen climbed the Grand in a pair of cowboy boots, and Betty Woolsey, a 1936 Olympic skier and dude ranch owner. Somewhere in the 1990s it "tipped" to become a community of wealthy mavens with few roots or a sense of place in Jackson history.

Between 1990 and 2000, Jackson's population grew from 11,172 to 18,251. It was the magnitude of the change and the nature of the change that altered Jackson's character. Most saw it coming, but kept thinking that time was on their side. It wasn't. Two lane roads became four lane highways. Local restaurants became "chop houses," and espresso and martini bars. Country Western jukeboxes gave way to disco and reggae nights. The wildness and adventure of the place gave way to a determination to build as many high end commercial and residential properties as possible. Even today some of the latecomers like to urge the preservation of historic Jackson, open space, and scenic views. These are laudable statements, but twenty-five years too late.

During the next twenty years, Sublette County and Pinedale are unlikely to evolve into another Jackson. Their change will come from another direction: mainly through the expansion of the Jonah Field, Pinedale Anticline, and possibly the Wyoming Range. The magnitude of the population change obviously matters. But whether it is five hundred or two thousand, it will raise the question of whether the housing, sewer, water, health care, schools, police or sheriff, fire protection, courts, social services, day care, and the roads and bridges can manage the change. If not, how much will the adjustments cost? Will the costs exceed the revenues generated by the gas industry? And how much will those "improvements" change the quality of life?

For example, in 2003 the two major state highways that service the Jonah Field and Pinedale Anticline, Highways 191 and 351, carried well over a thousand vehicle trips a day, and those vehicles were not compact cars. Not only will those roads need regular repair and improvement, but the County and town roads designed for much less traffic will need repaving and routine enhancements. Since the Wyoming Department of Transportation may be planning a four lane highway from Rock Springs to Pinedale, perhaps it is time for the state, county and energy companies to consider "park and ride" networks for the two growing gas fields.

Without a much better understanding of the nature of past change, future change is difficult to predict. For example, the 2000 Census shows that Sublette County had 3,552 total housing units and the number of vacant units was 1,181 or thirty-three percent, a very sizable vacancy rate. New construction over a six year period even added more housing units.

A housing study conducted by the Wyoming Housing Database Partnership and completed in February, 2006, showed that the supply of housing in Sublette County grew significantly between 2000 and 2004. During these four years the number of housing units increased by 8.4 percent compared to a 3.92 percent for the state.

Despite the recent increase in housing supply, the few hundred living in the man camps, and more than a hundred soon to be living in company constructed or sponsored hotels, the county has recently approved 250 new lots within a one mile radius of Pinedale.

Reflecting a real or presumed shortage of available housing, rents and home sale prices have increased. But why? Only 643 people settled in the County between 2000 and 2004 and when adjusted for average family size, the number needing housing drops to about two hundred families. Some of those built their own homes, and the others should have been able to find suitable housing in the over a thousand vacant units or the newer homes built between 2000 and 2004.

Anomalies like this abound, and if the Census Bureau could afford to update all of the socio-economic data for rural counties, it would be easier to solve this riddle. Of course, Sublette County could conduct its own scientific housing survey.

A few other questions illustrate how little the county, its officials, and its residents understand about the nature of change. Of those who will arrive during the next decade, how many will be families with the financial capability and interest to relocate? How old will their children be, and how many will need day care or attend school? What level of education have the parents attained? How many newcomers will be single or without their families? Where would they prefer to live? What state will they be moving from and will they plan to return and, if so, when? How many will be more transient workers, and what challenges will they pose to the schools and social services?

The 2010 Census will help pinpoint some of this change, but by then it will have already happened, and the genie of change can't be put back in the bottle. But public opinion surveys could begin to answer these questions tomorrow. By using a question to identify or "screen" new arrivals and by ensuring an adequate sample of them as well as longer term residents, much can be discovered and many of these questions answered.

What about the tipping point for Sublette County? Without better data, computer models and public opinion data, I can only raise questions about the prospective challenges. First, and similar to Jackson Hole, if the county population increases by seventy percent or more over the next decade, that will begin to squeeze the tipping point trigger. That would be on top of the change that has already occurred. This growth of two thousand new residents would bring the total population increase to eighty-five hundred or an average of two hundred more people per year. The July 1, 2005 population estimates for Sublette County show 6,926 people—a 272 person increase from 2004.

An accelerated annual population growth rate began in 2003. At that pace the county's housing stock, health care, education, police, courts and fire protection would be stretched thin, if not overwhelmed. In 2005, an increase of just twenty-six new kids in the Pinedale elementary school was considered unprecedented growth. At best, the county would face a constant process of catch up. By 2014, about half of the current adult work force will have retired and the new residents will take over the higher paying jobs. The county's service industry will be unable to find qualified American workers who will accept their hourly wages and the influx of Spanish speaking and other foreign workers will take those jobs. As some ranchers will retire and others subdivide, much of the county's most scenic open space could be lost.

Without Jackson's world class mountain resort, the Tetons, Teton National Park and many other amenities, Sublette County could assume the character of an energy and industrial town sprawled in a mountain valley. If it tips that direction, then its attraction to seasonal residents, tourists, investors, fisherman, and hunters could well decline.

With the prospective decline in wildlife habitat and wildlife, its attraction and image as a "destination resort" or as a wild land of beauty will further erode. The environment has a tipping point just like social communities and, once it tips, the status quo cannot be restored. Of course, scientists, biologists, fish and wildlife experts can, and often do, disagree about the environmental consequences of public and private actions. But usually when major environmental changes are observed, a "prudent man" will take precautionary action to limit the damage.

Recent data on mule deer and sage grouse behavior on the Pinedale Anticline or Mesa, give such a cautionary warning. In 2005, the area's most definitive study of the development's impact on mule deer showed a forty-six percent decline in the Mesa's mule deer population. The study was industry-funded and conducted by the wildlife consultant, Hall Sawyer. Although the study found that · fawning ratios seem stable, increasing the number of wells from 293 to nine thousand, with all the companion roads and other disturbances, cannot help but adversely affect the deer.

A six year study conducted by University of Wyoming and funded by Encana and Ultra showed that if the winter restrictions were lifted, within four to six years the birds would leave their traditional breeding and nesting habitat. The author, Matt Holloran, noted that, "The birds are dispersing and declining. The data suggests that sage grouse populations are not sustainable in the gas fields."

The initial 2005 results from a five year study of antelope found the animals completely avoiding the Jonah Field. Although funded by Shell, the study is being conducted by Wilderness Conservation biologists, Kim Murray Berger and Joel Berger.

Even if subject to other interpretations or caveats, with greatly expanded drilling in the offing, it would be foolish to deny the obvious: century old patterns and populations of Wyoming wildlife in these areas have been and will continue to be greatly diminished, if not lost.

Perhaps even more threatening, is the matter of air quality degradation in the "air sheds," surrounding the two gas fields. Much controversy has surrounded the issue including a delay in issuing the BLM's Jonah Field's Final Environmental Impact Statement. That delay allowed a more in-depth modeling of air quality impacts, including the non-degradation standards for the surrounding Bridger-Teton Wilderness. The BLM's Supplemental EIS for the Mesa that was still under way in 2006 will also analyze air quality impacts. Many including a retired Air Force physicist, amateur astronomer and now air quality expert, Perry Walker, believe that Wyoming Department of Environmental Quality needs more air quality monitoring stations and stricter testing in the two gas fields. Currently three "live" ambient air quality monitors function near the two major gas fields—one in Boulder, one in the Jonah Field and one south of Daniel. Mr. Walker believes a minimum of nine are necessary to measure what is actually happening in contrast to the predictions of the air quality models. Further, historically the U.S. Forest Service maintained air quality monitors in the surrounding wilderness areas. While none are operating now, in 2006 BLM and industry have agreed to fund and restart the three air quality monitors in the nearby wilderness areas including the Bridger Wilderness Area. An ambient air quality monitor will also be placed in the Wyoming Range. Mr. Walker neatly summed up the environmental risks: "BLM with industry is turning this region into one big environmental proving ground." He might have added, "too little too late."

We are now coming to the end of this book and the end of this story about the cowboys and ranchers of Wyoming's Hoback Basin. It is time to tie them together. While much better information is required, the cumulative impacts of expanded development in the Jonah Field and the Pinedale Anticline could easily reach the social and environmental tipping points where the character and quality of both are dramatically changed. In view of those real and formidable risks, instead of rushing to develop the Wyoming Range, the U.S. Forest Service should have declared a moratorium on gas development in the Wyoming Range and Hoback Basin. That moratorium should last as long as the companies are producing gas in the two existing fields. Before leasing the Wyoming Range, U.S. Forest Service, BLM, the Environmental Protection Agency, the State of Wyoming, Sublette

County, and industry should know the cumulative social and environmental impacts of the two existing fields. All of that information, including environmental monitoring should be made public in a regular and understandable fashion.

As of spring, 2006, the U.S. Forest Service has decided to lease the Wyoming Range. Any rational plan will now come about as the result of protests, litigation or national legislation by environmental and citizens groups. A grass roots and public relations campaign directed towards local officials, state elected officials and particularly the members of the U.S. House and Senate who serve on the relevant subcommittees of the Appropriation and Energy and Natural Resources Committees, would strengthen the campaign. That campaign could also help leverage the shareholders and investors of energy companies that develop the Wyoming Range.

In mid-summer 2006, the success of Senator Conrad Burns, R-MT, in using an Interior Department appropriations bill to protect part of Montana's Front Range stands as one example of an approach commonly practiced by Washington lobbyists. A bipartisan House bill, first crafted by Rep. Tom Udall, D-NM, and passed overwhelmingly by the House, withdrew 101,000 acres in the Carson National Forest from mineral exploration or development. That acreage is known as the Valle Vidal and is used for grazing and recreation. It represents another very promising option for the Wyoming Range. Other recent national legislation creating new wilderness areas or designating more miles of wild and scenic rivers in California, Idaho, Nevada, Oregon, and Utah also jump out as examples of what can be accomplished when local citizens and their lawmakers work to find solutions.

That part of Wyoming Range extending north into the Hoback Basin remains one of the few mountain ranges and National Forests in the county and beyond that remains untouched by development. Its several hundred thousand roadless acres represent the largest roadless area in the seven hundred thousand acre Bridger-Teton National Forest. It is unspoiled.

The corridors into the Wyoming Range are also dotted with historic ranches, homesteads, and trails. They allow clear and uncluttered views of the mountains, sagebrush hills, and forested ridges.

The following facts are based on a 2005-2006 study by the Wilderness Society, *The Wyoming Range, Wyoming's Hidden Gem*. It highlights the unique features of the Wyoming Range:

The Wyoming Range moose herd, a subpopulation of the famous Sublette County moose herd, is the largest sub-herd in the state.

In terms of the land mass it inhabits, the Wyoming Range mule deer population, which has numbered close to fifty thousand, was one of the largest in North America. In 2006, that herd was 45.7 percent below its fifty thousand goal.

The Wyoming Range provides such excellent habitat for elk that it can be used as a model to design elk habitat.

Streams flowing from the Wyoming Range like Horse Creek serve as one of the last major strongholds for the Colorado River cutthroat trout. It is the only range in Wyoming with four species of native cutthroat.

Reflecting its richness as wildlife habitat, in 2004, twelve thousand hunting licenses for elk, mule deer, and moose were issued in and around the Wyoming Range.

It should then come as no surprise that the Wyoming Range generates tens of millions of dollars from recreation—part of a fifty million dollar economy built on wildlife in the Bridger-Teton National Forest.

We know that neither national security nor a limited and fragile natural gas supply require unrestricted development. Not even knowing the full range of social and environmental impacts of greatly expanded development, wisely or not, Sublette County has facilitated the growth of two gas fields encompassing tens of thousands of acres—a level of development that will ensure for the next twenty to thirty years no alternative use of those acres.

Under those circumstances, only greed or a case of collusion by the federal government can explain any interest in leasing the Wyoming Range. Preserving that incomparable resource will take the same measure of grit that characterized the early settlers, ranchers, and cowboys of the Hoback Basin. If change does come to the Hoback Basin, I hope it will be of their choosing and slow paced. Since the Basin does not have the housing, healthcare, transportation, work force or commercial facilities to support a large scale development, a faster pace would submerge it. But most importantly, Wyoming and the rest of the Rocky Mountain West should preserve a few places whose natural beauty, history, and authenticity have served the West and America so well for over a century. The Hoback Basin is one such place. It reminds us how the West was really won, and how tradition can endure.

PAUL JENSEN

Notes and Sources

Part One: A Guided Tour of Wyoming History

T.A. Larson's *History of Wyoming*, Second Edition, Revised (Lincoln and London, University of Nebraska Press, 1965, 1978) served as the primary source including the early Census data, pp. 108, 194, 262. The chapters that most informed Part One include *The Organization of Wyoming Territory*, pp. 64-94; *1870s—A Troubled Decade*, pp. 95-132; *Boom and Bust in Cattle*, pp. 163-194 and *Years of Struggle 1890-1897*, pp. 262-309.

A substantial complement to Larson's history was Howard R. Larmar's edition of *The New Encyclopedia of the American West*, (New Haven and London, Yale University Press, 1998.) It offered an easily accessible and rich reference on places, people and institutions that played major roles in Wyoming and western history.

Warren A. Beck and Yvez D. Haase, *Historical Atlas of the American West*, (Norman and London, University of Oklahoma Press, 1989) offered a supplementary source as did Candy Moulton, *Roadside History of Wyoming* (Missoula, Montana, Mountain Press Publishing Company, 1995.)

Velma Linford, *Wyoming Frontier State* (Denver, Colorado, The Old West Publishing Co., 1947) provided useful historical perspective.

Finally, Frederick Jackson Turner, *The Frontier in American History* (Tucson, University of Arizona Press, 1986) informed the last pages of this first part.

Part Two: The Place, Its Exploration and Ranching Heritage

David Lageson and Darwin Spearing, *Roadside Geology of Wyoming*, Revised Second Edition (Missoula, Mountain Press Publishing, 1991) contributed to the geology of the Hoback Basin as did D.L. Blackstone, Jr., *Traveler's Guide to the Geology of Wyoming* (Laramie, Wyoming, *The Geological Survey of Wyoming Bulletin 67, 1988.*)

Climate data was provided by the courtesy of Joe Sullivan, Chief Meteorologist with the National Weather Service office in Riverton, Wyoming, and the Wyoming weather web site he forwarded.

Topographical information was groomed from first hand experience, lessons from local ranchers, topographical maps and the periodic environmental assessments conducted by the U.S. Forest Service's Teton and Big Piney District Offices. The U.S. Forest Service's 1951 and 1981 inventory evaluations and the *1982 Decision Notice* provided the best topographical and historical information. As a result, they also served as a source for the overall history of the Hoback Cattle and Horse Allotment. They were augmented by shorter assessments of range conditions that often contained information about current members of the Association. Those began in the 1930s and continued through the 1970s.

The section on Wyoming Indian Tribes was drawn from John Upton Terrell, *American Indian Almanac* (New York and Cleveland, World

Publishing Company, 1971) and Virginia Cole Trinholm and Maurine Cavalry, *The Shoshones, Sentinels of the Rockies* (Norman, University of Oklahoma Press, 1964.) Again, Howard R. Lamar, ed., *The New Encyclopedia of the American West* (New Haven and London, Yale University Press, 1998) provided valuable resources on the Shoshone.

The history of the mountain men and John Hoback was drawn from Robert M. Utley, *A Life Wild and Perilous: Mountain Men and the Path to the Pacific* (New York, Henry Holt and Company, 1997.)

Other information on the early exploration came from the introduction to the *V-V Guest Book* and Velma Linford, *Wyoming Frontier State* (Denver, The Old West Publishing Co., 1947).

The early ranching history of the Basin was pulled from many sources. They are: Eunice Ewer Wallace, *Wyoming's Own*, (Boise, Idaho, Joslyn and Rentshler Lithographers, 1976); Jonita Sommers, *Green River Drift, A History of the Upper Green River Cattle Association* (Helena, Montana, SkyHouse Publishing, 1994); Robert G. Rosenberg, *Wyoming's Last Frontier*, Sublette County, Wyoming (Glendo, Wyoming, High Plains Press, 1990); Sublette County Artists Guild, *Seeds-Ke-Dee Revisited, Land of Blue Granite and Silver Sage* (Freeman, South Dakota, Pine Hill Press, 1998) and Hayden H. Huston, ed., Daniel, Wyoming, *The First Hundred Years, 1900-2000, Books One and Two* (Araska Books, 2000.)

The information on Johnnie Curtis was provided by Sandra Milleg of Big Piney, wife of Johnny Curtis' grandson, Bill Milleg.

The previously cited U.S. Forest Service documents provided much of the data on the Allotment. In addition, their actual annual Permit Allotment Sheets from 1930s-1950s proved invaluable as did their Basin homesteading records that began with 1901 entries.

Beyond the U.S. Forest Service documents, the public lands review was based on three sources. They include two earlier citations, T.R. Larson's *History of Wyoming* and Howard R. Lamar, ed., *The New Encyclopedia of the American West.*

The third source, and the most informative one, appeared as an article by Jim Huston, "The Public Domain," pages 32-39 in *Wyoming Wildlife, Volume LXVIII, Number 10,* October 2004 (Cheyenne, Wyoming, Wyoming Game and Fish Department, 2004.)

The information on Charles Dibble and other elements of early homesteading in northwest Wyoming was drawn from Fern K. Nelson's, *This Was Jackson's Hole* (Glendo, Wyoming, High Plains Press, 1994.)

Interviews with Bob McNeel, Grant Beck and Cheryl Johnston, who all ranched or rode for the Association, provided important first—hand information about the earlier ranching days and those times from the 1950s-1970s.

The true story on the Roundup Tradition and Fred Turner was told by Victor Mack, Sr., and his wife, Jo.

Last, more than a decade of reading Wallace Stegner has informed some of my thinking about the American West, particularly influential for this book were his essays in *Where the Bluebird Sings to the Lemonade Springs, Living and Writing in the West* (New York, The Modern Library, 1972.)

A few riders like Kent Snidecor and Tim Tolton rode for four or five years. Most rode for a year or two. In 1974 and immediately after Harve Stone, Roy Snow rode for several years. After Roy, Harve Stone's oldest daughter, Cheryl, and her first husband, Kent Snidecor, rode together for a couple of years. Kent rode with second rider, Tom Filkins, in 1980 and 1981 and then with Tim Tolton in 1982. Jim McKinney rode from 1983-1984 and Tolton rode from 1984-1989. Charlie Lopeman rode in 1990, and then in 1991 Mike Needham came aboard. Troy Seilback rode in 1992, and Charlie Lopeman had a return engagement in 1993. As noted, in 1994 Tom Filkins and his family moved back to the Basin from Cody, and ever since he has ridden for the Association

Part Three: Bondurant and the Basin: Its Earliest Pioneers

Two sources cited earlier provided the best initial background material. In order of value: Hayden H. Huston, ed., *Daniel, Wyoming, The First Hundred Years, 1900-2000, Book One and Two* (Agreka Books, 2000) and *Seeds-Ke-Dee Revisted, Land of Blue Granite and Silver Sage* (Freeman, South Dakota, Pine Hill Press, 1998.)

Three special publications gave direction and precision: first, Hayden Huston's Homesteading and Township Maps for Sublette County; second, Josephine Jons, *"The Hoback Basin in Sublette County, Wyoming,"* *Works Project Administration Collection, No. 1273* (Cheyenne: The Wyoming State Archives, Museums and Historical Department, Historical Research and Publications Division, n.d.); and third, an unpublished paper by Mrs. Pearl Oscar Bondurant, n.d.

In Part Three's history of the Sanford family, the current price of furs was calculated using the U.S. Bureau of Labor Statistic's CPI Inflation Calculator. Since the data series only goes back to 1913, I used the annual average increase from 1913 to 2006 and accordingly increased the base number, $341.20, so it roughly reflected the inflation adjusted price from 1890 to 2006.

The information on Sandy Marshall came from Richard Hecox's *Memories Of Kendall Valley* (Disney Krause Brunette in cooperation with the Sublette County Historical Society, Second Edition, 2005) pp. 211-217.

Telephone interviews and subsequent information provided by Dewey Bowlsby, his wife, Deanne, and his older brother, Bill Bowlsby, created the family's genealogical foundation.

Last, an unpublished paper on Shel E. Baker, initially given to Jesse Faris and retained by her granddaughter, Cheryl Johnston, provided the biographical data on him.

An earlier Green River Valley Museum interview with Jake Pfisterer provided background on his family. A telephone interview with Kay Buston supplemented Jake's interview.

The Jackson Hole Historical Society provided the background and newspaper records on Frank Van Fleck and Wallace Hiatt.

The story of Cleophas J. Dowd was based on an article, Cleophas J. Dowd, Utah's Most Enigmatic Lawman, by Kerry Ross Boren. Most recently, it was published in *Badges N' Badmen, the Utah Police Officer, Summer, 1992, Volume 69, Issue 2.* That article by Boren is part of a larger collection, *The Kerry Ross Boren Papers, 1853-1993,* held and copyrighted by the Utah Historical Society.

Information on the circumstances of Noah Booker's death was provided by Grace Van Winkle's family. The history and value of the Stradivarius was drawn from Guy Gugliotta's "Unlocking Stradivari's Sound," p.35, *The Washington Post National Weekly Edition, February 13-19, 2006.*

Personal interviews by the author with Sublette County residents Tuffy Davis, Louis Dapra, and Cheryl Johnston, who all rode in the

Hoback Basin, gave additional flavor to the section on the Basin's social life.

Background material provided by Richard and Gloria Thomas established the chronology of the Elkhorn's development.

Sublette County Homemakers, ed., *Sublette School Days* (Boise, Idaho, Joslyn & Rentschler, December, 1974), pp. 22-24 and 116-122.

Part Four: The Originals

Eunice Ewer Wallace's *Wyoming's Own*, (Boise, Idaho, Joslyn and R Lithographer, 1976, pp. 241-252) provided the biographical and anecdotal information on Charles Noble. That information was supplemented by interviews with Bob McNeel and Grant Beck who both rode for Charles Noble.

The Tarter story was based on Hayden H. Huston, ed., *Daniel, Wyoming, First Hundred Years, 1900-2000, Book One,* (Araska Books, 2000, pp. 293-313).

The section on Phil Marincic Sr. was based on Sublette County Artist Guild, *More Tales of the Seeds-Ke-Dee,* (Walsworth, 1976, pp. 340-354).

The information on Alex "Dead Shot" Swenson came primarily from Sublette County Artists Guild, *Seeds-Ke-Dee Revisited, Land of Blue Granite and Silver Sage,* (Freeman, South Dakota, Pine Hill Press, 1998, pp. 123-124.)

Supplemental background on "Dead Shot" and the information on Jim Williams were drawn from Hayden H. Huston, ed., *Daniel Wyoming,* p. 208.

The information on Danish history and the Mormon missions was provided by Rudolf J. Jensen, Professor, Scandinavian Studies, Grandview College, Des Moines, Iowa.

The history of the Butterfield Overland Mail Company was drawn from Howard R. Lamar's edition of *The New Encyclopedia of the American West*, (New Haven and London, Yale University Press, 1998, pp. 837-838.)

Austin Richardson's story was drawn from Hayden H. Huston, ed., Daniel, Wyoming, pp. 435-438, 638-640.

Clarence Webbs' biography was informed by the Sublette County Artist Guild's *More Tales of the Seeds-Ke-Dee*, pp. 161-178.

Gordon Jewett's account was based on Hayden Huston, pp. 447-449, and *More Tales of the Seeds-Ke-Dee*, pp. 245-267.

The Clure Smith story was based primarily on two interviews with his daughter, Marjorie Thurston. Supplemental information was provided by Hayden J. Huston, ed., Daniel, Wyoming, pp. 406, 448, 449, 678.

The information on Mother Williams and Charles Clyde was first drawn from interviews with Dan Budd and Gordon Mickelson, both from Big Piney ranching families who had hired Mother Williams and knew Charlie Clyde. This information was enhanced and complemented by an entry in the Sublette County Artists Guild, *Seeds-Ke-Dee Revisited, Land of Blue Granite and Silver Sage*, p. 128) and most importantly by interviews with Charlie Clyde's son, whose name is also Charlie Clyde.

Harve Stone's story was based on three separate interviews with his oldest daughter, Cheryl Johnston, a family tree, a transcribed oral history by Harve Stone, and Lois, his wife's obituaries obituaries. All of this information was generously provided by Cheryl Johnston. Interviews with Kevin Campbell and Gordon Mickelson added more insight into Harve Stone's character. Also the information on the Faris family was provided by Cheryl Johnston. This was later printed in *Seeds-Ke-Dee Revisited*, pp.319-324.

The information on Norm Pape was drawn from two interviews with Norm and Barbara Pape; an earlier interview with them recorded by the Green River Valley Museum, *More Tales of the Seeds-Ke-Dee*, pp. 65-73, and Hayden Huston, ed., Daniel, Wyoming, pp 489-491 and 499-503.

The story on John Peck May was based on Hayden Huston, p. 482 and an interview with Norm and Barbara Pape.

Part Five: The Cowboys

From June 1, 2005 to November 1, 2005, the author rode for the Hoback Stock Association. In fall, 2005, he also rode roundup for the Pape Ranch, and he rode roundup for their ranch in 2003 and 2004, too. His first hand experience and conversations with the "cowboys" shaped Part Five's Introduction and the subsequent profiles.

Interviews with Kevin Campbell; his brother, Lennie; his sister, Katherine; and his mother, Pat, painted a clear yet colorful portrait of the family and its individual members. Prepared by Katherine Campbell, two family genealogies added more chronological detail to the family painting. However, a narrative history of the Campbell family, including photos and newspaper articles, gave a remarkably rich texture to its history. That history, *The Homestead*, was prepared by Walden Campbell's sister, Lila LuPreal. Her daughter, Sonja Box, helped compile and edit the history.

Interviews with Gerry and Rusty Endecott, conversations around their kitchen table, short genealogies, and very thoughtful answers to a few prepared questions furnished the material for their profile. With respect to the history of the Little Jennie Ranch, the archivist at the *Salt Lake City Tribune* generously provided the background on the Kearns family. The Kansas City, Mo., Public Library similarly prepared the biographical information on Bob Wagstaff, and Bob's son, Tom, graciously enhanced that history with facts, anecdotes and his family's memories.

Months of conversations with Tom Filkins at cow camp or on horseback formed his profile. Of course, conversations with his wife, Marilyn, and their sons, Jake and Wade, gave more insight to Tom's personality. An interview with Scott Jackson added historical fact and flavor to Tom's horse wreck in 2004.

Riding fall roundups with Victor Mack, Jr. and listening to his stories about the Hoback Basin offered a special look into his life and values. Adding pleasure and information to this story were interviews and conversations with his mother, Jo, and father, Vic, Sr. Of course, his wife, Lucy, and his daughter, Megan, shaped his life even more than the Hoback Basin.

Part Six: A Glance into the Future

The ranch land data and value of Sublette County agriculture were based on the 2002 Agricultural Census. Later in Part Six, the economic value of the county's travel and tourism business came from the Wyoming Travel Industry's *2003 Impact Report* published by Wyoming's State Travel and Tourism Office.

All of the population and other demographic data throughout Part Six were drawn from the U.S. Census Bureau's online data bases, including the State & County Quick Facts file.

The real estate data for Jackson, Teton County, Idaho, and Wyoming's Star Valley were based on 2005 annual report prepared by David Viehman of Jackson Hole Real Estate and Appraisal. That report was available on Viehman's Web site jacksonholereport.com. The Sublette County data was initially drawn from a *Pinedale Roundup* article, "Sublette County's Real Estate Market is Hot," by Rob Shaul, p. 3, April 14, 2005. The article was prepared for the *Roundup's* supplement, *Build It*. That data was updated by the Sublette County Assessor and printed in the July 27, 2006, issue of the *Pinedale Roundup* on page 7A.

Most of the information of the Jonah Field development and its impacts came directly from the Bureau of Land Management, Pinedale and Rock Springs Field Offices' Draft *Environmental Impact Statement, Jonah Infill Drilling Project, Sublette County, Wyoming, Volume 1 and 2, February, 2005*. That data was supplemented by the BLM's Jonah Infill Drilling Project Final EIS.

The Mesa or Pinedale Anticline drilling data and plans were based on a *Pinedale Roundup* article, "Ultra plans 2,800 wells on the Anticline," by Noah Brenner, p. 4A, October 13, 2005, and a *Pinedale Roundup* report by Rob Shaul, p. 24A, November 3, 2005.

Both the gas reserves estimates and well numbers for the Jonah Field and the Pinedale Anticline were reviewed with Don Likwartz, Oil and Gas Supervisor of the Wyoming Oil and Gas Conservation Commission.

The information on air quality was drawn from the February, 2005 report of the BLM's Pinedale Anticline Working Group on Air Quality and very informative conversations with Terry Svalberg, Bridger-Teton National Forest Air Quality Specialist. Terry also provide helpful comments on the entire draft of Part Six. The three live ambient air quality monitors mentioned in Part Six can be accessed through www.wyvisnet.com.

The information on the U.S. Forest Service plans for the Wyoming Range were first based on numerous newspaper articles including a 2005 series in the *Jackson Hole News and Guide* written by regular columnist, Todd Wilkinson. He can be reached at tawilk@aol.com. The other articles were a *Casper Star Tribune* article, "Groups protest leases in the Wyoming Range," by Whitney Royster, November 23, 2005, and a *Pinedale Roundup* article, "Wyoming Range lease draws heated protest," by Noah Brenner, p. 10, *Roughneck* supplement, November 24, 2005. In 2006, articles in the *Casper Star Tribune*, the *Pinedale Roundup*, and the *Sublette Examiner* reported on the subsequent of leases and other developments. They can all be found on-line at the respective Websites of some of those publications or in the computer or hard copy records of the Pinedale and Big Piney libraries.

The state, national and international information on the natural gas market was based on the Energy Information Administration's online data bases and reports, including *Natural Gas Basics, Natural Gas Information Sheets*, and EIA's online *Annual Energy Outlook* scheduled to be published in 2006.

The Pinedale Middle School mobility statistics came from an unpublished report prepared by the Middle School's administration.

The information on the wildlife and recreational values of the Wyoming Range were drawn from a 2006 brochure entitled *The Wyoming Range, Wyoming's Hidden Gems*. It was available from the Wilderness Society and specifically brian_maffly@tws.org.

The information on recent national legislation came from the Senate Interior Appropriations Committee staff and the office of Rep. Tom Udall, D.-NM The help of those staff members was augmented by a *Casper Star Tribune* article, "House approves wilderness for California, Oregon, Idaho," by AP writer, Matthew Daly, July 25, 2006, p. B6.

About
the
Author

   Paul Jensen resides in ranch country near Daniel, Wyoming where he moved over three years ago from Washington, D.C. He traded in a thirty year career in national politics and business for a life-long dream of living and working as a cowboy in the West. Since arriving in Wyoming, Paul has worked as a cowboy, substitute teacher, a ski-lift operator and most recently as director of Rendezvous Pointe, a senior and community center in Sublette County. He lives and enjoys his life with his wife, Sherrill, a middle school teacher, and eight-year old daughter, Lily.

Printed in the United States
202470BV00002B/106-147/A